REAL Computing
Made
REAL

REAL Computing Made REAL

Preventing Errors in Scientific and Engineering Calculations

FORMAN S. ACTON

Princeton University Press
Princeton, New Jersey

Copyright © 1996 by Princeton University Press
Published by Princeton University Press, 41 William Street,
Princeton, New Jersey 08540
In the United Kingdom: Princeton University Press,
Chichester, West Sussex

Library of Congress Cataloging-in-Publication Data
Acton, Forman S.
REAL Computing made real : preventing errors in scientific and
engineering calculations / Forman S. Acton.
p.   cm.
Includes Index.
ISBN 0-691-03663-2 (alk. paper)
1. Error analysis (Mathematics) 2. Numerical analysis—Data
processing. I. Title.
QA275.A25 1996
519.4'0285'51—dc20   95-10606
CIP

This book has been composed in Stempel Schneidler, Flintstone and Lucida Sans

The publisher would like to acknowledge Forman Acton for providing the
camera-ready copy from which this book was printed
Text Design by C. Alvarez

Princeton University Press books are printed on acid-free paper and meet the
guidelines for permanence and durability of the Committee on Production
Guidelines for Book Longevity of the Council on Library Resources

Frontispiece: Courtesy of the Freer Gallery of Art, Washington, D.C. 98.423:
An Actor in Character by Katsukawa Shunko (1743-1812) Japan, Edo period.
Detail from a painting; color, lacquer black on silk: 58.7 x 26.8 cm.

All other photographs courtesy of Phisit Phisitthakorn

Printed in the United States of America
by Princeton Academic Press

1 2 3 4 5 6 7 8 9 10

CONTENTS

> Make fewer errors! (Errors are hard to find.) We need help — but much software obscures! — A kind of *Kyrie*.

ACKNOWLEDGMENTS

Altho A.P.C. long served to cure headaches, the present team of Acton, Phisit, and Carmina have here delivered a book that may produce them! Let me therefore quickly declare that the designer, Carmina Alvarez, is responsible for wonderfully turning the author's penchant for oriental statues into a coherent visual style that uses some of the seventy-three photographs taken, on very short notice, by my friend Phisit Phisitthakorn, architect, of Bangkok. But neither of them can be blamed for the verbal content, which was created entirely by your author.*

I would also like to thank Jane Low who led the production team at the Princeton University Press and Trevor Lipscombe, the Physical Sciences Editor, who gallantly sponsored the book even after I concluded that a few Shavian simplified spellings were too ingrained by my fifty-five years of use to be expunged now.

*Of course the text is error-free — but you report any you find to acton@princeton.edu.

AN EXHORTATION

AVE ATQUE VALE!

This book addresses errors of the third kind. You've never heard of them? But you've made them; we all make them every time we write a computer program to solve a physical problem.

Errors of the first kind are grammatical — we write things that aren't in our programming language. The compiler finds them.

Errors of the second kind are our mistakes in programming the algorithms we sought to use. They include $n-1$ errors, inversions of logical tests, overwriting array limits (in Fortran) and a lot of other little technical mistakes that just don't happen to be ungrammatical. *We* have to find them.

Then, *mirabile visu,* the program runs — and even gives the correct answers to the two test problems we happen to have already solved.

Errors of the third kind are the ones we haven't found yet. They show up only for as-yet-untested input values — often for quite limited ranges of these parameters. They include (but are not limited to) loss of significant digits, iterative instabilities, degenerative inefficiencies in algorithms and convergence to extraneous roots of previously docile equations. Since some of these errors occur only for limited combinations of parameter inputs they may never disturb our results; more likely some of them will creep into our answers, but so quietly that we don't notice them — until our bridge has collapsed!

Exhaustive searching for these errors after a program is written is time consuming, computationally expensive and psychologically frustrating — after all, they may not really be there! We can identify with the chap who lamented

> As I was going up the stair
> I met a man who wasn't there.
> He wasn't there again today.
> I wish, I wish he'd stay away!

A more productive strategy is to develop thought habits and programming techniques that will prevent frequent occurrence of these errors of the third kind. It is cheaper to prevent than to cure. (And we would only cure those errors whose effects we had detected.)

This book is your author's attempt to raise your consciousness about errors of the third kind, mostly by way of simple examples — then to give you the opportunity to practice sensible error avoidance via a generous supply of problems for solution. Reasonably detailed solutions are provided, but obviously it is better if you at least attempt your own before peeking. There is considerable redundancy here, both in the examples and in the problems — you don't have to do them all! And you certainly don't have to read the whole book; the chapters are largely self-contained.

The greatest space is given to the preserving of significant digits. The disappearance of those digits usually pinpoints an algorithmic weakness that needs fixing. After many years of helping engineers and physicists debug their deviant programs, I am sure that this difficulty is as alive and well today as it was in 1949 when I began programming in absolute machine language — there being no other. Standard programming texts do little to help. They necessarily concentrate on errors of the first and second kind — their readers are interested in getting programs to <u>run</u>. REAL correctness is a later, more sophisticated concern. I hope, Dear Reader, that you have reached this later stage, that you have been bitten by errors of the third kind once too often and are now seeking help — not to fix the deficient past but to improve the future. This book is an imperfect instrument, but it is offered in the belief that it will help.

"Should I use Mathematica to solve my problem?"

The answer to this question is the same as J. P. Morgan's answer about how much it cost to run a yacht: "If you have to ask, you can't afford it." If you already are fluent in Mathematica^{TM} then obviously you already will be using its considerable manipulative powers to help you analyze your problem — perhaps even exploiting its nearly infinite-precision arithmetic (which runs nearly infinitely slowly). But if you have not used it, don't begin with a difficult problem you do not yet fully understand!

Mathematica is a huge system of remarkable capabilities cloaked in a stupefying variety of commands. But after six months of frequent experimentation, I still find that three-quarters of *my* time goes into trying to discover why I got an error message instead of the answer I was expecting.*

Similar questions arise about what language to use for the problem at hand. ("Should I learn C?") Again, if you are happy with a language, use it. BASIC is limited, but you can do the essentials with it. Spend your intellectual energies on the current problem — not on fancy tools. When the volume and sophistication of your problems demand these weapons you will know it. That is the time to learn a new tool — and learn it by re-doing an already-solved problem, not a new one.

---

*This experience may not be universal. I am not a touch typist, so long identifiers of mixed upper- and lowercase characters combine with visual confusions of many nested brackets, braces and parentheses to produce obstacles over which I regularly stumble — distracting me from the logic I should be pursuing.

Avoiding major algorithmic errors

While this book necessarily treats the picky little difficulties that plague scientific computing — instabilities, disappearing digits, extraneous roots of equations — it largely ignores the biggest waster of computational energy: the use of an incorrect algorithm. Or worse, the use of an algorithm that is correct but quite inappropriate for the problem.

A major logical flaw in an algorithm will almost always show itself when you run a few test examples to which you know the answers. Detecting troubles that appear only for special numerical conditions or extreme parameter values requires patient logical thought, systematically followed by special debugging runs to verify your analysis. (It is easy to indulge in wishful thinking disguised as logical thought.) Anybody who launches massive computer runs without these tests deserves the numbers he gets.*

But what about the *big* error — choosing the wrong tool for the job? Of course you should at least glance thru the literature. If two authors seem to have taken quite different algorithmic paths, you would do well to ponder why. Finally, if you can persuade a friend or two to listen, *explain your problem* and your algorithmic approach. Even if they don't raise deep questions or offer enlightening suggestions, the mere act of organizing your thoughts for the presentation will often illuminate an obscurity in your approach that may conceal a fatal flaw.

The human interface

Our chances of creating erroneous programs greatly increase whenever we adopt a convention that conflicts with our personal habits. All programming languages contain constructs that will push the user against her history — and they should be resisted. For example, as my friend likes to point out, most of us were not taught by our mothers to count on our fingers starting with the thumb as *zero!* Accordingly, you will probably make fewer $n-1$ errors if you do not use zero subscripts when dealing with matrices. (Of course, if your mother was

---

*I once received an irate letter accusing *me* of wasting thousands of DOD dollars by including (in a 1970 book) a public algorithm that lacked a crucial minus sign! A small test case would have caught the problem for the user and allowed a more temperate note advising me of my omission.

sufficiently foresighted ...)   Also it is wise to include a comment if, for compelling reasons, you decide to store a vector starting with zero or some even more unnatural subscript.

Thruout this text I recommend small practices that I have found effective in reducing my errors. I believe they may help you — but perhaps I'm less typical than I fondly suppose. These suggestions sometimes run against standard pedantry — and will perhaps incite professional ire. Why, for example, do I adopt $x^2 + 2bx + c = 0$ as my standard form for the quadratic? Because it eliminates two factors of 2 in the solutions — and factors of 2 get lost in my programs more often than anything except minus signs. I find that <u>important</u>; you may not. But whatever form you prefer, stick to it. Don't switch promiscuously. Fear not; at least in matters of programming style Consistency is *not* the hobgoblin of little minds. It is a virtue of the highest order.

And now with these exhortations to consistency and perseverance, combined with careful thought and judicious scepticism, you are on your own. I must take my leave. Only my hopes and good wishes can follow you.

REAL Computing Made
REAL

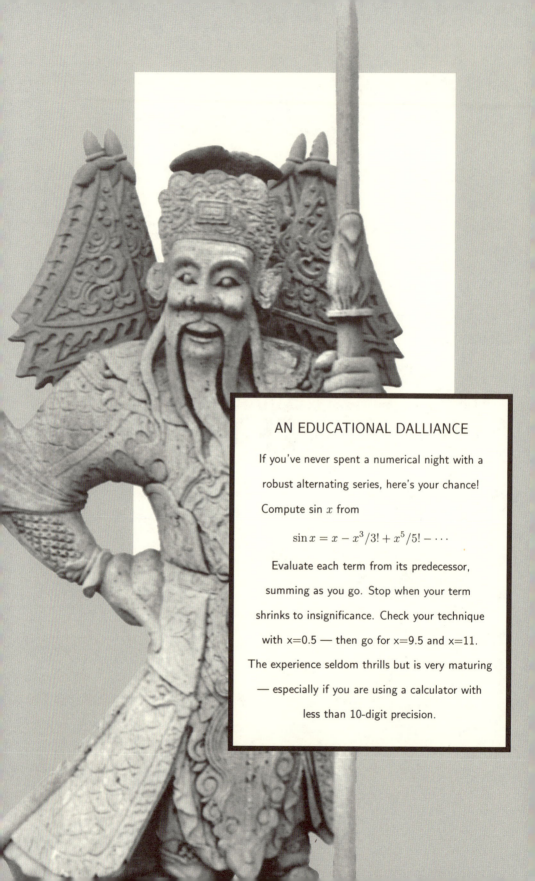

AN EDUCATIONAL DALLIANCE

If you've never spent a numerical night with a robust alternating series, here's your chance! Compute sin x from

$$\sin x = x - x^3/3! + x^5/5! - \cdots$$

Evaluate each term from its predecessor, summing as you go. Stop when your term shrinks to insignificance. Check your technique with x=0.5 — then go for x=9.5 and x=11. The experience seldom thrills but is very maturing — especially if you are using a calculator with less than 10-digit precision.

Chapter 0

TOOLS OF THE TRADE

"There is always work, and tools to work withal
—for those who will."
Lowell

How does one solve transcendental equations? How do sticky definite integrals get evaluated correctly? These, at first glance, seem to be the principal concerns of this book. But since first glances can deceive, let me quickly say that these topics are also the vehicle for teaching something more important: *how to visualize the shape of a function* and, ultimately, how to use that shape to construct algorithms that process that function accurately and efficiently. Geometry is as important as algebra and calculus here, with constant switching of the viewpoint between them. Does a curve have a minimum? (Where is the slope zero?) Does it have a vertical asymptote? (How rapidly does it go to infinity there?) Are the several roots clustered or are they dependably separated? (How to find good starting approximations?) Is the integrand seriously non-polynomic? (Does it try to go vertically somewhere?) Thruout the book you are urged — nay, implored — to *sketch* the functions and curves to discover their shapes and to quantify their critical behavior. We emphasize the dangerous geometries as well as the dangerous arithmetics: nearly parallel intersections and losses of significant figures.

The tools needed for the book are seldom more than school algebra and a first course in the calculus, altho the way we *use* those tools can at times become rather sophisticated. This chapter summarizes the most important tools. You are probably familiar with much of the material; feel free to browse and skip. When in doubt, do an exercise (without peeking at the answer first) to test your current competence. If you find that you need a bit of practice on the topic, do another exercise or two. Most are short, with reasonably complete answers in the back of the book.

As already stated, sketching functions realistically is crucial for understanding most nonlinear numerical problems. Richard Hamming long ago correctly proclaimed,

> *"The purpose of computing is insight, not numbers."*

He equally well could have added that gaining insight is an *iterative* process. You begin by:

(A) trying to visualize the problem; you get a rough sketch; you evaluate a few points — getting numbers. They are wrong! Or only partially right. [When you think this step gives good data, go to **B**.] Anyway, you have another fact to help you visualize the problem so go to **A**. This loop lies inside a larger iteration:

(B) Having a "correct" sketch (you hope), you choose a tentative algorithm, trying it on a pocket calculator — getting more numbers. They are wrong! Or they are right but the process is inefficient. You refer the algorithm back to your sketch to see why it did *not* work as expected — and find that the sketch is still wrong at some crucial point. (Go to **A**!)

People who omit the sketch from these iterations throw away the most important problem-solving tool they possess — *geometric intuition*. They handicap themselves at the beginning of what is, at best, a difficult process — gaining insight. Thus we urge you *not* to skip the last section of this chapter, A Workshop for Practice in Sketching Functions. And be sure to do a reasonable number of those exercises. The rewards are immense.

Quadratic equations

There is no one method for solving quadratic equations that is universally superior; in this book at least three are used regularly. But here we recommend one technique for algebraic exploration and, usually, for hand evaluations by pocket calculator or even approximate mental arithmetic. The crucial step: Always put the equation into our "standard" form

$$x^2 + 2bx + c = 0 \qquad \text{(note the '2')} \tag{1}$$

by dividing thru by the coefficient of the x^2 term and then cutting the new x-term coefficient in half to get b. This form simplifies the schoolboy formula to

$$x_\pm = -b \pm \sqrt{b^2 - c} \tag{2}$$

with the added feature that the *product* of the two x values is c. With a calculator the button-pushing is simplified and getting rid of one parameter and some factors of 2 and 4 helps a lot with mental arithmetic. The discriminant is easily tested to show whether the roots are real. If, as is usual in this book, b or c contains a parameter, the interesting discriminant questions concern the parameter values that give real or double roots.

   In order to preserve significant figures one should always first evaluate the *larger* (in absolute value) root of (2) numerically *by using the sign that avoids a subtraction*, that is, use $-$ if b is positive and $+$ if it is negative. Then get the smaller root from the relation

$$x_+ \cdot x_- = c. \tag{3}$$

For some algebraic purposes it is useful to write (2) as

$$x_\pm = -b\left[1 \pm \sqrt{1 - c/b^2}\right]$$

but I do not recommend this form for numerical evaluation. (After all, b might be zero.) Also, some people prefer to define (1) as

$x^2 - 2bx + c = 0$, which removes the first minus in (2). It's your choice, but whichever system you choose, stay with it. Factors of 2 and lost minus signs are major causes of wrong answers!

Plotting a "simple quadratic"

Suppose we need a plot, y versus p, of

$$py^2 - 2y + 2 = 0. \tag{4}$$

Any sensible engineer would solve this equation for p, then plug in various values of y and plot the results, one point for each y. Zero for y is awkward but no other problems arise.

Here, however, we are eager to use our quadratic equation solver, so we shall choose various p values and solve (4) for the corresponding y's — only real solution pairs being of interest. Thus we write

$$y^2 - \frac{2}{p}y + \frac{2}{p} = 0 \tag{5}$$

hence

$$y_{\pm} = \frac{1}{p} \pm \sqrt{\frac{1}{p^2} - \frac{2}{p}} = \frac{1}{p}\left[1 \pm \sqrt{1 - 2p}\right] \tag{6}$$

both forms being ultimately useful. We immediately see that if p is negative there are always two real y values, but once p grows beyond

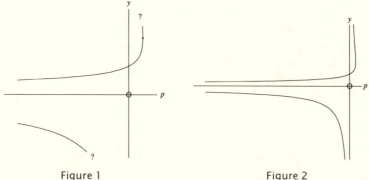

Figure 1   Figure 2

$+1/2$ no real solution exists. *At 1/2 there is a double root, $y = 2$.* At $p = -4$, y is either 1/2 or -1 while at -12, y is 1/3 or $-1/2$. Zero for p is not nice in (6) but (4) shows that $y = 1$ will satisfy our equation there. We can now do a partial sketch (figure 1) that leaves us with some questions. It is clear that as p goes out left toward $-\infty$, both roots approach zero, with the positive y being slightly closer to the p-axis than is the negative y. The questions concern what happens when p is very small. The second form of (6) shows that when p is small the radical shrinks to 1; hence the larger root behaves like $2/p$ — that is, it goes toward $-\infty$ when p is negative and toward $+\infty$ when p is positive — thus allowing us to complete our plot (figure 2). Note that (1) is a *quadratic* equation even when p is zero, so it must have *two* roots whose product is $2/p$ [the constant term in (5)]. One of those roots is 1, so the other must be $2/p$ — a confirmation of our previous results obtained from (6).

The student who finds all this a little strange might now consider getting figure 2 the sensible way — from $p = 2(y-1)/y^2$ — and note that he has to deal with the location of the maximum value, as well as resolve questions about how rapidly p is going to $-\infty$ as y approaches zero from either side.

Exercise

To appreciate why the smaller root should be computed from the larger, solve the extreme quadratic $x^2 - 20000x + 1 = 0$ on a pocket calculator using the quadratic formula (2) for *both* roots.* Then recompute the smaller root from the larger. How many digits agree? [If your calculator only handles 8 digits, change the 20000 to 2000.]

Power series

Most of the common transcendental functions have power series representations that are extremely useful for getting rid of the function when its argument is very small. Thus, $\sin x$ in an awkward place in an equation can frequently be replaced to good effect by x, or perhaps by $x - x^3/6$, provided we don't need too much accuracy and are reasonably sure that x will remain smaller than about 0.1. We have approximated $\sin x$ by one, or two, terms of its power series. There are many more terms, but their usefulness rapidly decreases and becomes disastrous if x gets larger than about 3. Don't *ever* com-

---

*But for such an extreme equation the efficient solution method for the smaller root is the iteration $x \leftarrow (1+x^2)/20000$ — which does not even require square roots! For this root it is really a *linear* equation with a small quadratic fungus.

pute with 100 terms of a power series even if mathematicians quote theorems about its guaranteed convergence! More about that later.

We give here our minimal collection of standard series that one really ought to know.

The exponential trio:

$$e^x = 1 + \frac{x}{1!} + \frac{x^2}{2!} + \frac{x^3}{3!} + \cdots$$

Good for all positive x — but for negative x larger than 3 it loses significant digits thru subtractions.

$$\cos x = 1 - \frac{x^2}{2!} + \frac{x^4}{4!} - \cdots$$

Again, alternating signs produce increasingly worse values for $x > 3$; but who needs it beyond $\pi/4$?

$$\sin x = x - \frac{x^3}{3!} + \frac{x^5}{5!} - \cdots$$

Ditto.

The harmonic duo:

$$\operatorname{atn} x = x - \frac{x^3}{3} + \frac{x^5}{5} - \cdots$$

Inefficient beyond $|x| = 0.5$ — and a disaster at 1. (No factorials to help.)

$$\ln(1 + x) = x - \frac{x^2}{2} + \frac{x^3}{3} - \cdots$$

Ditto — but note that the argument x is a *deviation from unity.* $\ln(0)$ is not nice!

The algebraic twins:

$$\frac{1}{\sqrt{1 + x}} = 1 - \frac{1}{2}x + \frac{1 \cdot 3}{2 \cdot 4}x^2 - \frac{1 \cdot 3 \cdot 5}{2 \cdot 4 \cdot 6}x^3 + \cdots$$

Again, $|x| < 0.5$ is the practical range.

$$\sqrt{1 + x} = 1 - \frac{-1}{2}x + \frac{-1 \cdot 1}{2 \cdot 4}x^2 - \frac{-1 \cdot 1 \cdot 3}{2 \cdot 4 \cdot 6}x^3 + \cdots$$

Same range. Looks terrible but is quite nice, really.

Many other series can be looked up when needed (AMS-55* has an extensive collection) but these are needed often. First terms of series are also useful reminders about how their functions behave near the origin. When sketching the sine curve, that x should stand in our

---

Handbook of Mathematical Functions by Abramowitz and Stegun (National Bureau of Standards, Applied Mathematics Series 55).

mind's eye, making sure that we draw the curve thru the origin with a 45° slope — and not, as so many students do, with a slope of 2 or 3. Series also help resolve most indeterminate expressions more expediently than L'Hospital's rule.

Evaluating a systematic series

Most series evaluations start with the zeroth term, compute the next from it, and keep going — adding each term to the sum as soon as it is available and stopping when the next term is small enough. But if one is evaluating a power series *and if one knows how many terms are needed,* there is a better way: Treat it like a big polynomial and evaluate it "inside-out." As a short example, consider evaluating

$$S = a_0 + a_1 x + a_2 x^2 + a_3 x^3 + a_4 x^4$$

which we parenthesize as

$$S = a_0 + x\{a_1 + x[a_2 + x(a_3 + xa_4)]\}.$$

Then we start with a_4, multiply by x, and add a_3 — continuing in the obvious way. This order and technique take fewer total operations (because one does not evaluate the powers of x explicitly) and the procedure is often slightly less "noisy" with respect to the propagated errors. If the series has factorials in its terms, a minor variant accommodates them efficiently:

$$F = a_0 + a_1 \frac{x}{1!} + a_2 \frac{x^2}{2!} + a_3 \frac{x^3}{3!} + a_4 \frac{x^4}{4!}$$

becomes

$$F = a_0 + \frac{x}{1}\left\{a_1 + \frac{x}{2}\left[a_2 + \frac{x}{3}\left(a_3 + \frac{x}{4}a_4\right)\right]\right\}$$

again via the inside-out approach.

Finally, note that an *alternating* series

$$A = a_0 - a_1 + a_2 - a_3 + a_4$$

can easily be summed, downwards, via the iteration

$$A \leftarrow a_n - A \qquad n = N, N-1, \cdots, 1, 0$$

starting with $A = 0$. (Try it, by hand.) You can even play the same game upwards, altho it is annoying to have to remember to flip the sign of the sum if N was odd. Of course, one can always take the absolute value of the final A if one is sure the result has to be positive.

tan x — the power series

Altho everybody knows that it is the continued fraction for $\tan x$ that is regular and easily generated systematically, the continued fraction is not very useful inside an integral or if we wish to make analytic manipulations. For those purposes (if the ratio of sine over cosine won't do), a power series is better. Unfortunately, the power series for $\tan x$ is not as regular as those for $\sin x$ and $\cos x$ or $\ln(1+x)$, being

$$\tan x = x + \frac{1}{3}x^3 + \frac{2}{15}x^5 + \frac{17}{315}x^7 + \frac{62}{2835}x^9 + \cdots$$

$$\cdots + \frac{(-1)^{n-1}2^{2n}(2^{2n}-1)}{(2n)!}B_{2n}x^{2n-1} \quad (7)$$

to give the usual version (AMS-55). Worse, the Bernoulli numbers, B_{2n}, have no simple rule for generation — so this "general term" is not helpful. In fact, it is downright obscurant! The general term *really* is

$$\frac{4}{\pi} \cdot \left(1 - \frac{1}{2^{2n}}\right)\zeta(2n) \cdot \left(\frac{x}{\pi/2}\right)^{2n-1} = \frac{4}{\pi} \cdot \left(\frac{1}{1^{2n}} + \frac{1}{3^{2n}} + \frac{1}{5^{2n}} + \cdots\right) \cdot z^{2n-1}.$$

But if we rewrite series (7) in terms of the variable $x/(\pi/2) = z$, we can express the series as

$$(\pi/4) \cdot \tan z = a_1 z + a_3 z^3 + a_5 z^5 + \cdots \quad (8)$$

with the table of the a_{2n-1} showing interesting regularities.

	a_{2n-1}	$a_{2n-1} - 1$		
1	1.23370 055014	2.3370 055014E−1	13	2.0924 E−7
3	1.01467 803160	1.4678 031604E−2	15	2.3237 E−8
5	1.00144 707664	1.4470 766409E−3	17	2.5814 E−9
7	1.00015 517903	1.5517 902530E−4	19	2.8681 E−10
9	1.00001 704136	1.7041 363045E−5	21	3.1867 E−11
11	1.00000 188585	1.8858 485831E−6	23	3.5407 E−12

It is clear that if we merely take a_{2n-1} to be unity for $2n-1 > 9$ we will commit an error of less than 1 in the 9th decimal place whenever $z < 0.5$ — and we are not apt to use the series for larger arguments — especially as reciprocal transformations make angles larger than $\pi/4$ accessible in terms of their complements. But if you want greater accuracy, the a_{2n-1} can be approximated quite well by

$$a_{2n-1} \approx 1 + e^{-13.18113} \cdot e^{-2.2(n-6)} \qquad \text{for} \qquad n \geq 6$$

or by

$$1 + e^{-10.97987} \cdot e^{-2.2(n-4)} \qquad \text{for} \qquad n \geq 4.$$

Still, you are probably better off using the ratio of sine over cosine in most applications where analytic manipulations suggest a series approach.

More exponential functions

The functions e^x and e^{-x} have no symmetries. They go thru the y-axis at 1 with a 45° slope and are monotonic, which is about all you can say, there. And as x increases, e^{-x} approaches the positive x-axis.

In problems with a symmetric geometry, it often helps to replace the simple exponentials with the *hyperbolic* functions $\sinh x$, $\cosh x$, and $\tanh x$. The first two are:

$$\cosh x = \frac{1}{2}(e^x + e^{-x}) = 1 + \frac{x^2}{2!} + \frac{x^4}{4!} + \cdots$$

$$\sinh x = \frac{1}{2}(e^x - e^{-x}) = x + \frac{x^3}{3!} + \frac{x^5}{5!} + \cdots$$

and there is a useful Pythagorean relation

$$\cosh^2 x = \sinh^2 x + 1.$$

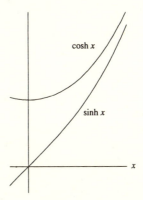

Figure 3

There are many other identities, all similar to the familiar trigonometric ones but with some signs changed. If you need them you really ought to get yourself a copy of AMS-55, the indispensable heavy reference that has everything in it about the common (and not-so-common) functions. As their graphs imply (figure 3) $\cosh x$ and $\sinh x$

have even and odd symmetry, respectively — facts reflected in their series of even and odd powers. Further, these series are simply those of the cosine and sine *without any negative signs* — so obviously they grow large with x, quickly!

The geometry of $\tanh x$ near the origin is best deduced from the first term of its series, x, and from its exponential form when x is big, where it approaches unity from below — hence its curve (figure 4).

As with $\tan x$, the power series for $\tanh x$ is not conveniently systematic. We give enough terms for use with quite small x:

$$\tanh x = \frac{\sinh x}{\cosh x} = \frac{e^x - e^{-x}}{e^x + e^{-x}} = x - \frac{1}{3}x^3 + \frac{2}{15}x^5 - \frac{17}{315}x^7 + \cdots .$$

For systematic manipulations that might need more terms, it is better to replace $\tanh x$ by $\sinh x/\cosh x$ and use their series, which are trivial to program and (unlike the sine and cosine series) do not suffer significant figure loss as x increases — merely a loss of efficiency as you need more and more terms.

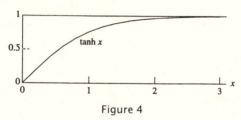

Figure 4

Like their trigonometric cousins, the hyperbolic functions have *inverses* and some of them appear in some programming languages and even show up as buttons on scientific calculators. One needs a bit of caution here, however, because the easy way to implement these inverses is not the accurate way. Consider what you would do if given a value of a $\sinh x$ or a $\cosh x$ and wished to find x. You would probably observe that since $\cosh x + \sinh x = e^x$ then $x = \ln(\cosh x + \sinh x)$, and Pythagoras has allowed you to compute the other hyperbolic function. But be alert for possible significant figure loss in the subtractions *and* in the evaluation of the logarithm when x is small. An example: If $y = \cosh x = 1.01234$ then $x = \ln(1.01234 + \sqrt{(1.01234)^2 - 1})$ and we foresee trouble! (Remember that $\ln(1 + \epsilon)$ should be evaluated from ϵ — which will be noisy because of *two* nasty subtractions.) If we need a precise solution we need to be given the *deviation* of y from *one* and then act to preserve that deviation via an iterative solution that uses the *series* for cosh x — completely avoiding the logarithm and the sinh functions. (We suspect that your calculator and your Fortran inverse hyperbolic functions do *not* do it this way! Check them by computing arccosh(1.012345) to see if they give you the correct single-precision value, 0.1569693. And things get worse as the argument y shrinks toward unity.)

Looking at the inverse problem for $\tanh x$, we see troubles at both ends, tho arguments near unity give the real trouble — the curve being so flat at large x. If we are given ϵ in $1 - \epsilon = \tanh x$, then we have no problem. We note

$$\tanh x = \frac{e^x - e^{-x}}{e^x + e^{-x}} = 1 - \frac{2e^{-x}}{e^x + e^{-x}} = 1 - \epsilon = y$$

hence

$$\epsilon = \frac{2}{e^{2x} + 1} \qquad \text{so} \qquad e^{2x} = \frac{2}{\epsilon} - 1$$

and finally

$$x = \frac{1}{2} \ln\left(\frac{2}{\epsilon} - 1\right).$$

Of course if you only have y you must evaluate

$$x = \frac{1}{2} \ln\left(\frac{1+y}{1-y}\right)$$

with y slightly less than unity — which is noisy because of the unavoidable subtraction.

Delicate numerical expressions

When you evaluate a mathematical expression on a computer, there is usually one value of the variable that requires special treatment. The ratio $\sin x / x$, for example, is a very stable pleasant function on the range $(0, \pi/2)$ that declines slowly from 1 at the origin to about 0.64 at $\pi/2$. You and I know it is 1 at the origin, but the computer does not. So we have to provide special code to tell the computer its value at zero. But if we are going to do our job correctly, we have to provide not only an alternate computation for $\sin x / x$ at zero but *near* zero too. If 0/0 is a complete computational disaster, then (nearly-0)/(nearly-0) is not exactly reassuring. (Remember that computer numbers move in small discrete jumps, so we might not like the results of a small number that just happens to be zero dividing a small number that just happens to be not quite zero!) Fortunately, the cure here is simple: a few terms of the sine series give us

$$\frac{\sin x}{x} = 1 - \frac{x^2}{3!} + \frac{x^4}{5!} - \cdots \tag{9}$$

and we have our alternative computation that is not only stable and completely correct at zero, but also *efficient near zero* since it avoids the evaluation of the transcendental function there. We only have to decide what accuracy we want and choose the number of terms we are going to use. These two facts will fix the largest x value for which we can use this alternate expression. Thus, if we use (9) as written, we neglect $x^6/7!$, so if we want errors smaller than 10^{-7} we must then restrict x to less than about 0.3 since $(0.3)^6/7! = 1.45 \times 10^{-7}$. If 10^{-14} is our error tolerance, then we must limit x to under 0.02 or use more terms of the series.

Most indeterminate forms yield to similar treatment, but sometimes interesting alternatives suggest themselves. Consider, near zero, the expression

$$\frac{1 - \cos x}{x^2} = \frac{1}{2!} - \frac{x^2}{4!} + \frac{x^4}{6!} - \cdots \tag{10}$$

where the cosine series yields this form. A half-angle identity, however, gives

$$\frac{2(\sin(x/2))^2}{x^2} = \frac{1}{2}\left[\frac{\sin(x/2)}{x/2}\right]^2 = \frac{1}{2}\left[1 - \frac{(x/2)^2}{3!} + \frac{(x/2)^4}{5!} - \cdots\right]^2 \tag{11}$$

while Pythagoras urges

$$\frac{1 - \cos^2 x}{x^2(1 + \cos x)} = \frac{(\sin x/x)^2}{1 + \cos x} = \left[1 - \frac{x^2}{3!} + \frac{x^4}{5!} - \cdots\right]^2 \Big/ (1 + \cos x)$$

all capable of serving nicely for smallish, and zero, arguments. Most of us will probably prefer (10) because it is easier to code, but (11) delivers marginally more precision with the same number of terms. Pythagoras, unfortunately, is merely "interesting."

Avoiding dangerous subtractions

Very often, mathematical expressions will lose significant digits at some value of x by subtracting nearly equal subexpressions. If accurate answers are needed, then you must provide alternate evaluations at least for the region of the difficulty. (The numerator $1 - \cos x$ of the previous section is an example. All three of the alternatives got rid of that subtraction — altho that was not the primary objective there.) Now let us consider

$$\sqrt{1 + x} - \sqrt{1 - x}$$

when x is small. We would probably multiply above and below by the sum of the radicals to produce

$$\frac{1 + x - 1 + x}{\sqrt{1 + x} + \sqrt{1 - x}} = \frac{2x}{\sqrt{1 + x} + \sqrt{1 - x}}$$

altho two applications of our series for $\sqrt{1 + x}$ gives

$$1 + \frac{1}{2}x - \frac{1}{2 \cdot 4}x^2 + \frac{1 \cdot 3}{2 \cdot 4 \cdot 6}x^3 - \cdots - 1 + \frac{1}{2}x + \frac{1}{2 \cdot 4}x^2 + \frac{1 \cdot 3}{2 \cdot 4 \cdot 6}x^3 + \cdots$$

$$= x + \frac{2 \cdot 1 \cdot 3}{2 \cdot 4 \cdot 6}x^3 + \frac{2 \cdot 1 \cdot 3 \cdot 5 \cdot 7}{2 \cdot 4 \cdot 6 \cdot 8 \cdot 10}x^5 + \cdots$$

which is systematic and avoids two square roots. It also reveals that our expression is slightly *larger* than x — a fact not obvious from the first treatment.

A similar expression

$$\sqrt{x + 1} - \sqrt{x}$$

has significant figure problems when x is big and the cure is similar — get rid of the square roots so that the subtraction can be performed algebraically instead of numerically. Thus

$$(\sqrt{x + 1} - \sqrt{x}) \cdot \left(\frac{\sqrt{x + 1} + \sqrt{x}}{\sqrt{x + 1} + \sqrt{x}} \right) = \frac{1}{\sqrt{x + 1} + \sqrt{x}}$$

which is well-behaved for *all* positive values of x.

We treat more of these dangerous expressions later in this chapter and still more in chapter 2. But the reader might well try a few examples here.

Exercises

(Answers or hints for most of the *numbered* exercises are in the back of the book.)

1. How would you evaluate

$$\ln \sqrt{x+1} - \ln \sqrt{x}$$

for large x without losing significant figures? Compare your method with direct evaluation on a 6-digit calculator for $x = 1088.03$.

2. Find the behavior of

$$\ln \left[\frac{\sqrt{1+x^2} - x}{\sqrt{1+x^2} + x} \right]$$

a) for large x
b) for x near zero

and then suggest how the function should be evaluated.

3. Try evaluating

$$\frac{1 - \sin x}{\pi/2 - x} \quad \text{near} \quad x = \pi/2$$

and

$$\frac{\cosh x}{2 - \cos x} \quad \text{near} \quad x = 0$$

— accurately!

4. What are the limiting behaviors of

$$\frac{\sin x}{1 - \cos x} \quad \text{and} \quad \frac{\sinh x}{\cosh x - 1}$$

as x approaches zero (from each side).

5. Evaluate
$$w(x) = 1 + 0.5 \tanh(x^2) - \cosh x$$

for $x = 0.1$ (a) as expressed here; (b) from a series expansion. Keep all arithmetic to 10 decimals. Where and how does the error arise?

6. Now try

$$v(x) = 1 + 2\left(\tanh \frac{x}{2}\right)^2 - \cosh x$$

for $x = 0.1$ (a) as expressed here; (b) from a series expansion; and (c) from an exact expression that involves no damaging subtractions. (This last expression will require the application of several identities.)

7. Try

$$1 - \cos x - (\tan x)^2 / 2.$$

Altho this expression can be handled by brute force (series expansions of everything after tangents are re-expressed in sines and cosines), it is much more elegant if you can use a few identities to reduce the problem to a product of well-behaved factors and *one* further factor, $\cos(x/2) - 1$, that yields to series nicely.

8. This one requires force:

$$1 - \cos x - \frac{1}{2} \tan(x^2).$$

9. Show that when x is small compared to b

$$b - \sqrt{b^2 - x^2}$$

can be represented by either

$$\frac{b \cdot g}{1 + \sqrt{1 - g}} \qquad \text{or} \qquad \frac{bg}{2}\left[1 + \frac{g}{4} + \frac{g^2}{8} + \frac{5g^3}{64} + \cdots\right]$$

where $g = (x/b)^2$.

"Significant" digits — and the loss thereof

Life would be simpler if we could avoid the term "significant digits." Too much has been written in attempts to define precisely what is often only a simple intuitive concept. Indeed, the *useful* idea is "loss of significant digits." But if you can lose them, they once must have existed; hence the semantic quagmire around which we are gingerly treading. Fortunately the important concept is easy to demonstrate: in the subtraction $1.23456 - 1.23444 = 0.00012$ we say that we have lost four significant digits.

> *A subtraction of two nearly equal quantities*
> *loses significant digits.*

Significant digits (or significant figures, if you prefer) are lost off the *front (left) end* of a number and are usually lost *suddenly* in a single subtraction. (Loss of precision, in contrast, is erosion by repeated rounding errors. It sneaks slowly in from the *right* end — the least significant digits being eroded away first.) There are more complicated ways to lose significant digits — by summing the terms of a series with alternating signs, for example — but they all involve *subtractions*. Multiplications and divisions with REAL numbers do not lose significant digits.

Altho a process can lose significant digits, it is less clear *how many* significant digits one has in any given number. An abstract decimal number stored by Fortran as REAL holds the binary equivalent of approximately seven decimal digits in its mantissa. Similarly, on a piece of paper 0.999986 is a six-digit number but it is dangerous to say that all six digits are significant because nobody has specified what these digits are to be used for. One needs to ask, "Significant for what?" — or better yet, avoid the term. It's just a six-digit number. But the next section shows that any attempt to solve $\cos x = 0.999986$ on a six-digit pocket calculator will lose four of those digits in a subtraction — leaving the quite nervous value 0.000014 with which it must determine x. Said x will thus be known accurately to only two figures, even tho our calculator will say, perhaps, 0.00529151. So, does 0.00529151 have six significant figures — or two? Don't ask! Just throw those trash figures away quickly and say your answer is $x = 0.0053$. You don't have to dignify the garbage digits by the term insignificant.

An ill-conditioned problem

Look at the two pictures in figure 5, both of which show a horizontal line intersecting with the first quadrant part of the cosine curve, and consider for a moment how well their points of intersection are determined. And just to be clear about it: we are asking a *geometrical*

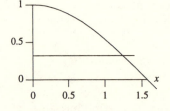 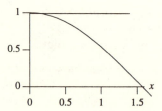

Figure 5

question about how much the *points move* if we shift the horizontal
lines up a little (say, one millimeter). Clearly, the point in the right-
hand picture moves a lot more than the one in the left picture. Of
course we all know from our calculus how to evaluate the slope of
the cosine curve — but our concern here is the geometric one: the
point in the right-hand picture is not nearly as *well determined* by our
knowledge of the position of the line because the two curves are
nearly parallel where they intersect. The problem on the right is
geometrically ill-conditioned — and we see it instantly when we look
at the picture. As always, a geometric artifact has its algebraic and
computational counterparts. We are asking how well x is determined
in the equation

$$\cos x = b \qquad (12)$$

when we are given b-values of 0.321098 (on the left) or 0.987654
(on the right). Of course if we are given our b's to more than six
figures, our x's will be more precisely fixed — but that is not the
question. Here we only have six-figure b's; the next bigger values
of b our six-figure pocket calculator can recognize are 0.321099 and
0.987655, respectively. If we solve for x for all four b's we get the
data of table 1 and we now have quantitative confirmation of our
geometric observation. A move of one unit in the least significant
figure of b causes a move of about one unit in x in the left problem
but produces a change of six units in the less well-posed problem on

b	x	b	x
0.321098	1.243908	0.987654	0.157299
0.321099	1.243907	0.987655	0.157293
−0.000001	0.000001	−0.000001	0.000006

Table 1

the right. (Try this experiment on your own pocket calculator — being sure first to find out, experimentally, just how close two numbers
can be before your calculator thinks they are identical. Usually this is
1 in the last digit shown in the display *after you add zero* to something
like 1.23456789123.)

For these b's and x's we are probably not too concerned by the
imprecision we find, but clearly the problem grows worse as b approaches unity. Consider the values in table 2.

b	x	x
0.999985	.005477 23	.005477
0.999986	.005291 51	.005292
−0.000001	.000185 72	.000185

Table 2

We see that here our x changes by 185 in units of the sixth decimal place when b changes by only 1. Thus six correct figures in b are not adequate to produce six correct figures in x — indeed they produce only *two*. To put it differently: if we only know that b lies between 0.999985 and 0.999986, then we only know that x lies between .00548 and .00529. *And there is nothing we can do about it* unless we are given more precise values for b.

A slightly different (but a much better-conditioned) problem

Suppose that we still can handle only six-digit quantities but that our problem is to find x from

$$\cos x = 1 - \epsilon \quad \text{with} \quad \epsilon = .0000142345 \qquad (12a)$$

If we rashly subtract our ϵ from 1, we are immediately back to our ill-conditioned equation (12)

$$\cos x = 0.999986$$

hence x is .00529151 on a good floating-point six-figure calculator (and only .005292 on a fixed-point clunker).

But suppose we rephrase our problem so as to preserve the ϵ but *get rid of the 1!* A straightforward way is to replace $\cos x$ by the first few terms of its power series, whence

$$1 - \frac{x^2}{2!} + \frac{x^4}{4!} - \frac{x^6}{6!} + \cdots = 1 - \epsilon$$

and the 1's disappear — leaving an equation in x^2

$$x^2 \left(\frac{1}{2} - \frac{x^2}{24} + \frac{x^4}{720} - \cdots \right) = \epsilon \qquad (13)$$

that equates the *small* quantities ϵ and (more-or-less) $x^2/2$ instead of the original form (12) that equates (almost-1) with (almost-1). Equation (13) is easily solved iteratively for x^2 from

$$x^2 \leftarrow \frac{\epsilon}{1/2 - x^2/24 + x^4/720}, \qquad \text{starting with} \qquad x^2 = 0, \qquad (14)$$

to give

$$x^2 = 2.84691(10^{-5}) \quad \text{hence} \quad x = .00533564.$$

These 6-digit answers to equation (14) and hence (12a) were obtained on a 6-digit calculator and *all 6 digits of x are correct!* The x^4 term in the denominator is not even needed as it is of order 10^{-12} and is added to 1/2.

Note that it is the *deviation of b from unity* that really determines x accurately and that in this problem that discrepancy, ϵ, was given to six-figure accuracy. Our task was to preserve that accuracy by using ϵ in an equation that equated only similarly-sized small quantities. In solving equation (14) we have no need for an extended-precision calculator; a six-digit machine will handle all the precision we have. (A fancier ten- or twelve-digit calculator will produce more *digits* in its x answer but not a more *precise* x — since ϵ is given only to six figures.)

Significant figure loss in function evaluations

Altho most arithmetic expressions evaluate accurately and efficiently on a digital computer, some do not. Consider the expression $(1 - x^2)/(1 - x)$ for x values close to 1. The subtractions will cause small losses of significant figures, while the subsequent division will produce a rather "noisy" result. Of course the whole problem can be avoided simply by reducing the expression algebraically to $(1 + x)$ — and should be. When trigonometric functions appear in the expressions, however, inaccurate arithmetic becomes more common and requires constant vigilance lest one lose too much information. Again, the cure is analytic manipulation via trig identities or expansion in series.

The expression

$$1 + \frac{1}{2}\tanh(x^2) - \cosh x \qquad (15)$$

clearly goes to zero with x and there seems little that can go wrong. If, however, you evaluate it for $x = 0.1$ on a pocket calculator as it stands (try it!) you will probably not get the correct answer, $-4.3347222\mathrm{E}{-6}$,* to anything like the number of digits that your calculator claims to keep. The difficulty is a tremendous loss of significant figures in the subtraction, where two numbers slightly greater than 1 manage to produce a difference that is about 0.0000043. Six figures is a lot to lose on a twelve-digit machine like the HP-28S — and it is an absolute disaster on a seven-figure device (like the IBM-370 systems)! Worse, most computers give no warning that anything is amiss. They happily shift the digits that survive to the left, adjust the exponent, and proceed to use this somewhat shaky result in subsequent calculations. Unless you specifically test for the loss, you probably will never discover it. Of course a hand calculation with tables reveals the problem immediately — but who does those willingly today? The student should verify that (15) has a series expansion beginning

$$-x^4/24 - (1/6 + 1/720)x^6 + O(x^8).$$

Sometimes you can get a closed form that avoids the subtraction, thereby permitting precise evaluation without resort to series — altho series may actually be more efficient. Thus

$$1 + 2(\tanh \frac{x}{2})^2 - \cosh x$$

is mathematically identical to

$$-2\frac{(\sinh \frac{x}{2})^4}{1 + (\sinh \frac{x}{2})^2}$$

but at $x = 0.1$ finite arithmetic precision will give them rather different values.

Exercise

10. Try evaluating the following expressions for $x = 0.1$ both as they stand and after rearranging or expanding to eliminate subtractions.

a) $1 + \frac{1}{2}(\tanh x)^2 - \cosh x$
b) $1 + \tanh \frac{x^2}{2} - \cosh x$
c) $\tanh x - \arctan x$

*Henceforth we usually will use this representation for $-4.3347222 \times 10^{-6}$.

Preserving small quantities

Most people evaluating $\sin x$ for x near $\pi/2$ are aware that $\cos(\pi/2-x)$ is more efficient because the argument for the cosine series will be small, but they are not apt to worry about the potential loss of significance inherent in either calculation. After all, one loses either in the explicit subtraction in the argument for the cosine or in the same subtraction performed by the sine function inside the software package (most of the standard sine-cosine routines reduce the argument) — so it's a no-win situation that seems not very important anyway unless x is *very* close to $\pi/2$. If one cannot prevent the loss, why worry?

But these losses frequently *can* be prevented. Examination of physical problems in which trig functions arise shows that many arguments close to $\pi/2$ actually arise originally as *deviations* from $\pi/2$. Thus they are, or can be, originally available as small numbers, say 0.00068522679 on an eight-figure machine rather than as the less useful argument 1.5701111 that on subtraction from $\pi/2$ becomes 0.0006852x, where "x" is a mysterious digit produced by the rounding properties of the machine. Thus the proper way to keep full machine accuracy is to *preserve the original small arguments,* reformulating the problem so that you give names to (and hence store) the small quantities that are needed. Accurate large arguments can always be produced by adding small numbers, but accurate small numbers cannot be got by subtracting large, nearly equal big numbers. Hence our second mantra:

Store small variables!

The sensitive-argument principle should be applied whenever trig functions occur in transcendental equations that are being solved. If, for example, one is given a small quantity ϵ with a need to solve

$$\epsilon = 1 - \sin x \tag{16}$$

it is clear that x is going to be slightly less than $\pi/2$ (if a first-quadrant root is wanted). Get rid of the dangerous subtraction by letting $x = \pi/2 - u$ then rewriting (16) as

$$\cos u = 1 - \epsilon \tag{17}$$

which was solved previously. [See (12a) and (14), replacing the symbol x with u there.]

If iterations offend, one can rewrite (17) as

$$\sin u = \sqrt{1 - (1 - \epsilon)^2} = \sqrt{2\epsilon - \epsilon^2}$$

or

$$\tan u = \frac{\sqrt{2\epsilon - \epsilon^2}}{1 - \epsilon}$$

and invoke either the arctangent or the arcsine function with a reasonably small argument.

Exercise

11. How does one avoid significant figure loss in solving:

a) $\tan x = 485.32$
b) $x \cdot \cot x = 1 - \epsilon$, ϵ small?

An ill-posed problem

Many problems contain forms that behave badly for at least some values of the variable. The equation

$$\frac{\arctan x}{\tanh x} = b \qquad 1 \le b < \pi/2 \tag{18}$$

has a unique solution for every value of b on the range $(1, \pi/2)$ but near both limits the value of x is quite poorly determined. (Draw the graphs of arctan x and tanh x — then you should see why we have a problem.) For b near 1 the equation should be rearranged to permit the explicit subtraction of the two functions and the equating of the difference to the *small deviation* of b from unity. Letting $b = 1 + \beta$ we write

$$\arctan x = (1 + \beta) \tanh x \qquad \text{hence} \qquad \arctan x - \tanh x = \beta \tanh x.$$

For expanding in series, sinh x and cosh x are better than tanh x, so we substitute, getting

$$\arctan x \cdot \cosh x - \sinh x = \beta \cdot \sinh x$$

then

$$\left(x - \frac{x^3}{3} + \frac{x^5}{5} - \cdots \right)\left(1 + \frac{x^2}{2!} + \frac{x^4}{4!} + \cdots \right) - \left(x + \frac{x^3}{3!} + \frac{x^5}{5!} + \cdots \right) = \beta \sinh x$$

so

$$\frac{x^4}{3(5)} - \frac{x^6}{3(6)} + \frac{x^8}{3(7.0064)}^\dagger - \frac{x^{10}}{3(8.113)} + \cdots = \beta \frac{\sinh x}{x}$$

† It is dangerous to predict the general term of a series merely from the first two terms!

which can best be solved iteratively (for small x^2) as

$$x^4 \leftarrow \frac{3\beta\left(1 + \dfrac{x^2}{3!} + \dfrac{x^4}{5!} + \cdots\right)}{\dfrac{1}{5} - \dfrac{x^2}{6} + \dfrac{x^4}{7.0064} - \dfrac{x^6}{8.113} + \cdots}$$

using the obvious starting value of $x^2 = \sqrt{15\beta}$.

For large x both $\tanh x$ and $\arctan x$ become asymptotically constant, so the deviations from their asymptotic values are the sensitive quantities. And, as for small x, it is the deviation of b from its limiting value that is crucial. If we express $\arctan x$ as $\pi/2 - \arctan(1/x)$ we get the small complementary angle expressed in terms of the small argument $1/x$. The hyperbolic tangent in its exponential form is easily rewritten to give

$$\tanh x = \frac{e^x - e^{-x}}{e^x + e^{-x}} = \frac{1 - e^{-2x}}{1 + e^{-2x}} = 1 - \frac{2e^{-2x}}{1 + e^{-2x}}$$

so we see that the deviation from unity is a small exponential. Letting

$$b = \pi/2 - \gamma$$

equation (18) becomes

$$\pi/2 - \arctan\frac{1}{x} = \left(\pi/2 - \gamma\right)\left(1 - \frac{2e^{-2x}}{1 + e^{-2x}}\right).$$

Replacing $1/x$ by u in the arctangent (but not in the exponentials) we have

$$\arctan u = \gamma + 2be^{-2x}/(1 + e^{-2x})$$

and finally

$$u = \frac{\gamma + 2be^{-2x}/(1 + e^{-2x})}{\arctan u/u} = \frac{\gamma + 2be^{-2x}/(1 + e^{-2x})}{1 - u^2/3 + u^4/5 - \cdots}$$

where the second form is preferable when $1/x = u$ is very small. This iteration is both precise and rapidly convergent, the result containing as many significant figures as are available in γ — which clearly is the quantity that should be generated and stored (rather than b) if at all possible. The starting value is $1/x = \gamma$. Chapter 2 gives more sophisticated examples of simplifying expressions to avoid deleterious subtractions.

Exercise

12. Find the leading terms of the behavior for small x of:

a) $\sinh x - \tan x = b$
b) $\sinh x / \tan x = b$
c) $\text{arcsinh } x / \arctan x = b$
d) $1 + \arctan x - \tanh x = b$
e) $\tanh x / \arctan x = b$
f) $e^{-x^2} - (\cos x)^2 = b$

Partial fractions — Friend or Foe?

The technique of partial fractions is usually learned in a calculus course, where it separates an integrand that is a ratio of two polynomials into the sum of integrands with simpler denominators — often permitting analytic integration of the several parts, separately. In that use it is a classical divide-and-conquer tool. We have more to say about partial fractions when we discuss quadratures in chapter 3, but here we would warn against their uncritical use *numerically*.

Consider the standard example

$$\frac{1}{(x+a)(x+b)} = \left(\frac{1}{x+a} - \frac{1}{x+b}\right)\bigg/(b-a) \qquad (19)$$

which is so simple that the formal machinery of partial fractions can be ignored. Just write the two simpler fractions, put them (mentally) back over their common denominator, and immediately discover that we need to divide by $(b-a)$ to give the original expression. Thus, we have separated a single fraction with a *quadratic* denominator into the sum of two fractions with *linear* denominators. A great improvement! ...Or is it?

Clearly no judgements can be offered in a vacuum. What were we trying to do with that quadratic expression? Let us suppose that x, a and b are all positive quantities with x being variable, a and b fixed at 2 and 4 — and we are interested in the behavior of our expression as x is varied. Now the separation into two fractions is suddenly less attractive; the original expression is easier to evaluate numerically and to plot.

Looking more carefully at (19) we realize that we have separated a moderately *small* quadratic fraction into the *difference* of two fractions, each of which is *larger* than the original. We have created a potential loss of significant figures by asking for the subtraction of nearly equal quantities. Potentially dangerous, but surely not always bad. Still, going from a clean expression with *no subtractions* on the left to *two* on the right cannot reassure the man who computes. He sniffs danger in the air.

Specializing a bit further: suppose a and b are *nearly equal.* Suddenly the right-hand world falls apart as we approach the indeterminacy of 0/0. Numerically, both small quantities become imprecise, being differences of larger numbers that are nearly equal. This is the route to numerical suicide and we can only say, STOP! GO BACK! You didn't know when you were well-off! (But there is an often useful expansion of the quadratic fraction that we discuss next.)

A less well-known but more informative rearrangement

When a and b are nearly equal, we can usefully indulge in some algebraic acrobatics by playing with their sum and difference as fundamental parameters. But to make clear our maneuvers we retain the original parameters for a while, even tho it complicates the typography. Noting the identities

$$\frac{a+b}{2} + \frac{a-b}{2} = a$$

$$\frac{a+b}{2} - \frac{a-b}{2} = b$$

we then write

$$(x+a)(x+b) = \left[\left(x+\frac{a+b}{2}\right) + \left(\frac{a-b}{2}\right)\right] \cdot \left[\left(x+\frac{a+b}{2}\right) - \left(\frac{a-b}{2}\right)\right]$$

$$= \left(x+\frac{a+b}{2}\right)^2 - \left(\frac{a-b}{2}\right)^2.$$

Now, letting

$$s = \frac{a+b}{2} \quad \text{and} \quad d = \frac{a-b}{2},$$

we can write

$$\frac{1}{(x+a)(x+b)} = \frac{1}{(x+s)^2 - d^2}.$$

Factoring out the first term, we get

$$\frac{1}{(x+a)(x+b)} = \frac{1}{(x+s)^2\left[1 - \left(\dfrac{d}{x+s}\right)^2\right]}$$

$$= \frac{1}{(x+s)^2}\left[1 + \left(\frac{d}{x+s}\right)^2 + \left(\frac{d}{x+s}\right)^4 + \cdots\right]$$

(20)

where the series is useful when d is small, that is, when a is nearly equal to b. Thus the original fraction is the reciprocal of the parabola $(x+s)^2$, with the magnification factor $[1 - d^2/(x+s)^2]^{-1}$ that is almost ignorable when d is small.

If our purpose is *analytic simplification*, either of the forms in (20) will retain more of the geometric character of the original fraction than does the partial fraction representation — nor do they introduce dangerous tendencies toward indeterminacy. Indeed they are solidly exact when a equals b.

If *approximation* is our need, then these forms again often serve well. Suppose both a and b lie on the range $(2, 2.4)$ and are often nearly identical. Suppose further that x varies over the entire range of $(0,1)$. In the worst case, where $a = 2$, $b = 2.4$, we can fix the x inside the brackets at 0.5 to produce

$$\frac{1}{(x+2.0)(x+2.4)} \approx \frac{1}{(x+2.2)^2[1 - 0.04/(2.7)^2]} = \frac{1.00552}{(x+2.2)^2} \quad (21)$$

which is never farther from the original function than 0.0006 and on average is within 0.0002.

Alternatively, the truncated *series* (in which x is kept as a variable everywhere)

$$\frac{1}{(x+2.2)^2}\left[1 + \left(\frac{0.2}{x+2.2}\right)^2 + \left(\frac{0.2}{x+2.2}\right)^4\right]$$

is in error by approximately $(0.2/(x+2.2))^6$, that is, -1.2×10^{-7} when x is zero and -5.8×10^{-9} when x is unity.

"But why approximate such a simple expression *at all?*" I hear you cry! Most of the answers lie buried in tomes on theoretical physics and hydrodynamics — where this simple piece of algebra turns up under impressive-sounding names. But here we give a partial answer by integrating both parts of (21) to get

$$\int_0^t \frac{dx}{(x+2.0)(x+2.4)} \quad \text{and} \quad 1.00552 \int_0^t \frac{dx}{(x+2.2)^2}$$

hence

$$\frac{1}{0.4}[\ln(1 + t/2) - \ln(1 + t/2.4)] = \frac{1}{0.4}\ln\left[\frac{1 + t/2}{1 + t/2.4}\right]$$

and

$$\frac{1.00552t}{2.2(t + 2.2)}.$$

If this integral occurs inside a larger scientific formula so that further *analytic* manipulation is needed, the approximate form is apt to be more convenient — while for repeated *numerical* evaluations it is much more efficient, having no logarithm. Nor is it teetering on the brink of indeterminacy. [Evaluate the approximation and the analytic closed form on a pocket calculator for several t on $(0, 1)$ to find out how many significant figures get lost. Then repeat with $a = 2$ but $b = 2.04$.]

How to solve a cubic

An algorithm to find the real roots of a cubic is a useful tool. There are many; you may already have one. But in this section we construct one anyway, partly to illustrate the type of geometric-algebraic analysis we favor and partly because we feel that everyone should have a cubic-solver that they understand.

Every generation in this century, it seems, has developed a cubic-solver — or at least espoused one that was proclaimed to be superior to its predecessors. These superiorities, when real, came from a change in the arithmetic tools available: mechanical desk calculators supplanted mental arithmetic and tables of square roots (1930); mechanical square roots were added (1949); and now electronic computers make *iterative* calculation not only efficient but psychologically acceptable. (A person using pencil and paper and multiplying numbers in his head prefers a finite algorithm — the finiter the better! Iteration, even if actually shorter, had two strikes against it in the nineteenth century.)

So, since we can now all iterate happily, our cubic algorithm will be Newton's method. The only problems are the starting values, which need to be "reasonably close." The rest of this section is devoted to the starting value problem. Oh yes — and whether our cubic has one or three real roots. That's important too!

First we reduce the cubic to *our* standard form (note the sign of b and the position of c)

$$x^3 - bx = c \tag{22}$$

by:

1. *Normalizing* the coefficient of the cubic term to 1* by dividing thru by it so that the cubic now reads

$$u^3 + a_2 u^2 + a_1 u + a_0 = 0. \tag{23}$$

2. Then *shifting* the curve horizontally by $a_2/3$ either by repeated synthetic division or by using the equivalent formulæ

$$b = a_2^2/3 - a_1 \qquad \text{and} \qquad c = \frac{a_2}{3}\left(a_1 - \frac{2}{9}a_2^2\right) - a_0, \tag{24}$$

which eliminates the quadratic term.

Of course we must save the shift, $a_2/3$, because any x-roots of (22) must have this quantity subtracted from them to give the u-roots of (23) that are also the roots of our original cubic. Indeed, it is our *starting value* that we should translate, then execute Newton's iteration on the original equation — thereby avoiding any imprecision that might have been introduced by the reduction to (22).

The plot of the left side of (22),

$$x^3 - bx = x(x^2 - b), \tag{25}$$

is nearly trivial. We show its two forms in figures 6p and 6n in which b is *positive* and *negative*, respectively. If you have momentary doubts about which sign of b is associated with which geometry, reflect that the *slopes* of (25) are given by

$$3x^2 - b$$

and hence at the origin the slope is $-b$. Temporarily leaving aside the geometrically dull figure 6n, we note that the three x-intercepts and the two extrema are all simple functions of b, as shown in figure 6p.

---

*But see the final paragraph of this section.

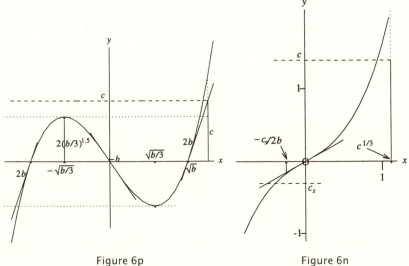

Figure 6p   Figure 6n

Also available are the *slopes* of our curve at each of the three inter-cepts. These five numbers not only let us sketch the curve quickly and accurately — they will also enable us to get reasonable first approximations for the roots of (22) when we put c in the picture.

From figure 6p we see that if c lies between $\pm 2(b/3)^{1.5}$ our cubic has three real roots, otherwise only one. (And in figure 6n only one real root regardless of c.) For the three-root geometry it is also clear (figure 6p) that reasonable first approximations can be got by extending the three tangents at the three intercepts to the horizontal line at c. From each of those abscissae Newton can "see" only one root; hence convergence is guaranteed. The only danger is that of a double root — again an obvious geometry that will have been tested while deciding whether we have one or three roots. We give most of a flow diagram.

Turning to the one-root geometries, we see that when $|c|$ is "large" then $c^{1/3}$ is apt to be a good first approximation since the term bx will be less important than x^3 in (22). When c is "small" a better approximation is about half the intercept of the line tangent at the origin, $-c/(2b)$. A reasonable definition of "small" here is when $c^2 < |b|^3$. Our flow diagram bears all these starting values with the term "*near*" implying a call to Newton's method with the given function of b and c as the first approximation. [Of course for a totally mindless algorithm the front end should be elaborated to make sure that one

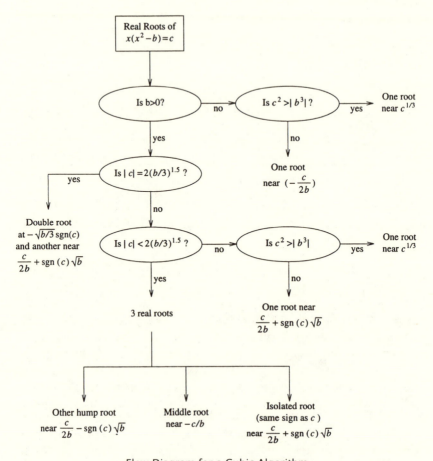

Flow Diagram for a Cubic Algorithm

actually has a cubic — not merely a linear or quadratic equation that happens to have a very small cubic perturbing term. Thus

$$0.001x^3 - 2x = 4$$

is, if it arises from a physical problem, almost certainly *not* a cubic. It has one interesting root near -2 that is best found by iterating

$$x \leftarrow -2 + 0.0005x^3.$$

This is a problem that should never be turned over to a cubic algorithm for solution. (The other "roots" are 45.7 and -43.7.)]

A WORKSHOP FOR PRACTICE IN
SKETCHING FUNCTIONS

Since most school mathematics programs give little practice in visualizing the shapes of any but the most elementary functions, here is a short set of worked examples. Few of them are trivial, but they require only persistent application of school mathematics. Each is followed by similar problems that you are strongly urged to do for yourself *before* consulting the sometimes extensive answers that lie at the end of *this* chapter. The few Mystery Problems, for which no answers are provided, are so noted — allowing the faint-of-heart to avoid them.

How to sketch functions

Most engineers tend to think pictorially — they look at an equation and say, "What is the *shape* of the curve it defines? What does it *look* like?" But many other people look at an equation and think, "How can I *solve* this equation? How can I transform it into an analytical solution? What substitutions can I make?" — without a geometric picture entering their minds.

The picture-seekers are far ahead when it comes to the process of solving real numerical problems. They will see the trouble spots that must be addressed; they will see the one or two profitable strategies for solution displayed via a sketch. The symbol-manipulators, on the other hand, being faced with many opportunities for variable substitutions and series expansions, will tend to bog down in largely unmotivated symbolic thrashing that sometimes hits upon an effective algorithm but more often ends in frustration and dropped factors of 2. (Minus signs and factors of 2 are the principal culprits to be suspected in computer programs that "run OK, but the numbers seem wrong." A picture will usually challenge a wrong sign; a *good* picture will often catch a factor of 2.)

Having exhorted you to sketch your equation (and, later, your integrand) it is only fair to entertain the question, "How?" Of course there is no universal answer, nor even a fairly satisfactory one. But one must at least try. The major strategies are:

1. *Divide and conquer.* If the equation contains two distinct parts that are equated — or can be pushed into such a state — then draw the two parts on the same graph. Thus $x \cdot \sin x = 0.987654$ is easily recast into $\sin x = 0.987654/x$, permitting the sine curve and the hyperbola to be plotted without much effort. (x_t in figure 7 marks where both curves have the same slope.) But if a sketch is to be helpful, it is important that it be reasonably accurate. Unfortunately many student

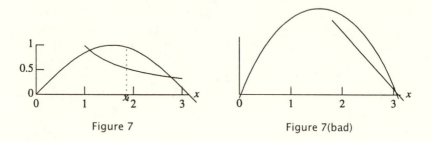

Figure 7   Figure 7(bad)

"sketches" of the sine curve look more like figure 7(bad). Everybody locates the sine and cosine *intercepts* correctly, but they forget that these curves cross the axis at 45° and that the height of the arch, being unity, should only be about one-third of the span. If the line in figure 7(bad) is supposed to be $y = 3.1 - x$, the viewer will see that the curves probably intersect near π but will miss the fact that they are *parallel* there — a property crucial in designing an efficient root-finding algorithm.

If an equation contains a single transcendental function, it is wise to try isolating that function on one side of the equation — a strategy employed with the previous example. The equation

$$\frac{1 - \cos x}{x^2} = 1 - x$$

is easily rewritten as

$$\cos x = 1 - x^2 + x^3 \tag{26}$$

then plotted (figure 8).

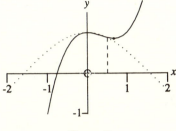

Figure 8

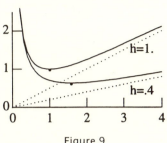

Figure 9

2. *Plot polynomials from their critical points.* Our cubic in (26) clearly cuts the y-axis at 1 and passes thru $(1,1)$ and $(-1,-1)$. It also has zero slope at $x = 0$ and again at $3x = 2$, where it is roughly 0.85, then heads off to infinity in the northeast and southwest directions almost as soon as it can. This is enough information to produce a quite accurate sketch with minimal trouble. Of course if you have one of the fancier pocket calculators that plot these things for you, take advantage of it. (But it might take you longer if you don't use it often and forget the precise instructions. Still, somebody else's correct picture is better than your own wrong one.)

3. *Plot algebraics from their asymptotes, minima, and zeros.* Consider

$$y = \frac{1 + hx^2}{2x} = \frac{1}{2x} + \frac{hx}{2}$$

where we see from the second form that it is almost $hx/2$ for large x with the $1/2x$ term adding a steadily smaller quantity as x increases. For small x, however, the first term dominates and takes the curve off to infinity at the origin. Clearly there must be a minimum that is easily found from $1/x^2 = h$ to lie at $(1/\sqrt{h}, \sqrt{h})$. Figure 9 shows the first quadrant part of the curve for two different values of h. (Since our function has odd symmetry, the part in the third quadrant presents no new geometry — only a reversal of signs in both x and y.)

An extravagant example

The system of equations

$$\left.\begin{array}{l} 4x - 3y + kx\cos y = 7 \\ 2x + 6y - ky\sin x = -2 \end{array}\right\} \quad \text{for various } k$$

shows the futility of seeking a universal solution method. If we rewrite the equations so as to separate the variables, we get

$$x = \frac{7 + 3y}{k \cos y + 4} \quad \text{and} \quad y = \frac{2 + 2x}{k \sin x - 6}. \qquad \text{(27) (28)}$$

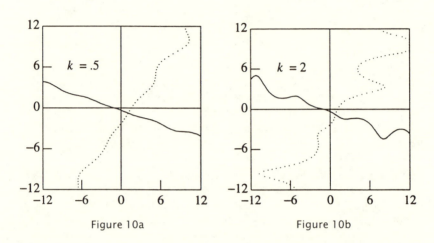

Figure 10a   Figure 10b

Qualitatively, for small k these are nearly straight lines. [When k is zero this is exactly true, with an intersection at $(6/5, -11/15)$.] As long as the denominator cannot become zero, the oscillations of the trigonometric terms only make these two lines wiggle locally — seen from afar they are still straight lines. (See figures 10a and 10b, where $k = .5$ and $k = 2$.)

But once k grows large enough to produce periodic zeros in a denominator, we get asymptotes and hence multiply branched curves — with multiple solutions nearly inevitable. Equation (27) develops asymptotes when $k = 4$, while equation (28) waits until $k = 6$. We look at $k = 5$ as an interesting compromise. Equations with asymptotes are always easy to sketch, so we begin with (27). The denominator goes to zero whenever $\cos y = -4/5$, that is, at $y \approx \pm 2.5, \pm 3.78$ and at intervals of 2π from each of these four values. Curve (27) crosses the axes at obvious places, so now we can sketch the principal branch (figure 11). Since the numerator remains continuous, the several transits of the asymptotes cause an alternation in sign, and the fact that the cosine goes thru an absolute extremum between asymptotes means that the denominator has *no* change of sign there;

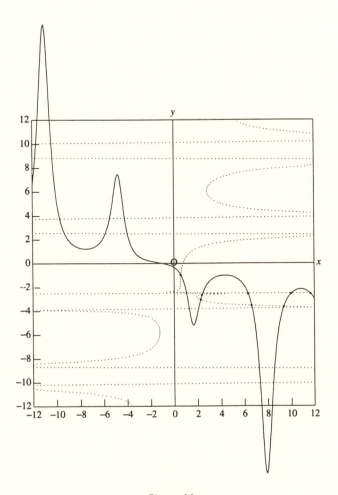

Figure 11

except for the principal branch, the curves exit in the same direction from whence they enter. Thus, we need only evaluate x for $y = n\pi$ to get a rather good idea of how close to the y-axis the turning points lie. [Of course the extrema do not lie exactly at $n\pi$, so a little more exploring is required for the branches that turn suddenly and thus have rather pointed shapes there.]

Plotting equation (28), however, is *not* easy. k is too large for the straight-line geometry to be visible, but it is not quite large enough to generate the asymptotes that would split the curve into multiple branches. It is clear that the curve will be trying to get off the page near the places that the asymptotes would develop — that is, at $k = 6$, $x = \pi/2 \pm n\pi$, so we look for bumps there — near $x = 1.6$ and -4.7. In those regions you have to evaluate several points and plot them if the position of the curve is needed with any precision. The two intercepts are, of course, trivial. We show the curve (solid) on figure 11, along with the previously discussed equation (27) and its asymptotes — (dotted).

It is clear from the figure that there are at least nine roots in the fourth quadrant — and no others are likely except farther to the southeast on lower branches of equation (27). We should, however, check how far up equation (28) comes in its next approach to the x-axis — near $x = (4 + \frac{1}{2})\pi$.

In any problem arising in the physical world we will have *a priori* information that will tell us which branches of (27) are interesting and which we can ignore — except insofar as they may introduce false roots that we must avoid in our algorithm. Nevertheless, it is clear that designing an algorithm to find even a third of the roots that have appeared will require much effort — and the further appearance of more roots when curve (28) becomes branched increases the total complexity of the program to the point that you will ponder quite a while about whether this exercise is really necessary! Fortunately most real problems have simpler geometries than this one — tho their equations are often much longer.

Which term dominates — and when?

Consider plotting

$$\frac{y^2 \cos x}{\sqrt{(\pi/2)^2 - x^2}} - x^2 y = 4 \tag{29}$$

using only the positive square root — a fairly easy exercise in relative magnitudes that you ought to undertake before reading beyond this paragraph. Clearly only values of x lying between $\pm\pi/2$ are of interest, and a second glance reveals that the entire equation is *even* in x, tho not in y, so that you need examine only $0 \leq x \leq \pi/2$. ...Take it from here! (Read the rest after some careful thought.)

At x equal to zero everything is finite and the second term disappears, so we find y to be $\pm\sqrt{2\pi}$ with the even symmetry producing zero slopes there. At $\pi/2$ the indeterminacy must be resolved. L'Hospital's rule can be used but it is more informative to change to a small local variable, δ, via $x = \pi/2 - \delta$, after which we have

$$\frac{y^2 \sin \delta}{\sqrt{\delta(\pi - \delta)}} - y(\pi/2 - \delta)^2 = 4$$

and we see that the $\sin \delta$ shrinks to zero faster than $\sqrt{\delta}$ in the denominator. If y is finite, the second term survives while the first disappears, so we obtain $-y\pi^2/4 = 4$ or $y = -16/\pi^2$.

Except at $\pi/2$, equation (29) is a quadratic in y whenever x is fixed. Picking $\pi/4$ as a convenient value we have

$$y^2 - \frac{\pi^3 \sqrt{6}}{64} y - \pi\sqrt{6} = 0 \qquad \text{hence} \qquad y = \begin{cases} -2.24 \\ 3.43 \end{cases}$$

a process that must *always* produce a positive and a negative value for y. The only missing link now is the behavior of the positive curve near $\pi/2$. At $\pi/2$ the quadratic equation (29) suddenly becomes linear, but *near* $\pi/2$ it is still quadratic. Further, if a quadratic is written with leading term y^2, the product of the two roots is the third term. Writing the local form of the equation with the unimportant δ's dropped and $\sin \delta$ approximated by δ, we have

$$\frac{y^2 \sqrt{\delta}}{\sqrt{\pi}} - y\frac{\pi^2}{4} - 4 = 0 \qquad \text{hence} \qquad y^2 - \frac{\pi^2 \sqrt{\pi}}{4\sqrt{\delta}} y - 4\sqrt{\frac{\pi}{\delta}} = 0$$

so the product of the roots gives

$$-\frac{16}{\pi^2} y_+ = -4\sqrt{\frac{\pi}{\delta}} \qquad \text{or} \qquad y_+ = \frac{\pi^2}{4}\sqrt{\frac{\pi}{\delta}} \to \infty$$

which, altho approximate, agrees well at $x = 3/2$ where exact roots are -1.604 and 16.435 (while δ, being 0.070796, gives 16.436). In this way we obtain the asymptotic behavior of the positive branch near $\pi/2$. In the unlikely event that we need a more accurate analytic expression in δ, the dropped δ's can be retained, as well as the $-\delta^3/3!$ term from the $\sin \delta$ expansion, and then the quadratic solved algebraically for the larger root.

The final sketch shows a negative branch that moves horizontally from -2.507 at $x = 0$, then drifts slowly upward to -1.621 when $x = \pi/2$. The positive branch starts horizontally at 2.507 but curves upward fairly quickly, reaching 4.32 at $x = 1$, 16.4 at 1.5 and $+\infty$ at $\pi/2$.

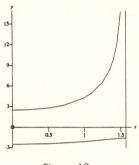

Figure 12

Exercises

(Except for a few Mystery Problems, answers to sketching exercises are at the end of *this* chapter.)

S1a. (This one is easy.) Find the critical behavior of

$$y^2 - \frac{2y}{\sin x} - 4 = 0$$

and sketch it over $0 \le x \le \pi$. Note that it has two branches almost everywhere.

S1b. Now try

$$y^2 - \frac{2y}{\sin x} + 4 = 0$$

— which doesn't.

S2. Plotting most of

$$y^2 \sin x - \frac{xy}{\cosh x} = 4$$

ought to be easy too ... now.

A two-way cubic

What does the graph of

$$x^3 - 3y^3 + 4x^2 - 3y^2 = 12 \tag{30}$$

look like? Pick a value for either variable and this becomes a cubic in the other variable. The brute force approach is to dust off a reliable cubic-solver and start plotting points. But considerable information can be got by simpler measures. The variables are separable, so write

$$x^2(x+4) = 12 + 3y^2(y+1) \tag{31}$$

and also, dividing by the left side and 3,

$$\frac{1}{3} = \frac{4}{x^2(x+4)} + \frac{y^2(y+1)}{x^2(x+4)} \tag{32}$$

from which we see that for large $|x|$ we have

$$\frac{1}{3} \approx \frac{y^2(y+1)}{x^2(x+4)} = \frac{y^3(1+1/y)}{x^3(1+4/x)} \approx \left(\frac{y}{x}\right)^3.$$

Thus, we know that the curve exits via the first and third quadrants — approaching an asymptotic slope of $(1/3)^{1/3} = 0.69336$ — the dotted line in figure 13.

The x and y intercepts are fixed by the cubics (from 31)

$$y^2(y+1) = -4 \qquad \text{hence} \qquad y = -2, \tag{33}$$

and

$$x^2(x+4) = 12 \tag{34}$$

which can be solved by iterating

$$x \leftarrow \sqrt{12/(x+4)} \tag{35}$$

to give $x = 1.4778$. It is clear from (31) that this same equation (34) also holds for x when $y = -1$, and that (33) also applies when $x = -4$. (This same iteration, $x \leftarrow \sqrt{const/(x+4)}$, effectively solves (31) for most human-sized positive values for y, i.e., between 0 and 10, and the analogous iteration $y \leftarrow \sqrt{const/(y+1)}$ often succeeds in solving it when we choose less felicitous values of x.)

Turning to *slopes*, differentiation gives

$$\frac{dy}{dx} = \frac{x(3x+8)}{3y(3y+2)} \tag{36}$$

from which it is clear that slopes of *zero* occur at $x = 0$ and $x = -8/3$, while *vertical* slopes exist when $y = 0$ and $y = -2/3$.

After solving for the other coordinates and slopes of these critical points we have:

x	y	slope
−4	−2.0	0.667
−8/3	−1.417694	0
0	−2.0	0
1.4798	0	∞
1.5036975	−2/3	∞
1.4798	−1	6.136

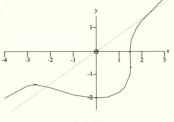

Figure 13

so it is easy to produce the sketch of figure 13. Questions remain about how the curve approaches the asymptote, but the critical geometry is nicely fixed. Two or three more points should resolve the remaining distant behavior. At $x = 10$, y is 7.42 — clearly above the asymptote. Indeed, even at $x = 100$, y is still noticeably above it at 69.9165. But then asymptotes, like porcupines, should be approached cautiously.

Exercises

S3. Find the shape of

$$x^3y - 3x^2y^2 + xy + 2x = 4$$

— exploring asymptotes and critical points. (It is cubic only in x.)

S4. Find the critical points and sketch

$$x^3 + 3y^3 + 4x - 3y = 12.$$

Fairly easy, but needs your cubic-solver.

S5. (Mystery Problem) Another equation that needs the cubic-solver is

$$x^3 + 3y^3 - 15x - 15y = 12.$$

Sketching extreme behavior

Most of the effort needed to produce an accurate sketch of any curve more complicated than a conic or a cosine will go into finding the critical points, especially the *extrema*, that is, the places where either the curve or its slope is *zero* or *infinite*. Not only do these places tend to fix the global shape of the curve, allowing us to sketch in the ordinary parts that lie between, but most of the mathematical and numerical troubles that arise in root-finding with these curves can be avoided if the behaviors at these extrema are understood before we choose our algorithms. Here we examine a fairly complicated curve to illustrate the various techniques.

Consider

$$\frac{x^2 y}{\sqrt{1 - x^2}} + xy^2 = 4 \tag{37}$$

in which we are to use only the positive square root. Obviously all the curve lies on $(-1 \le x \le 1)$, but inspection shows little else except that y must go to infinity as x nears zero, while intuition suggests it may do the same near the endpoints — altho that remains to be explored. Setting y to zero yields no solution for x except possibly at the endpoints, where the first term will be indeterminate — a possible counter to our previous hunch. Unless we are to fall back on brute force plotting of many points, we need to do some analysis. We can differentiate to find the slope, hoping to find places where the curve is horizontal or vertical, but the prospect does not please, as the derivative threatens to be worse than the curve itself (we explore this gambit later) — and then we notice that for any fixed x our equation is a *quadratic* in y! After writing

$$y^2 + \frac{x}{\sqrt{1 - x^2}} y - \frac{4}{x} = 0 \tag{38}$$

the quadratic formula gives

$$y = -\frac{x/2}{\sqrt{1 - x^2}} \pm \sqrt{\frac{x^2/4}{1 - x^2} + \frac{4}{x}} \tag{39}$$

and the interesting questions concern where the argument of the large square root is nonnegative (and finite).

For *positive* x the only troubles arise at 0 and 1 — between which there will be both a positive and a (somewhat larger) negative value for y. As x shrinks toward zero, all terms except the last tend to zero so that near zero the first approximation shows y approaching infinity as

$$y_{0+} \to \pm 2/\sqrt{x} \to \pm\infty.$$

Near $x = 1$ equation (39) has two large terms nearly equal in magnitude so we need a magnifying glass to see what happens when they are subtracted. Shift the origin to 1 by letting $x = 1 - \delta$, preferably in the original equation (37), to get

$$\frac{(1 - \delta)^2 y}{\sqrt{(2 - \delta)(\delta)}} + (1 - \delta)y^2 = 4 \tag{40}$$

that for small δ is well approximated by

$$\frac{y}{\sqrt{2\delta}} + y^2 = 4 \tag{41}$$

and we see that if the left side is to remain finite as δ approaches zero, y must also go to zero — or just possibly go to $-\infty$ in some way so that the two terms on the left differ by 4. The first option gives

$$y_{1+} \approx 4\sqrt{2\delta}$$

which yields 4 from the first term while making the y^2 disappear. The local curve here is thus a *parabola lying on its side* with its vertex at $(1,0)$ — only the positive part being pertinent. The other root is

$$y_{1-} = -\frac{1/2}{\sqrt{2\delta}} - \sqrt{\frac{1/4}{2\delta} + 4} = -\frac{1}{2\sqrt{2\delta}}\left[1 + \sqrt{1 + \frac{8\delta}{1/4}}\right]$$

$$= -\frac{1}{2\sqrt{2\delta}}\left[1 + \sqrt{1 + 32\delta}\right] \approx -\frac{1}{\sqrt{2\delta}}$$

— a large negative approach to $-\infty$.

Perhaps it is time to evaluate a few intermediate points on (37) and sketch what we now know. We get figure 14 and see that there is a missing critical point — the extremum near $(0.7, -2.5)$ which we should now find. Differentiating (37) produces

$$\frac{dy}{dx} = -\frac{y}{x} \frac{\left[\frac{x}{\sqrt{1 - x^2}} \cdot \left(\frac{2 - x^2}{1 - x^2}\right) + y\right]}{\left[2y + \frac{x}{\sqrt{1 - x^2}}\right]} \tag{42}$$

and we wonder where it is zero. Obviously we need the square bracket of the numerator to be zero, which gives an expression for y in terms of x with which we can eliminate y in (37).

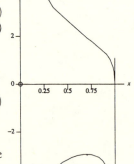

Figure 14

After some algebra we get the sextic

$$x^6 - x^5/4 - 3x^4 + x^3/2 - 1 = 0$$

which has only two real roots: -1.26099 and 0.70208, the first being of no real interest. Solving for the y corresponding to the second we find the horizontal point of the curve to be at $(0.70208, -2.93025)$. We now know enough to be able to decide how to solve, for example, for the positive intersections of this curve with straight lines or even circles of various diameters — or at least we can see the approximate configurations that will demand special care and further exploration.

Turning to *negative values* of x, examination of (39) shows that most values of x on $(-1, 0)$ give a negative discriminant, for which no solution for y exists. Indeed, even if you substitute $-0.1, -0.2, \ldots$, -0.9, you find no positive argument for the square root and might therefore conclude that no solutions exist for negative x. But the careful worker will solve to find *where* the discriminant becomes zero, obtaining the cubic

$$x^3 - 16x^2 + 16 = 0$$

which clearly has one real root slightly less than 16. We find it to be 15.937005. On dividing it out we get a quadratic with roots at 1.033967 and -0.97097184. So suddenly we see that (37) has another curve in the very thin strip $-1 \le x \le -0.97097$. Whether or not this part can be ignored depends, of course, on the context in which (37) has arisen. Here, for its instructional value, we will pursue our tale by making the independent variable in (38) and (39) small via $x = -1 + u$. Formal substitution gives

$$y^2 - \frac{1 - u}{\sqrt{(2 - u)u}} y + \frac{4}{1 - u} = 0 \tag{38'}$$

and

$$y = \frac{1 - u}{2\sqrt{(2 - u)u}} \pm \sqrt{\frac{(1 - u)^2}{4(2 - u)u} - \frac{4}{1 - u}} \tag{39'}$$

from which we can extract the critical behavior. Asking where this discriminant becomes zero, we get the cubic

$$u^3 - 19u^2 + 35u - 1 = 0$$

that gives the more accurate

$$u_0 = 0.02.90281546248$$

for which

$$y_0 = 2.02967582144.$$

On substituting this point into the denominator of (42) we find that

$$2y + \frac{x}{\sqrt{1 - x^2}} = 0$$

so the curve has infinite slope there — expected, but a reassuring check. For the rest of the strip we have two values of y, the larger of which is given accurately by (39') using the positive sign, but the smaller is better evaluated by noting that the product

$$(y_{small})(y_{large}) = \frac{4}{1 - u}. \tag{43}$$

Neglecting u where it is subtracted from 2 or 1 in (39') we have

$$y_{large} = \frac{1}{2\sqrt{2u}} + \sqrt{\frac{1}{8u} - 4} = \frac{1}{2\sqrt{2u}}\left[1 + \sqrt{1 - 32u}\right] \to \frac{1}{\sqrt{2u}}$$

that defines the asymptotic behavior of y_{large} at -1. Then from (43) we get

$$y_{small} = \frac{4\sqrt{2u}}{(1 - u)} \to 4\sqrt{2u}$$

and we see that again y is, at least very briefly, the top part of a recumbent parabola. Note that these last two formulae are usable numerically only for *very* small values of u, say, less than 0.001. Their purpose, rather, is to define the functional behavior of y as it approaches its limiting values. Figure 15 thus completes the exploration of our curve, which is finally seen to have three branches. Each of them might have to be considered when solving for its intersections with another equation.

Figure 15

Exercises

S6. Find the critical points of $y\sqrt{1 - x^2} - y^2x = 4$ and sketch the curve. (Use only the positive square root.)

S7. The analysis of

$$\frac{xy^2}{\sqrt{1-x^2}} + x^2y = 4$$

is somewhat harder.

S8. Sketch $xy - y^2\sqrt{1-x^2} = 4$ after finding the critical points. (Positive square root.)

S9. (This one is fairly difficult.) Explore and sketch

$$\frac{x^2y}{\sqrt{1-x^2}} + x\sqrt{y^2+1} = 4.$$

S10. (Mystery Problem)

$$\frac{xy}{\sin x} + y^2\cos x = 4.$$

Brute force plots are necessary — sometimes

Consider how to plot

$$xy(2x^2 - y^2) + 16(x + y) = 48 \qquad (44)$$

within ± 5 for both x and y. We easily see that both positive axes are crossed at 3 — but nothing else seems to help fix the geometric picture. Algebraically, if we hold one variable constant, we have a *cubic* in the other. So we know that along any coordinate line (vertical or horizontal) there is at least *one* and perhaps *three* points on our curve — but never only two (why?). But that information still fails to give us a useful picture. We cannot simplify our equation by neglecting minor terms. A conversion to the polar coordinates $x = r \cdot \cos\theta,\ y = r \cdot \sin\theta$ gives

$$r^4 \cdot \cos\theta \cdot \sin\theta \cdot (2\cos^2\theta - \sin^2\theta) + 16(\cos\theta + \sin\theta) \cdot r = 48$$

which seems to say that for any ray thru the origin we have a quartic in r that will yield 0, 2 or 4 points on our curve. Worse! But then we see that the quartic has the form $ar^4 + br = c$ which has a *unique* point with zero slope via

$$4ar^3 + b = 0 \qquad \text{hence} \qquad r_{min} = \left(-\frac{b}{4a}\right)^{1/3}$$

and thus looks more like a parabola than a quartic, so for various c there are 0 or 2 roots — never 4. That's reassuring but still not much help.

So finally we must turn to brute force: evaluate our equation (44) on the grid $-5 \leq x, y \leq 5$ at the integer values and sketch it. (If you have a sophisticated graph plotting package on your computer, you can try that — but most of them require you to write your equation as $y = f(x)$ — something we cannot do.) The plot is shown as figure 16 (where we have added a circle of radius 4 to help visualize the scale) and we see that our curve has 4 branches. Further refinement of the grid in useful places suggests that some of the tails could be asymptotic to the axes — a suggestion we should now explore. What happens when x or y becomes large? Clearly, if x becomes big without a comparable increase in y, the second term in each parenthesis of (44) is unimportant, giving

$$xy(2x^2) + 16x = 48$$

hence

$$2x^2 y + 16 = \frac{48}{x} \to 0.$$

As x increases, the right side approaches zero, so y must behave like

$$y = -8/x^2$$

showing that it approaches zero from below, no matter whether x is positive or negative. (What happens if y grows while x is small?)

This analysis clarifies the behavior of four of the tails of our curves as they exit the local scene. The other four seem to be heading more-or-less toward the $45°$ points of the compass. How can we check on that suspicion? Divide (44) by xy to get

$$2x^2 - y^2 + 16\left(\frac{1}{y} + \frac{1}{x}\right) = \frac{48}{xy}. \tag{45}$$

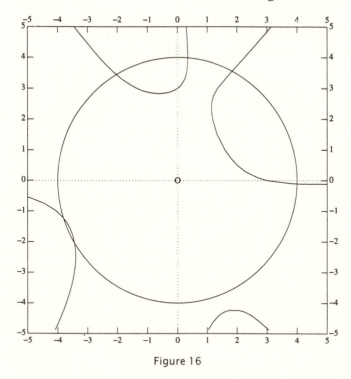

Figure 16

What happens here if x and y *both* become large with whatever signs? So the slopes turn out to be $\pm\sqrt{2}$ — not exactly toward rational points on the compass, after all. [Turn the magnification of your numerical-analytical microscope up a notch to find from which side the curves approach these $\sqrt{2}$ asymptotes. Watch your signs! If you have doubts about your analytical reasoning, try substituting $x = 16$ and $y = 16\sqrt{2}$ into the "unimportant" terms of (45).]

Odds and ends

To get the roots of

$$\ln\left(\frac{x}{\sqrt{x^2 - 1}}\right) = (\cos x)^2 \tag{46}$$

a superposition of the two graphs (figure 17) shows most of them to be pairs lying on either side of the odd multiples of $\pi/2$. Also, the intrapair distance steadily decreases as the logarithmic curve clamps down on the x-axis. There are no roots for any x less than unity (Why?) and the first root is isolated, lacking a sibling. Get it by any

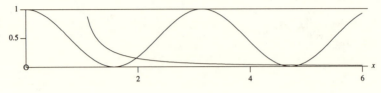

Figure 17

method, but start worrying about the later roots, because equation (46), as it stands, requires the evaluation of a cosine that is small from an x that is large — a situation that could lead to a nasty loss of significant figures. Of course, the problem is avoided by shifting to local coordinates via $x = (k + \frac{1}{2})\pi + \delta$.

The logarithm, too, is a source of worry for the experienced computor since its argument is approaching unity with growing x and algorithms that evaluate logs will subtract 1 and then compute the log from whatever remains — again a loss of significant figures. It is much safer to do the subtraction yourself, analytically, getting an equation that contains the essential information in variables that are small. Thus we have

$$(\sin \delta)^2 = \ln\left(\frac{1}{\sqrt{1 - 1/x^2}}\right)$$

which, on invoking series, becomes

$$\delta^2 \left[1 - \frac{\delta^2}{3!} + \frac{\delta^4}{5!} \cdots\right]^2 = -\frac{1}{2}\ln\left(1 - \frac{1}{x^2}\right)$$

$$= \frac{1}{2x^2}\left[1 + \frac{1}{2x^2} + \frac{1}{3x^4} + \cdots\right]. \qquad (47)$$

This replacement of the logarithm is usually more efficient than the library function and has the advantage that *you* control its accuracy by the number of terms you keep. The nasty subtraction has disappeared. Equation (47) can be put into a form for iterative solution by dividing by the squared-bracket coefficient of δ^2 and taking the square root of both sides. Choosing the plus or minus sign consistently will produce two algorithms for the value of δ — one for each root of the pair.

Exercises

S11. Sketch $\cos x = x/\sqrt{x^2 + 1}$. Now square it, subtract both sides from unity, then take the square root to get $\sin x = \pm 1/\sqrt{x^2 + 1}$. Compare the sketches of the problems. Are they equivalent?

S12. Sketch

$$(\cos x)^2 + \ln\left(\frac{x}{\sqrt{x^2 + 1}}\right) = 0$$

and consider how to find the roots efficiently.

S13. Tired of asymptotes? Try symmetries instead. Consider

$$\sin x + \sin y = 0.40.$$

To get you started: For small x and y this is almost the straight line

$$x + y = 0.40$$

down in the corner of the first quadrant — but something must ultimately quit growing since sines cannot exceed unity. Consider, then Reflect — carefully.

S14. (Since we don't want to end on 13!) Now try

$$\sin x + \sin y = 1.40.$$

Answers to Most of the Sketching Exercises

S1a. The equation

$$y^2 - \frac{2y}{\sin x} - 4 = 0$$

has *odd* symmetry about the origin and *even* symmetry about $x = \pi/2$ so only $0 \leq x \leq \pi/2$ needs to be explored. It can also be written as

$$\sin x \cdot (y^2 - 4) = 2y \quad \text{or} \quad y = \frac{1}{\sin x}\left[1 \pm \sqrt{1 + (2\sin x)^2}\right].$$

$$\text{(S1a.1), (S1a.2)}$$

This last form shows that two real roots exist almost everywhere, the positive root being the larger. When $\sin x$ is zero, (1a.1) shows one root to be zero, hence the other is infinite. More precisely: for x small but positive, equation (1a.1) becomes

$$x(y^2 - 4) = 2y$$

so y is small; hence y^2 is neglectable compared to -4. Thus we finally deduce that y behaves approximately like $-2x$ very near the origin. And since the constant term in the quadratic is -4, the other branch must behave roughly like $-4/(-2x) = 2/x$ there. The turning points, by symmetry, must lie at $\pi/2$ where the ordinates are 3.24 and -1.24.

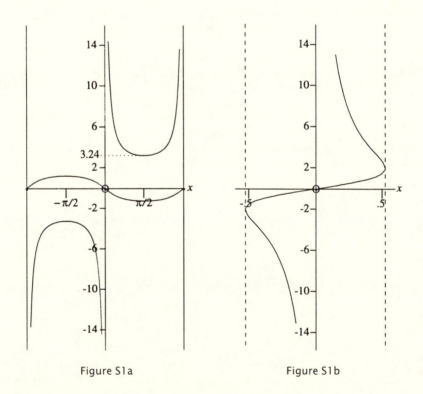

Figure S1a   Figure S1b

We can now produce the sketch figure S1a, altho it may help to evaluate a point or two on the tails of the upper branch if you need to represent the approach to the asymptotes accurately.

S1b. This equation clearly differs from the previous only in the sign of the 4. But a glance at the argument of the square root in

$$y = \frac{1}{\sin x}\left[1 \pm \sqrt{1 - (2\sin x)^2}\right]$$

shows that now there are x values where no roots exist — specifically, whenever $\sin x > 0.5$. Thus, we must explore only $0 \le x \le 0.5236$, the symmetries being the same as before. And, as before, the limiting behavior for small x is the same except for the changes in sign. At the critical value 0.5236 the ordinate is 8. Hence our sketch looks something like figure S1b. (But note that to fit the figures on the page we have compressed the vertical scales.)

S2. For fixed x this equation is a quadratic in y except at integer multiples of π. Formal solution gives

$$y = \frac{x/2}{\sin x \cdot \cosh x}\left[1 \pm \sqrt{1 + \left(\frac{4\cosh x}{x}\right)^2 \sin x}\right]$$

from which we see that whenever $\sin x \ge 0$ the square root exists, but the *positive* y will become infinite when $\sin x = 0$. The *negative* y at that point comes from the *linear* form of the equation. It is $-4\cosh x/x$ when $x = \pi,\ 2\pi,\ \ldots$ so is finite.

The behavior at $x = 0$ is special because both x and $\sin x$ go to zero together. For small positive x our equation is $xy^2 - xy = 4$, hence $y^2 - y - 4/x = 0$ — which shows that $|y|$ becomes infinite. Ignoring y relative to y^2 we get $y \to \pm 2/\sqrt{x}$ as $x \to 0_+$.

We are left with the question: For $\sin x < 0$ are there any real solutions? Near $\pi,\ 2\pi,\ \ldots$ the expression $(4\cosh x/x)^2$ is large, but $|\sin x|$ *can* be small enough to make the product less than 1 in magnitude — so the answer is *yes*. The negative branch, tho finite at $k\pi$, continues briefly into the region of negative $\sin x$ on its way to $-\infty$. Since the equation is still a quadratic, it must still have two roots, but here the square root is less than 1, so both roots are negative. So the other branch comes in from $-\infty$ at π_+ and links up at the double root, which we now seek. Letting $x = \pi + \delta$, our equation becomes

$$y^2 + \frac{x}{\sin\delta\cosh x}y + \frac{4}{\sin\delta} = 0$$

whose discriminant becomes zero when

$$\left(\frac{x/2}{\sin\delta\cosh x}\right)^2 = \frac{4}{\sin\delta}$$

hence

$$\sin \delta \leftarrow \left(\frac{x/4}{\cosh x} \right)^2. \qquad (S2)$$

For an approximate solution let $x = \pi$ to get $\delta = 4.5906\text{E}{-}3$, whence the corresponding ordinate

$$y = -\frac{\pi/2}{\sin \delta \cosh \pi} = -29.5187.$$

(If accurate values are desired, you can iterate equation (S2) three times to get $\delta = 4.562264\text{E}{-}3$ with the ordinate -29.6101.)

The asymptotic behavior of the big branch is found by dividing the last term of our quadratic by the solution of the linear equation. Thus

$$y \approx \frac{4/\delta}{-4 \cosh \pi / \pi} = \frac{-\pi}{\delta \cosh \pi} = -0.271/\delta,$$

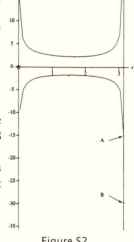

Figure S2

$\sin \delta$ having been replaced by δ.

This equation has no actual symmetries but is nearly periodic in its geometry. The spaces where $\sin x$ is negative, $(-\pi \le x \le 0)$, $(\pi \le x \le 2\pi)$, ... are *almost* empty — the only part of the curve that intrudes in figure S2 being a bulge that is so narrow it cannot be seen. (It starts at A, achieves its greatest excursion, B, at $x = 3.1462$, then heads rapidly south to become asymptotic to $x = \pi$.) In later branches this bulge lies at much greater y values and is even thinner. But even if it can't be seen, its mere existence can produce unexpected roots, hence unexpected behaviors in programs written by innocents.

S3. This equation is a quadratic in y so

$$y = \frac{1 + x^2}{6x} \left[1 \pm \sqrt{1 - 12 \frac{(4 - 2x)}{(1 + x^2)^2}} \right]$$

from which we see that for $x > 2$ there is both a positive root and a smaller negative root. At $x = 2$, y is 0 and 5/6. When $12(4 - 2x)/(1 + x^2)^2 = 1$ there is a double root at $(1.53266, 0.36419)$ and there are no roots for smaller x.

When x grows large, the radical tends to unity — so the positive y behaves like $(1 + x^2)/3x$ hence $x/3$. The behavior of the negative root for large x can be seen by writing the equation as

$$y = \frac{4 - 2x}{x^3 - 3x^2y + 2} \to \frac{-2}{x^2},$$

the domination of x^3 over the other terms giving the last expression. Since this shows the lower branch becoming asymptotic to the x-axis from below, there must be a minimum point. Unfortunately, precise determination of the minimum would require solution of the zero-slope equation $3x^2y - 6xy^2 + y + 2 = 0$ simultaneously with the original equation. It can be done, but for a sketch it is simpler to evaluate a few points! The minimum lies approximately at $(3.13, -0.0634)$. Our sketch is figure S3.

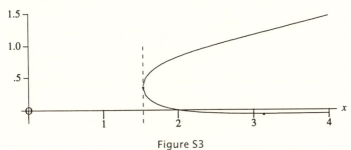

Figure S3

S4. Writing the equation as

$$x(x^2 + 4) = 12 + 3y(1 - y^2),$$

intercepts can be found at $(0, 1.796)$ and $(1.722, 0)$. From the derivative

$$\frac{dy}{dx} = \frac{3x^2 + 4)}{3(1 - 3y^2)}$$

we see that the curve is never horizontal but that it becomes vertical twice — at $(1.809, 1/\sqrt{3})$ and $(1.629, -1/\sqrt{3})$. As the curve exits the picture in the second and fourth quadrants, it is slowly approaching a slope of $-(1/3)^{1/3}$.

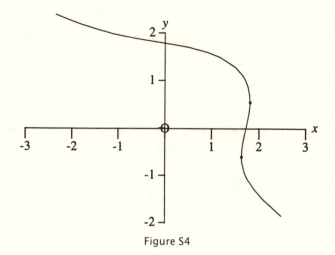

Figure S4

S5. (It's still a Mystery!)

S6. For any given x this equation is a quadratic in y; hence

$$y = \frac{\sqrt{1-x^2}}{2x}\left[1 \pm \sqrt{1 - \frac{16x}{1-x^2}}\right] \qquad \text{(S6)}$$

while the slope is given by

$$\frac{dy}{dx} = \frac{y^2 + \frac{xy}{\sqrt{1-x^2}}}{\sqrt{1-x^2} - 2xy}. \qquad \text{(S6s)}$$

From the original form of the equation we see that for $x = -1$, $y = \pm 2$ while at $x = 0$, y is 4 — and because the equation is still a quadratic we suspect an infinite y as well.

The discriminant of (S6) is nonnegative when $16x/(1-x^2)$ is less than 1, that is, for $-1 < x \le 0$ and also for positive x up to a solution of $1 - x^2 = 16x$. Solving, we get $x = -8 \pm \sqrt{65}$ so the relevant root is $1/(8 + \sqrt{65})$† $= 0.0622577$, where $y = 8$ and the slope must be infinite (because of the double root there). The condition for infinite slope from (S6s)

$$\sqrt{1-x^2} = 2xy \qquad \text{hence} \qquad y = \frac{\sqrt{1-x^2}}{2x}$$

† Where did this come from . . . and why?

is satisfied by $x \to 0$, with y going to infinity with the same sign as x. Substituting $x = \delta - 1$ in (S6s) will show that as x approaches -1 both the curves approach their finite value, ± 2, both with slope $-1/2\sqrt{2\delta}$ approaching $-\infty$. This is enough information to allow sketching of the curves near the y-axis and near $x = -1$.

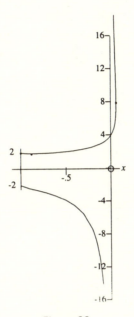

Figure S6

Evaluating y at $x = -0.5$ and perhaps one or two other points completes the sketch except for determining the location of the minimum

$$y^2 + \frac{xy}{\sqrt{1 - x^2}} = 0 \tag{S6m}$$

in the upper branch. For that we solve jointly with the original equation. After using (S6m) to eliminate y^2 and $y\sqrt{1 - x^2}$, we have

$$x^2 - \frac{x}{4} - 1 = 0$$

which has roots -0.88278 and 1.1328, the latter being irrelevant. Thus, we find the minimum to be at $(-0.88278, 1.8791)$. We could also find the inflection point in the lower branch, but that would contribute little to any use of this curve in a root-finding context. *Pax!*

S7. From the form

$$xy^2 + x^2y\sqrt{1-x^2} = 4\sqrt{1-x^2}$$

it is clear that there are no symmetries, that there are no solutions for $|x|$ greater than 1, and that at $x = \pm 1$, $y = 0$. The behavior near $x = 1$ is seen by letting $x = 1 - \delta$, getting

$$y^2 + \sqrt{2\delta}y - 4\sqrt{2\delta} = 0 \qquad \text{hence} \qquad \sqrt{2\delta} = \frac{y^2}{4-y}$$

so

$$y^2 \approx 4\sqrt{2\delta}$$

showing a vertical slope there. Since our equation is a quadratic we can also write

$$y = -\frac{x}{2}\sqrt{1-x^2} \pm \frac{1}{2}\sqrt{x^2(1-x^2) + 16\frac{\sqrt{1-x^2}}{x}}.$$

Near $x = 0_+$ only the last term is large, so

$$y_\pm \approx \pm\frac{2}{\sqrt{x}}.$$

Over $(0,1)$ the discriminant is positive, making the negative branch slightly larger in magnitude than the positive. When x is negative, however, that negative last term prevents real solutions. To see this clearly, write the equation as

$$\frac{1}{x\sqrt{1-x^2}} + \frac{1}{y} = \frac{4}{x^2y^2}.$$

Near $x = -1$ we have

$$(\text{big negative}) + \frac{1}{y} = \frac{4}{y^2}$$

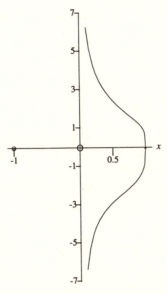

Figure S7

so y must be less than 1 for the left side to be positive. But as y shrinks toward zero, $4/y^2$ will increase faster than $1/y$, so equality will never be reached. Remember, however, that the *isolated* point $(-1,0)$ *does satisfy the equation* and could cause some unexpected results unless you keep global root-finders away from it.

S8. This equation has solutions only at some *points* — which we let you find.

S9. (The picture is omitted — to discourage peeking!) Near $x = 1$ let $x = 1 - \delta$ to get $y/\sqrt{2\delta} + \sqrt{y^2 + 1} = 4$, from which it is clear that y must be small. Thus the second term is unity — giving $y \approx 3\sqrt{2\delta}$. Letting $x = -1 + \delta$, the analogous behavior near $x = -1$ is $y \approx 5\sqrt{2\delta}$. For $0 < x < 1$ the rearrangement

$$y \left[\frac{x^2}{\sqrt{1 - x^2}} + x \frac{\sqrt{y^2 + 1}}{y} \right] = 4 \tag{S9}$$

shows that for x near 0, y must be large — and for large y the expression $\sqrt{y^2 + 1}/y \to \operatorname{sgn}(y) \times 1$. Thus, for small x and positive y, (S9) becomes $y(x^2+x) = 4$ so $y \approx 4/x$ and for negative y we get $y \approx -4/x$.

At $x = 1/2$, y is 5.009 and -18.866 but at $x = 3/4$ only positive y exists (2.406). For *negative* y, suspecting an asymptote that would make the expression

$$\frac{x^2}{\sqrt{1-x^2}} - x = 0,$$

we find the critical x to be $1/\sqrt{2}$ and some analysis shows $y \approx -2/\delta$ for $x = 1/\sqrt{2} - \delta$.

For negative x, only a positive y-branch exists and that only for $-1 \leq x < -1/\sqrt{2}$. For $x = -1/\sqrt{2} - \delta$, $y \approx 2/\sqrt{\delta}$ — and we have already discussed the behavior at -1.

Both positive y-branches are monotonic, but the negative branch has a maximum. It can be found by combining the zero-slope equation

$$-\frac{\sqrt{y^2+1}}{y} = \frac{x(2-x^2)}{(1-x^2)\sqrt{1-x^2}}$$

with (S9) to produce $y = -4(1-x^2)\sqrt{1-x^2}/x^2$ that can be used to eliminate y. Ultimately we get the cubic (in x^2)

$$x^6 - \frac{7+1/16}{2}x^4 + \frac{7}{2}x^2 - \frac{1}{2} = 0$$

whose only real roots are $x = \pm 0.4134$. The negative root is irrelevant to our problem, so the maximum occurs at $(0.4134, -17.67)$. But it is undoubtedly easier to find the same result numerically by solving (S9) iteratively via

$$y \leftarrow \frac{4}{\dfrac{x^2}{\sqrt{1-x^2}} - x\sqrt{1+\dfrac{1}{y^2}}}$$

for several x until an approximate maximum y is found. (Note that since we are solving for the branch with negative y, she left her sign at the door when we moved her inside the radical.) Since the negative y's are large in magnitude, $1/y^2$ is small compared to unity. Thus, this iteration for y converges quickly for most x. Try it!

S10. (Another Mystery!)

S11. Except for an isolated first root (at 0.8603), $\cos x = x/\sqrt{x^2+1}$ has root *pairs* near $2k\pi$. The equation $\sin x = 1/\sqrt{x^2+1}$ has *isolated* roots at $k\pi$. For the equations to be equivalent they must each have the $\pm$ sign prefixed to their radical, giving each twice as many roots.

S12. The paired roots occur near $(2k+1)\pi/2$, beginning with $k = 1$. The first three roots are "well-separated" only if you have seen the picture. If you are playing blindman's buff, you will get one of them

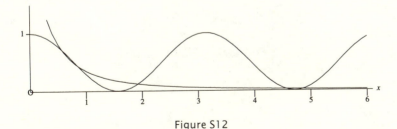

Figure S12

but will not be sure which one it is. As always, once you know where the roots are, it is easy to find them! (Consider what happens to the picture as we add a small constant to the logarithm in the equation.)

S13. It is a "diamond" with rounded corners centered at the obvious place. The easily found x-intercept (0.4115) and the extremum at $\pi/2, -0.6435$ suffice for an adequate sketch.

S14. It is nearly a circle. (Some people may prefer to move the center to the origin, then plot $\cos x + \cos y = 1.4$.) What happens to the shape as the right-side constant increases to 1.6?

GLOOMY MUSINGS:
Correctness, Efficiency and Responsibility in Computation

It was 1942 when I began serious scientific computing on a klunkety-klunk mechanical Monroe desk calculator — at about three multiplications per minute. It took time to enter each multiplier and to copy down the products. If you needed a cosine, you looked it up in a table; square roots were got by the divide-and-average iteration. An 0.8 power (there are a lot of those in Chemical Engineering) required a log table. The old Monroe was reliable; I was not! The errors were inescapably mine; errors of transcription mostly. Checking was occasional — done when things didn't look quite right.

I had the temerity to be numerically integrating a partial differential equation without being aware of existing methods for even ordinary differential equations — methods that seem, in retrospect, to have been known only to astronomers. In short, I was an undergraduate about to be drafted into the Army and I was in a hurry to finish my B.S.E. project. As it happened, my work got published. I still have a reprint — but I'm afraid to examine it carefully. Oh, the Big Picture is right enough, but those numbers probably won't stand much scrutiny. Fortunately it was the Big Picture that was important then — the Algorithm, as we would say today. The numbers were just a Numerical Example. Nobody was going to build a big Cylindrical Catalytic Converter based on *my* numbers. (It could have been a mini-Chernobyl! I didn't worry about it at the time; I was in the Infantry. But more recently I've sometimes dreamt about it.)

I'm still computing and, yes, it certainly has changed! I won't bore you with the fantastic speed-up statistics, the new algorithmic developments, the proliferation of helpful software — you know about them, are using them daily. But one thing has <u>not</u> changed: human error. Worse, some of these errors are *not our own* anymore — so we feel partially absolved from the responsibility of checking for them. Software has bugs — frequently quite obscure bugs that bite only rarely. (This kind of software is called "Reliable" or "Mature.")*

Even our own errors are now somewhat remote from our presence. A mistake in programming may not surface during the first 17 runs of our algorithm or our algorithm itself may be logically deficient only for a few parameter values. And when the error does occur it appears to spring from inside the computer — not directly from us. "Look what the <u>computer</u> did to me <u>this</u> time!" is a continual refrain in undergrad labs and, I fear, in the hearts of a great many of us more "mature" users of computer systems. We really don't want to accept this responsibility and the easiest way to duck it is to not see the errors when they occur. (Again in the student labs, it is always the roommate who can instantly spot the error altho the originator has been staring at it for some minutes with no recognition.) This psychological problem sits at the center of all error detection difficulties in serious computing. We just don't want to think that <u>we</u> were wrong. And when an error that trips us up turns out to be a system fault, that merely reinforces our reluctance to accept responsibility for *any* errors — even tho we weren't checking very well.

If errors remain so difficult to detect, what should the computor do? Strive mightily to make fewer of them is the obvious first command-

---

* New software is so notoriously buggy that at a recent convention a disgruntled Users Group was passing out buttons that read, "It's Not a Bug — It's a Feature"!

ment. The second remains, sadly, do a lot of checking both of your individual algorithms and of the finished results. If *anything* looks suspicious, take time to find out why — even if your boss wanted those results yesterday. Wrong answers are <u>your</u> responsibility and the fact that you delivered them on time does not improve them.

Checking the correctness of your program is slow grubby work and no theorem-proving software is ever going to lift it from your shoulders. If the numbers you are producing are critically important, the best advice I can give is to *compute them twice – by different algorithms*. If the results agree to 8 significant figures, they are very likely correct. And if they don't agree? Again: Find out why! Grim advice, but I can offer no better.

On error *prevention* I can be more optimistic. One can learn to program defensively: Develop a consistent style, avoid all fancy bells-and-whistles of your programming language, etc. — there is a lot of good advice floating around in print these days if you really need it. Happily, I can say that programs carefully crafted to be correct are often found also to be efficient. I'm unsure why these two desirable properties are linked, tho I suspect it lies in the psychology of the programmer — if he worries about the correctness of the details, he achieves a deeper understanding of his computational process that translates into the more efficient operations. Indeed, he often ends up with a <u>simpler</u> program that is correct instead of a kludge containing a lot of special-case testing. [If you are not familiar with *Programming Pearls* by Jon Bentley (Addison-Wesley, 1986), I commend it to you. What he discusses are pearls, not necklaces, but the point that I'm trying to make here sparkles thruout his book.]

The longer I have computed, the less I seem to use Numerical Software Packages. In an ideal world this would be crazy; maybe it is even a little bit crazy today. But I've been bitten too often by bugs in those Packages. For me, it is simply too frustrating to be sidetracked while solving my own problem by the need to debug somebody else's software. So, except for linear algebra packages, I usually roll my own. It's inefficient, I suppose, but my nerves are calmer.

The most troubling aspect of using Numerical Software Packages, however, is not their occasional goofs, but rather the way the packages inevitably hide deficiencies in a problem's formulation. We can dump a set of equations into a solver and it will usually give back a solution without complaint — even if the equations are quite poorly conditioned or have an unsuspected singularity that is distorting the answers from physical reality. Or it may give us an alternative solution that we failed to anticipate. The package helps us ignore these possibilities — or even to detect their occurrence if the execution is buried inside a larger program. Given our capacity for error-blindness, software that actually *hides* our errors from us is a questionable form of progress.

And if we do detect suspicious behavior, we really can't dig into the package to find our troubles. We will simply have to reprogram the problem ourselves. We would have been better off doing so from the beginning — with a good chance that the immersion into the problem's reality would have dispelled the logical confusions before ever getting to the machine.

How, then, do we persuade people to consider their problem formulations and algorithmic embodiments carefully *before* they write their programs? Afterwards is too late: by then the errors are in there, deeply embedded, usually hidden and psychologically undiscoverable. Further, the authors will have acquired a vested interest in their programs — will be determined to make them work, by patching. Clearly this is not the way to go. I can only suggest exposure to examples, coupled with exercises — but that medicine can be somewhat bitter. Until their computational lives have been threatened, they are not apt to take it.

Finally let us not forget System Software. Like it or not, we can't avoid it. Of course it too has its errors. Over the years I've used 5 or 6 major (modern) computers from as many manufacturers. On them I have run Fortran programs under maybe 10 compilers. In every compiler I have encountered a bug — and Fortran is about as standard and "mature" as computer languages come. Most of these bugs were minor (after I figured out what they were) and, of course, I learned to program around them. My initial sensitization to obscure system errors came in 1952 when I got crazy results because the square-root function on a 10-digit decimal machine gave correct roots for all fractions between zero and one except for the four arguments 0.9999999996, 0.9999999997, 0.9999999998 and 0.9999999999 — for which it returned the "root" 0.5000000000! I didn't discover this bizarre behavior until I happened to run an iteration that should have converged to unity from below. I hope it hadn't done too much damage to other work before we fixed it. That was long ago, in era BF,* but subsequent system errors have given my error sensitivities numerous booster shots. And, not entirely by the way, if you are one of those people who like to think that such errors are isolated relics of

*Before Fortran.

a bygone age, you might reflect on those 4 million Pentium^{TM} chips with very slightly defective division algorithms that were knowingly released upon the unsuspecting public in the Fall of 1994. They're still out there!

A PILLOW PROBLEM

Find the smallest positive root of

$$\frac{1}{1 + e^{-2x}} + \cos x = 0.$$

Three student proposals for solving this equation were:

(1) $\quad x_{i+1} \leftarrow \arccos\left[-\dfrac{1}{1 + e^{-2x_i}}\right]$; $\quad x_0 = 3$

(2) $\quad x_{i+1} \leftarrow \dfrac{1}{2}\ln\left[\dfrac{-1}{1 + 1/\cos x_i}\right]$; $\quad x_0 = 3$

(3) Newton's method, starting with $x = 3$.

Who did well — and did you do any better?

Chapter 1

NONLINEAR EQUATIONS

*"Thou hast damnable iterations, and art
indeed able to corrupt a saint."*
Falstaff

Nonlinear equations are divided into *transcendental* equations (strictly, equations containing a transcendental function — but often loosely applied to almost anything nasty), *algebraic* equations (things with square and cube roots or other fractional powers) and *polynomial* equations. Of these, polynomials are sufficiently specialized to warrant separate treatment. This chapter is concerned with the rest.

Before spending time trying to solve an unfamiliar nonlinear equation carefully, plot it! Or sketch it with some care. And look at it. You may be surprised at what you see. In the event, you will probably see enough of its geometry to suggest a reasonable solution method and, conversely, to rule out other methods you might have tried. We cannot overemphasize this advice:

Look at your equation's geometry first!

Nonlinear equations usually have several roots and they require iterative algorithms that will not work well unless started "geometrically near" a root. Without a good start, most methods will bounce all over the numerical landscape before either generating the machine equivalent of infinity or else settling down to laboriously deliver a root you probably did not want. (Newton's method is more efficient than most, but efficiency in getting a wrong answer is not a virtue. Don't turn Newton loose unchaperoned.)

Black-box equation solvers

Before turning to specific examples, we ought to say a few cautionary words about equation "solvers" that are now available in several mathematical software packages on PC's and mainframe computers and, more recently, in top-of-the-line pocket calculators. Most of them are quite accurate for cleanly posed problems, that is, for problems where an uncritical application of Newton's method will succeed. They do not invent a suitable starting value — that is a job they leave to you, with "If at first you don't succeed ...". They do, however, have two faults: they are frequently brute-force inefficient and they do not have the ability to reformulate an ill-conditioned problem — or even to detect its troubles. They just give you a poor answer, without comment. *Caveat emptor!*

A sine and a line

Let's explore a simple example: Find the smallest positive root of the equation system

$$y = \sin x \qquad \text{and} \qquad y = 0.1 + x/2 \qquad (1)\ (2)$$

which, being the sine curve and a straight line with slope 1/2 and a small intercept, 0.1, is easy to sketch (figure 1). Since the line is fairly flat, an iterative procedure comes to mind:

Step 1. Having an x, we move vertically to the line via

$$y \leftarrow 0.1 + x/2.$$

Step 2. Using this y we move horizontally to the sine curve via

$$x \leftarrow \arcsin y$$

then go to Step 1.

We show one possible iteration, starting at 0.48, in our figure 1. In practice we usually will combine the steps to execute

$$x_{step} \leftarrow \arcsin(0.1 + x/2).$$

Altho we can do better for a starting value than by setting x to zero, we try our procedure from there — producing the numbers in the column labeled x_{step}. It works, but not very efficiently. So we try Newton's method via

$$x_{newt} \leftarrow x - \frac{0.1 + x/2 - \sin x}{1/2 - \cos x}$$

again from zero, getting the x_{newt} of the second column. Good; very few iterations (but twice as many transcendental function evaluations per iteration — and they can take perhaps 50 arithmetic operations each).

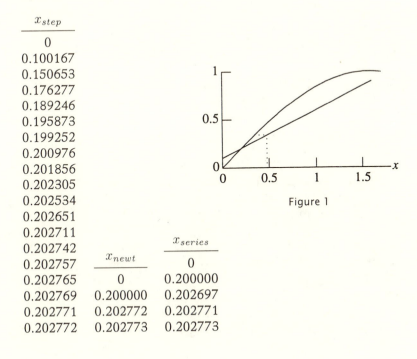

Figure 1

x_{step}	x_{newt}	x_{series}
0		
0.100167		
0.150653		
0.176277		
0.189246		
0.195873		
0.199252		
0.200976		
0.201856		
0.202305		
0.202534		
0.202651		
0.202711		
0.202742		0
0.202757		0.200000
0.202765	0	0.202697
0.202769	0.200000	0.202771
0.202771	0.202772	0.202773
0.202772	0.202773	

Finally, since the root we seek is near the origin, we might try replacing $\sin x$ by the first few terms of its power series to give

$$\sin x = x - \frac{x^3}{3!} + \frac{x^5}{5!} - \cdots = 0.1 + x/2.$$

Collecting the x terms on the left and factoring out x we get

$$x(1/2 - x^2/3! + x^4/5!) = 0.1$$

so

$$x_{series} \leftarrow \frac{0.1}{1/2 - x^2/6 + x^4/120}$$

which, still starting at zero, gives the x_{series} of the third column. One more iteration than Newton and *no* transcendental function evaluations — clearly more efficient at six arithmetic operations per iteration.

In summary, if you need one numerical root of a simple transcendental equation, the procedure is straightforward:

1. Make a reasonably careful plot of the equation (with the help of a pocket calculator where necessary) — then LOOK AT IT!

2. Note the approximate location of the root and, if there are several, make sure that this is the one you want.

3. Still looking at the plot, devise an iterative procedure to find it more accurately — then do it.

   a) If you can't come up with your own method, try Newton's — you already have a starting value that probably will work.

   b) If you don't trust Newton, try evaluating a point on either side of your best estimate of the root, then evaluate one halfway between them and keep on — thereby halving the interval each time. (This is known as the "Binary Chop.")

4. Make sure the answer you get lies reasonably close to the value with which you started. If not, find out why! (Check your plot.)

But if this were the only scenario involving transcendental equations, we would not be devoting two chapters to them. The interesting questions usually involve a *family* of similar equations, usually equations containing a *parameter* that will be supplied repeatedly by some other computer program and for which we need the root of the corresponding equation. Thus we are not just concerned with solving one equation once, nor with one geometry, nor with one algorithm.

Let us resume our exploration by considering our problem with the line in a slightly different position — with intercept 0.2 and slope 1/10. The picture (line A in figure 2) is not much different and our three algorithms give the numbers shown below in the same relative order, Newton in the middle. The stepping iteration is noticeably more efficient than before (the line is flatter, so y improves more dramatically at each vertical step) but stepping still does not successfully compete with Newton or our series iteration — which retain much the same relation as before, Newton being *less* efficient because of the sine and cosine evaluations.

Finally, suppose our current rather flat line has its intercept increased, moving it up to the position of line B in figure 2. From the

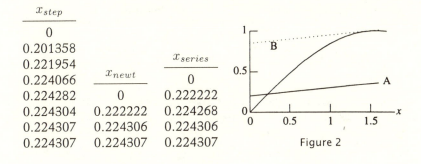

x_{step}	x_{newt}	x_{series}
0		
0.201358		
0.221954		
0.224066		
0.224282	0	0.222222
0.224304	0.222222	0.224268
0.224307	0.224306	0.224306
0.224307	0.224307	0.224307

Figure 2

picture it is not clear whether the line intersects with the sine curve at all, or if it does, how we should proceed. There are several related problems introduced by this near-tangency geometry that we discuss in chapter 2. Here we merely call attention to the considerable geometric change that can be produced by a quite small change in a parameter — from no positive root to two close positive roots merely by changing the intercept from 0.84792455 to 0.84792454 — and the close roots are not all that close, being 1.4705 and 1.4707. And of course lines with other slopes will produce other geometries that imply other solution methods.

If we are to construct a program that will handle all these various geometries correctly, we must explore the several typical ones, one at a time, by hand, until we feel sure that we understand the job to be done. The person who simply invokes a black-box computer program that "solves equations" without having done this kind of homework will have disaster on her hands at electronic speeds.

Exercise

Find the root just beyond $\pi/2$ for the equation pair (1) and (2). Try both Newton and stepping algorithms (both in the original variable and in deviations from $\pi/2$).

Another sine-line

Thus far our experiments with a straight line intersecting the sine curve suggest that simple *stepping* is rather slow but dependable, that Newton is fast and dependable, and that an iteration devised to take advantage of closeness to the origin is most efficient of all. Of course we have only looked at two quite similar configurations; a third might be helpful.

Look at the geometry of

$$\sin x = x - h = y$$

for h at 0.234567 and, more importantly, for h=0.000123456 — both problems being supplied with a six-digit value for h (figure 3). We can dismiss the point A as quite ordinary. That root lies near 1.2 and

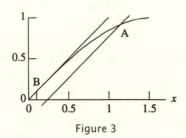

Figure 3

can be found by *stepping* vertically to the sine curve then horizontally to the line with

$$y \leftarrow \sin x \qquad \text{and} \qquad x \leftarrow 0.234567 + y$$

or, combining, by the iteration

$$x \leftarrow 0.234567 + \sin x.$$

If you prefer Newton's method, it works excellently there — requiring a cosine evaluation (or a square root) in addition to the sine function each iteration, but fewer iterations. And your favorite black-box calculator routine should also suffice.

Point B has near-tangential geometry; the curves are nearly parallel and very close together. Again, stepping will ultimately succeed, but the small spacing between the curves forces the algorithm to take such small steps that the process just takes too long to be practical. We show the progress of our iteration via occasional samples from

$$x_{step} \leftarrow 0.000123456 + \sin x. \tag{3}$$

Notice that it yields only three correct digits after two thousand iterations! We also show two faces of Newton and results from equation (5).

Newton is satisfactory *only* if you start him out properly, and he suffers from another difficulty: loss of significant figures (not visible here). The driving force in Newton's iteration is our equation written as $f(x) = 0$. Thus

$$x_{newt} \leftarrow x - \frac{x - h - \sin x}{1 - \cos x}$$

where both the numerator *and* the denominator are very small quantities (small even compared to x which itself is small) that become small by the subtraction of much larger nearly equal quantities.

And now, having realized that a small change in x produces *nearly the same change* in $\sin x$, we become retroactively worried about our stepping equation (3), which suffers from the same ill-conditioning as the numerator in Newton. In both we are trying to match the small quantities $x - \sin x$ with h but are computing the first by subtracting much larger, nearly equal items. The answers they produce may be good or not — a machine with double-precision arithmetic helps here — but for certifiably accurate answers we need a better way. Again a series resolves our difficulty

$$x = h + \sin x = h + x - \frac{x^3}{3!} + \frac{x^5}{5!} - \cdots \tag{4}$$

so, cancelling the x, we can equate the smaller quantities

$$\frac{x^3}{3!} - \frac{x^5}{5!} + \cdots = h$$

which, on factoring out x^3, can be expediently solved via the iteration (in x^2)

$$x^2_{series} \leftarrow \frac{h^{2/3}}{\left[\dfrac{1}{3!} - \dfrac{x^2}{5!} + \dfrac{x^4}{7!} - \cdots\right]^{2/3}} \tag{5}$$

and we see that for six correct digits we need keep only thru the x^4th term in a denominator whose magnitude is fixed by its first term, 0.166667. (*All* subtractions are not dangerous! Only when the items are nearly equal do we worry.)

step	x_{step}
0	0.0
29	3.58E$-$3
30	3.70E$-$3
129	1.59E$-$2
130	1.60E$-$2
529	6.003E$-$2
530	6.011E$-$2
1029	8.5095E$-$2
1030	8.5116E$-$2
2029	9.03978E$-$2
2030	9.03982E$-$2

Properly started, Newton works, but we should be a bit worried about how good our answer really is.

x_{newt}	x_{newt}	x^2_{series}
0.2	.00012	0.
0.1394	17146.7	8.18670E$-$3
0.1056	$-$1595492.0	8.18894E$-$3
9.256E$-$2	$\cdots$	8.18894E$-$3
9.0538E$-$2	Very	hence x is
9.04927E$-$2	Nervous!	9.04927E$-$2

So now what generalizations seem correct? Simple stepping is still "dependable" — but so slow as to be useless when squeezed into tight, nearly parallel geometries. This experiment does not rule out all stepping as useless; it only reinforces our exhortation to look at the geometry before choosing the algorithm. Newton's method, *when started properly*, can be very efficient, tho possibly imprecise — and can be a complete disaster when started at a wrong place. Finally, an iteration devised to circumvent anticipated significant figure loss by invoking a pertinent series is clearly both more efficient and more precise but cannot retain its efficiency when the root wanders too far from zero. (Why?) Choosing an algorithm is not trival; it requires thought and good judgement. Planning a comprehensive computer function that chooses the appropriate algorithm requires even more care.

A sine-hyperbola

In order to sketch

$$x \cdot \sin x = h$$

more easily we shall probably rewrite it as

$$\sin x = \frac{h}{x} = y$$

and produce something like figure 4. Altho the sine curve and the hyperbola go on forever in both directions and have many intersections, we shall limit our present interest to the pairs of roots, if any, that lie on the range $(0, \pi)$ and, since they can exhibit quite different geometries, we begin with the *smaller* of the pair. Thus, we wish to find the root r, s, or t — which is produced by different values of h, given in our examples to six-digit accuracy as 0.987654, 0.00123456 and 1.81234, respectively. For the roots r and t the sine curve seems to have a flatter slope than the hyperbola, which suggests a stepping algorithm: vertical to sin x, horizontal to the hyperbola

$$y \leftarrow \sin x \qquad \text{then} \qquad x \leftarrow h/y$$

or

$$x \leftarrow \frac{h}{\sin x}$$

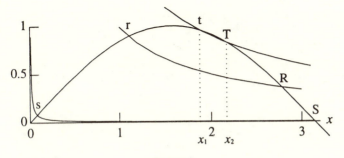

Figure 4

and, indeed, this iteration works with reassuring dependability — altho not always with gratifying celerity. For stepping to be quick we need one of the curves to be quite flat or one to be quite steep. (Why? Draw a sketch.) Thus, at t things go smoothly (try it) but at r we have a somewhat slow spiral convergence. Still we get there and without any numerical disasters.

Newton will also get there — much faster — but we must be careful about where we start him. The appropriate picture for Newton is *not* figure 4. It is figure 5, and now we see that there are two places where this curve has *zero slope* — and slope is the denominator in Newton. Further, these places (0 and close to 2) are numbers that the unwary are apt to choose to start Newton's method! (Fortunately for them, the other common choice, 1, works well here. Sometimes Murphy isn't looking — but one-in-three are not good odds. Don't gamble. Draw the picture and look at it!)

For root s, down near the origin, the hyperbola and the sine curve cross in a nearly perfect X. Stepping is obviously a poor strategy, but since successive iterates bracket the root almost symmetrically, it can be forced to work if we average each pair of iterates to get the next x. And Newton here is mucking about in a very flat part of his curve. He will work but, once again, don't start him at zero! We need to invoke the pseudoconstant gambit.

The pseudoconstant gambit

A better way to solve the sine-hyperbola problem when h is small depends on the fact that the function $\sin x/x$ varies quite slowly over $0 < x < \pi/2$ and is *very* close to 1 when x is small. Thus, we can neutralize $\sin x$ by dividing it by x — remembering to compensate by multiplying x by x — to produce

$$x^2(\sin x/x) = h = 0.00123456$$

then divide by our *pseudoconstant* to produce the iteration

$$x^2 \leftarrow \frac{0.00123456}{(\sin x/x)} \qquad \text{hence} \qquad x_s \leftarrow \frac{0.0351363}{\sqrt{\sin x/x}}$$

and *begin with* $(\sin x/x)$ *equal to unity.* We get

x_s
0.0351363
0.0351399
0.0351399 — convergence with celerity!

This is an example of neutralizing a transcendental function by turning it into a slowly varying function that we then temporarily treat as a constant, a pseudoconstant, thereby reducing the equation to an algebraic one (in this example a particularly simple one) that we may know how to solve. Since $\sin x/x$ shrinks slowly from 1 at the origin and is still relatively large (0.63) at $\pi/2$, this algorithm works rather well even for root r, but Newton is better there. We show numerical results by both techniques for x_r.

x_r	x_r Newton
0.99381	0.987654
1.08218	1.10605
1.10021	1.10527
1.10415	1.10527
1.10502	
1.10522	
1.10526	
1.10527	
1.10527	

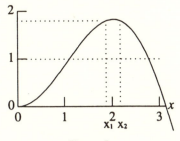

Figure 5

The roots at t and T are approaching each other at a point of tangency, x_{tan}, between the hyperbola and the sine curve. This geometry is definitely dangerous for all algorithms that ignore its special shape, and altho both stepping and Newton will yield values for these roots, their accuracy is less than we might wish — the problem as given being ill-conditioned. Geometrically, this is just a slightly tilted version of our $\cos x = 0.999986$ problem in chapter 0 and has the same numeric difficulties. If all we know is $h = 2.01234$, the roots t and T are determined to only a few correct digits, but if, on the other hand, we know the *deviation*, ϵ, of h from $h_{tan} = 2.0287598$, the h-value that produces actual tangency between the two curves, we can then get accurate roots. It is ϵ that precisely determines the *deviations* of x_t and x_T from x_{tan} (the location of the tangent point). If we need accurate results we need ϵ and we shall have to work rather carefully to recast our equation so that it equates ϵ to these deviations. It is an important but confusing and slightly esoteric art that we postpone until chapter 2 — preferring to discuss the more tractable problems first.

Finally, what about the roots S and R out near π? Since the hyperbola is quite flat there, stepping is clearly efficient. This time we move vertically to the hyperbola then horizontally to the sine curve. Beware the small boobytrap of simply using the arcsin button on your calculator without reflecting on the fact that it will give you an angle between 0 and $\pi/2$ — not really what you want! The correct stepping equations thus are

$$y \leftarrow h/x \qquad \text{and} \qquad x \leftarrow \pi - \arcsin y$$

or

$$x \leftarrow \pi - \arcsin(h/x) \qquad \text{starting with} \qquad x = \pi.$$

Newton also works — but again you want to be careful to tell him which quadrant you are exploring.

Exercises

1. How many roots does

$$\frac{1}{1 + x^2} = \cos x - b$$

have on $(0, \pi)$ for various values of b? Derive (and try) an iterative algorithm that is effective for small b. How many points of tangency between the two curves are possible on this range? Find it/them. (This problem is discussed fully in the Answers — but don't peek until you have done all the analytic and numerical exploring you can.)

2. And just in case you *did* peek, here is a similar one that we don't discuss in detail: How many roots and tangency points are possible for various values of b with

$$\frac{1}{\sqrt{1 + x^2}} = b + \cos x?$$

And how to find them, too. Indeed, find them!

An arctangent and a line

Looking at a line intersecting an arctangent*

$$\text{atn } x = x/2 - 3 \tag{6}$$

*We prefer the shorter abbreviation, atn — especially in equations.

we see (figure 6) that the root lies somewhere out near 9, which is not small. Nevertheless, the near horizontality of the arctangent at the root suggests that the simple stepping algorithm

$$\left. \begin{array}{c} \text{atn } x \to y \\ 2(y+3) \to x \end{array} \right\} \qquad \begin{array}{c} \text{beginning with} \\ y = \pi/2 \end{array}$$

ought to do rather nicely — and it does — giving the numbers shown. We can even start with x at 0, altho $2(3 + \pi/2)$ or our guess, 9, will both work a little faster.

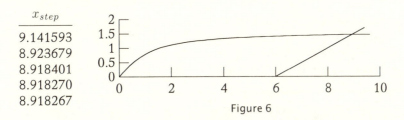

x_{step}
9.141593
8.923679
8.918401
8.918270
8.918267

Figure 6

But stepping is not the only possibility, and we remember that small variables are often better performers. Perhaps we should try to get one. Since the arctangent is not periodic, a simple shift of the origin to 9 would only complicate our equation. But arctangents have an affinity for *reciprocals* because, looking at a right triangle (figure 7),

$$\text{atn}(c/d) + \text{atn}(d/c) = \pi/2.$$

Figure 7

Letting $x = 1/u$, equation (6) thus becomes

$$\frac{\pi}{2} - \text{atn } u = \frac{1}{2u} - 3 \tag{7}$$

hence

$$u \cdot \text{atn } u - (3 + \pi/2)u + 1/2 = 0. \tag{8}$$

Since u is small we can now neutralize atn u, embalming it in a pseudoconstant by dividing it by u (and squaring the leading u to compensate) to produce

$$u^2 \left(\frac{\text{atn } u}{u} \right) - (3 + \pi/2)u + 1/2 = 0.$$

Denoting atn u/u by T and the constant $3 + \pi/2$ by P, we need to solve the pseudoquadratic

$$u^2 - \frac{P}{T}u + \frac{1}{2T} = 0 \qquad (9)$$

for its *smaller* root, which at first impulse might be evaluated from

$$u = \frac{P}{2T} - \sqrt{\left(\frac{P}{2T}\right)^2 - \frac{1}{2T}}$$

starting with $T = 1$. But being sensitive to unnecessary subtractions of perhaps nearly equal quantities [$(P/2T)^2$ is roughly 5, so subtracting 1/2 doesn't change it much], we heed the strictures of chapter 0 and so divide the constant term of (9) by the *larger* root to get

$$u = \frac{1/2T}{P/2T + \sqrt{(P/2T)^2 - 1/2T}} = \frac{1/P}{1 + \sqrt{1 - 2T/P^2}} \qquad (10)$$

with

$$P = 3 + \pi/2 \quad \text{and} \quad T = \left(\frac{\text{atn } u}{u}\right) = 1 - u^2/3 + u^4/5 - \cdots$$

more terms of the series being available if needed. Beginning with u equal to zero we find that our quadratic algorithm converges in two* iterations.

u^2	u	$x = 1/u$
0.	0.	
1.257570	0.1121414	
1.257573	0.1121294	8.918267

Is the more complicated algorithm justified? If we count arithmetic operations we find it needs 5 to get T, hence, if $1/P$ is stored, a total of eleven arithmetic operations and a square root for each iteration. Simple stepping takes 2 plus an arctangent. Thus, for this root stepping requires $8 + 8$ atn's and the quadratic needs 22 plus 2 square roots. Since the functions clearly dominate both algorithms and since the arctangent needs at least twice as many operations as

*Well ... *three* iterations if you count the one needed to duplicate our previous result.

the square root, we find *stepping requires about eight times as much computing* as the more complicated algorithm. If we need only one or two results, stepping is fine, but if we are using this root-finder inside nested loops of a big program, the savings are well worth it. (If you could cut the price of your new car by a *factor* of 8 by walking 10 miles to get it, would you remain at home and pay the full price? Remember, *somebody* is paying for your computer time!)

General principles? Useful techniques?

We have looked at some specific transcendental equations, drawn pictures, and tried algorithms that suggested themselves — but have any *general principles* emerged? Perhaps not, but some *useful techniques* certainly have. They are:

1. Rephrase your problems so that the root you are seeking is a *small quantity*.

2. Then replace the transcendental function by a *short* piece of its *power series*, if that helps.

3. Or try to neutralize the transcendental function by embedding it in a *pseudoconstant* — thereby reducing the problem to a probably simpler algebraic one that you know how to solve.

4. Remove large quantities from both sides of your equation so that it now equates small quantities, one of which is probably your *small* unknown x.

5. Try to put your equation into the form

$$x = f(x)$$

with an $f(x)$ that is *not very sensitive* to changes in x — then iterate

$$x \leftarrow f(x).$$

6. And, more negatively, use Newton, but only when you can start him "near" an isolated root and well away from the flat places of $f(x) = 0$. Pictures are essential here.

The details of these techniques vary. A root x that lies near 9.55 can be replaced by a small variable via

$$x = 3\pi + u \qquad \text{or} \qquad x = 1/v.$$

Obviously if the transcendental function is a sine or a cosine, we choose the translation of the origin to 3π; if it is an arctangent or other nonperiodic function, the reciprocal is usually more helpful. But the choice is not always clear-cut. Note that the nonperiodic e^{-x} becomes

$$e^{-3\pi} \cdot e^{-u} \qquad \text{or} \qquad e^{-1/v}$$

and while both these forms have their uses, the first is more likely to be effective.

Pseudoconstants are expressions like

$$\cos x \qquad \sin x / x \qquad \text{atn } x / x \qquad \ln(1 + x)/x \qquad \cosh x$$

but only *when x is near zero*. In each of these expressions the transcendental either is passing thru the origin with slope 1 so that division by x produces pseudoconstancy, or is itself nearly constant, being 1 with zero slope. We must be sure that x is small before invoking this gambit — one of the reasons for shifting the root to near the origin by a change of variable *first*. We can construct more complicated pseudoconstants like

$$\frac{(1 - \cos x)}{x^2} \qquad \text{and} \qquad \frac{1}{x} \cdot \frac{e^x - e^{-x}}{e^x + e^{-x}}$$

but the simpler set usually suffices.

We have alreaady seen simple examples of removing a large constant from both sides of an equation to create a more sensitive equation that equates small quantities — one of which is the root we seek. Thus, with $\cos x = 1 - \epsilon$ we replaced the cosine by its power series and cancelled the 1, leaving $x^2/2$ as the small quantity. With equation (4) the "large" quantity, x, was only large in comparison to some value of h — the relevant quantity of comparable magnitude was x^3. But the business of discovering and then removing larger quantities that mask the true carriers of the essential root information can be a complicated process for which general procedures simply do not exist. The sophistication that experience confers has no substitute. If your problem is large and expensive, get professional help.

An algebraic(⌘) equation

Suppose we need to find the real roots of

$$\frac{bx}{\sqrt{x^2 + 1}} = \frac{x}{2} - 3 \tag{11}$$

for various positive values of b. The right side is by now a familiar straight line, so we turn our attention to the left. Near the origin it behaves like bx. When x grows large it looks like $-b$ if x is negative and like $+b$ if x is positive. Figure 8 shows the geometry when $b = 2$ (solid) and it is obvious that there is only one real root — somewhere out toward 10. It also should be clear, after a moment's thought, that if b becomes sufficiently large, the negative part of the curve will dip down more steeply and will extend far enough to produce two additional roots. We show the curve for $b = 5$ (dotted) but shall confine our numerical efforts to the positive root for $b = 2$. (If algebraic problems amuse you, find the critical b_{tan}.)

A geometer looking only at figure 8 and seeing one or possibly three real roots might expect the equation to be a cubic, altho the present form of the plot does not look at all like a cubic. An algebraist, looking only at equation (11), would mentally square both sides and

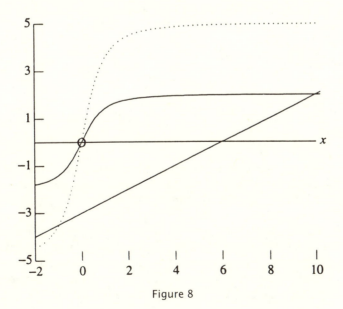

Figure 8

observe that on then multiplying thru by $x^2 + 1$ he would have a quartic — so obviously he would expect zero, two, or four real roots and thus would wheel out his polynomial-solving black box. Indeed, for $b = 2$ he would *get* two roots: near 9.9 and 2.3 — and be left wondering which he wanted.

The geometer, noting that the curve

$$y = \frac{2x}{\sqrt{x^2 + 1}}$$

is quite flat near the root, would propose the stepping iteration

$$x_{step} \leftarrow 6 + 4x/\sqrt{x^2 + 1} \tag{12}$$

beginning with 0, 6 or 10 — depending on how sophisticated a starting-value chooser he is. The iteration converges rather well from any of these three.

(No black box needed here to produce mild conumdrums.)

x_{step}	u
6.	0.
9.945576	0.1000000
9.979933	0.1001989
9.980069	0.1001997
9.980070	"

But then our geometer remembers that the arctangent problem, with similar geometry, did even better when a small root was sought. What if we try $x = 1/u$ here? We have

$$u \leftarrow 1 \Big/ \left(6 + \frac{4}{\sqrt{1 + u^2}} \right)$$

which gives the even shorter column of figures. (In the meantime, the algebraist is still searching for the instructions on the proper operation of his black box.) Get the message? If so, perhaps it is time for you to try some exercises.

Casual algebraic operations with an equation containing square roots can destroy the physical relation it was thought to tenaciously encapsule. Suppose we divide the numerator and denominator of $bx/\sqrt{x^2 + 1}$ by x. We get $b/\sqrt{1 + 1/x^2} \ldots$ Right?

Wrong! The first expression has *odd* symmetry; the new one is *even* — being positive for both positive and negative values of x. Of course our manipulation was wrong. The new $1/x$ factor in the denominator that we "moved" into the square root has to leave its sign at the door — rather like dirty shoes. Thus, the *correct* expression to use when x is large is $\mathrm{sgn}(x) \cdot b/\sqrt{1+x^2}$. Trivial — unless you forget it.

Exercises
(Answers or Hints to numbered exercises are in the back of the book.)

3. These equations are similar to the examples in this chapter. They will usually require different algorithms for different values of the parameter. Be sure to sketch them — maybe even recasting them somewhat. And try more than one method to gain a feeling for their relative efficiencies. There are few absolutes here; two people may well differ as to the best method. But whatever algorithms you devise, *be sure to try them on your pocket calculator.* And if two methods disagree even slightly, find out why!

a) $\cos x = b - x$ with $b = 1.57$ and $b = 2$.

b) $\cos x = 1 + b - x^2/2$ with $b = 0.001$ and $b = 0.24$.

c) $\tan x = x + b$ with $b = 10$ and $b = 0.01$.

d) $\mathrm{atn}\, x = x/10 - b$ with $b = 2$ and $b = -0.948$.

e) $\mathrm{atn}\, x + x = b$ with $b = 0.1$ and $b = 4$.

f) $x \cdot \mathrm{atn}\, x = b$ with $b = 0.01$ and $b = 25$.

g) $1 + b - e^{-x} = \sin x$ with $b = 0.001$. How large can b be before positive roots disappear?

h) For what r is the circle $x^2 + y^2 = r^2$ tangent to the curve e^{-2x}?

i) (Mystery Problem) How many roots does $b/(1 - x^2) = e^{-x}$ have for $b > 0$? For $b < 0$?

4. How to solve $b + x/(1 + x^2) = \sin x$ for small b? For what value of b does tangency occur?

5. Where are the intersections of $1/(1 + x^2)$ and $2\cos x - 1 + b$ for

$b > 0$? How should the first root be found if b is 0.001?

6. How many roots does $\cos x = e^{-x^2} - b$ have between 0 and π? Sketch both curves and make a geometric judgement about what happens as b moves from 2 down to $-1/2$. Can there ever be two roots? Three? Find an analytic-numeric way to settle these questions.

7. Consider the similar (but trickier) equation $\cos(x+0.2) = e^{-x^2} - b$ and answer the same questions as in exercise 6.

8. Find all positive roots of $e^{\sin x} = \ln x$. Try your favorite "black-box" or programmable pocket calculator by starting it at 10, 11 and 12. Do you get the results that you expected from your sketch? (My HP-28 does its own thing on this one.)

9. How would you find a value of b that will produce a double root for $e^{b \sin x} = \ln x$? Are there ranges of b values for which no double roots are possible?

10. Since the equation $e^{-ax} + e^{-bx} = 1$ has only one root for positive a and b, Newton is probably the reasonable algorithm. But it is fun to find iterative algorithms that don't use derivatives. Seek one that is effective when a and b differ widely — say 0.1 and 10 — and another when they are close, 2.0 and 2.2.

A superellipse and a cosine

Let us now look at the intersections of

$$y = b + \cos(x/2) \qquad \text{and} \qquad (x/3)^2 + y^4 = 1 \tag{13}$$

when b is small (say 0.01). Both curves are easily sketched (figure 9) and we see that one root lies just short of 3 and the other will be small, tho not as small as b. (Why?) The geometry near 3 suggests that stepping (horizontally to the ellipse and vertically to the cosine) should be satisfactory. But the small root needs a different treatment lest we lose significant figures in determining $x/2$ from a quite flat part of the cosine curve. It is the $\cos x = 1 - b$ type of difficulty again — and again a series is the proper tool.

We can eliminate y in (13) but raising $b + \cos x/2$ to the fourth power is unattractive. Further, since y will have a value near unity, it will

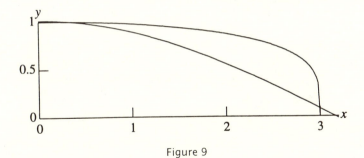

Figure 9

be $1 - y^4$ that determines the small quantity $(x/3)^2$. So we write

$$(x/3)^2 = 1 - y^4 = (1 - y)(1 + y)(1 + y^2)$$

and now we can get rid of the dangerous subtraction quite easily. Since the factors $(1 + y)$ and $(1 + y^2)$ will be pseudoconstants (nearly 2) when x is small, we get them out of the way by dividing to produce

$$\frac{x^2/9}{(1 + y)(1 + y^2)} = 1 - y = (1 - \cos(x/2)) - b = \frac{(x/2)^2}{2!} - \frac{(x/2)^4}{4!} + \cdots - b.$$

Factoring out $(x/2)^2$ and expressing the fraction in terms of that variable too, we get

$$b + \frac{\frac{4}{9}(x/2)^2}{(1 + y)(1 + y^2)} = \left(\frac{x}{2}\right)^2 \cdot \left[\frac{1}{2} - \frac{(x/2)^2}{4!} + \frac{(x/2)^4}{6!} - \cdots\right].$$

On combining and dividing we get our iteration, in the variable $(x/2)^2$

$$(x/2)^2 \leftarrow \frac{b}{\dfrac{1}{2} - \dfrac{4/9}{(1 + y)(1 + y^2)} - \dfrac{(x/2)^2}{4!} + \dfrac{(x/2)^4}{6!} - \cdots} \tag{14}$$

which, for $b = 0.01$, gives the data

$(x/2)^2$	$1 + y$	x
0.	2.010	0.
2.560545795E−2	1.997224566	0.3200341104
2.581582783E−2	1.997119831	0.3213460928
2.581757998E−2	1.997118959	0.3213569974
2.581759457E−2	1.997118952	0.3213570884
2.581759469E−2	1.997118952	0.3213570892

Notice that the pseudoconstant $1 + y$ isn't even very pseudo! These data come from having retained the $(x/2)^6/8!$ term. How wrong would they have been if only the terms shown in (14) had been used? Then the neglected term would be about 4×10^{-10}. Since the constant term in the denominator is about 0.4, the fractional error would be 1×10^{-9}, that is, one in the ninth figure of $(x/2)^2$.

Exercises

11. The same superellipse and b still small but with a different cosine

$$(x/3)^2 + y^4 = 1 \qquad \text{and} \qquad y = b + \cos 2x$$

poses interesting challenges.

12. (Rather easy.) Find algorithms for the roots of

$$\left(\frac{x}{2}\right)^2 + y^2 = 1 \qquad \text{with} \qquad y = b + \cos x$$

for $-2 < b < 0.5$.

13. How about

$$\left(\frac{x}{2}\right)^2 + y^2 = 1 \qquad \text{with} \qquad y = b \cos x$$

for various positive b, especially near 1?

14. Finally, try

$$x^2 + \left(\frac{y}{2}\right)^2 = 1 \qquad \text{with} \qquad y = b \cos x.$$

Consider, then reconsider

Suppose we need a computer program that will find all the roots of

$$bx = \frac{1}{1 - \cos x} \qquad 0.1 \le b < 10.0 \tag{15}$$

that are less than 10π. Since the cosine is periodic we suspect that these roots will lie approximately 2π units apart — sort of. So grab for Newton, start him at nice values — and hope! But let's draw a sketch first. Figure 10 shows a "typical" geometry (b is 0.2) in which the roots, except for the first, cluster in pairs on either side of $2k\pi$. The cosinely term *at* $2k\pi$ is infinite — we better be careful about just which "nice" values we use to start Newton! And then we notice that if b is 0.1 the straight line bx sneaks completely under the first branch of the other curve — so we have some homework to do to find out just how large b must be before we can safely seek roots on the range $(0, 2\pi)$.

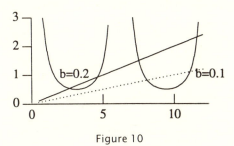

Figure 10

Perhaps we should consider a different formulation of our problem. So get rid of the denominator that can go to zero by writing (15) as

$$x(1 - \cos x) = 1/b \qquad (16)$$

and sketch it (figure 11, $b = 1$). It is a series of increasingly higher mountains with all the valleys hitting zero at $2k\pi$. The roots are all at the elevation $1/b$, which gives us a reasonable idea of where they

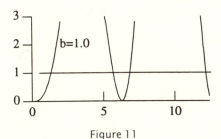

Figure 11

lie — unless b is so very small that $1/b$ misses the top of the first mountain entirely. But at least we won't have to worry about giving

Newton starting values that might land him on an infinity. Still, we might try another form of our problem, say

$$1 - \cos x = \frac{1}{bx} \tag{17}$$

giving us figure 12. Here we see a series of cosine hills, all alike, which helps when trying to visualize just what happens off the page to the right. The other curve, a hyperbola, usually will intersect all the hills and mostly very near the valleys at $2k\pi$ — but, of course, it *can* miss the first hill if b is near 0.1.

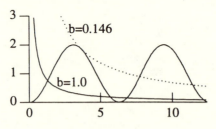

Figure 12

All three formulations of our problem give Newton-amenable functions that work efficiently if started with good values. But *we* have to come up with those good values. And *we* have to worry about when that first root pair disappears. First, the starting values.

Let us shift the origin to $2k\pi$ by substituting $x = 2k\pi + u$ in (17) to get

$$1 - \cos u = \frac{1}{b(2k\pi + u)}$$

and now u is usually small, so replace $\cos u$ with two terms of its series and ignore u entirely where it is added to $2k\pi$. We have

$$\frac{u^2}{2} \approx \frac{1}{2bk\pi} \qquad \text{or} \qquad u \approx \pm\frac{1}{\sqrt{bk\pi}}.$$

So good starting values for *any* iterative process should be

$$x = 2k\pi \pm \frac{1}{\sqrt{bk\pi}} \tag{18}$$

except for the first root.

The first root disappears when b is less than the value that makes the hyperbola tangent to the first hump. This occurs at the simultaneous solution of

$$1 - \cos x = 1/bx \qquad \text{and} \qquad \sin x = -1/bx^2.$$

(The second equation equates the slopes of the two curves.) Multiplying the second equation by x and adding it to the first to eliminate b gives

$$1 - \cos x + x \sin x = 0$$

to be solved for a root slightly beyond π — somewhere near 3.5 (figure 12, the dotted hyperbola). Since this is a solve-it-only-once equation, efficiency in the method is unimportant. Newton gives $x_t = 3.6732$, which leads directly to the critical value $b_t = 0.14621$.

Now we have most of the information essential for our program (which we leave to a programming course as an exercise). Observe, however, that all three formulations of the problem can be used to produce simple iterative algorithms of the up-to-curve-A-then-across-to-curve-B type. Some of these can challenge Newton for efficiency (but they also can deteriorate rapidly when the geometry becomes unfavorable). As an example, we use (17) to get

$$y \leftarrow 1/bx \text{ and } x \leftarrow \arccos(1 - y) \quad \text{hence} \quad x \leftarrow \arccos(1 - 1/bx)$$

which gives, for b and k equal to unity,

x_-	x_+
5.718996	6.847375
5.682846	6.830435
5.680880	6.831131
5.680773	6.831102
5.680767	6.831104

Notice how good the first approximation from (18) really is on this early pair of roots. For later roots it is even better.

Another reconsideration

Alternative formulations of an equation are usually worth exploring, but some care needs to be exercised to make sure that the reformulation really is equivalent to the original. Consider the equation

$$\tan(-\beta) = \frac{2\lambda\beta}{1 - (\lambda\beta)^2} \tag{19}$$

which immediately can be rewritten

$$-\beta = \text{atn}\left[\frac{2\lambda\beta}{1-(\lambda\beta)^2}\right] \tag{20}$$

then, using the identity for the sum of two arctangents, as

$$-\beta = \text{atn }\lambda\beta + \text{atn }\lambda\beta = 2\text{atn }\lambda\beta$$

and finally as

$$-\beta/2 = \text{atn}(\lambda\beta). \tag{21}$$

But this equation has only *half* of the roots of (19), as plots† of the two forms show — the roots of (21) being marked with o.

To get the missing roots, we must remember that since π can be added to the argument of a tangent without changing it, we can add π to the argument of tan in (19) to produce a second version of (21),

$$-\beta/2 + \pi/2 = \text{atn}(\lambda\beta), \tag{22}$$

as the other equation we need. It is the upper diagonal line in the second plot, the roots being marked with *.

Once we have the correct alternate equations we see that they simplify setting up systematic procedures for solving our problem (for various λ) — the geometric complications introduced by the vertical asymptote at $\lambda\beta = 1$ (dashed in the first plot) having vanished. Indeed, the intersections in the revised plot invite the simple iteration

$$x \leftarrow 2\lambda(k\pi/2 - \text{atn } x) \tag{23}$$

except possibly for the first, where an ×-configuration seems possible — suggesting the iteration

$$x \leftarrow \frac{\pi/2}{2.5 + \text{atn } x/x} \tag{24}$$

there.

We show the progress of the iterations for the first three roots, beginning the first with $x = \pi/2/3.5$ and the others with the not particularly felicitous $x = 2\lambda(\pi/2)(k-1)$.

† In both plots $\lambda=0.2$, and in the the second, $x=\lambda\beta$ to standardize the arctangent argument.

1	2	3
.448800	.62832	1.25664
.456632	1.03224	1.52556
.456882	.93614	1.48874
.456890	.95567	1.49323
.456891	.95153	1.49267
	.95241	1.49274
	.95223	1.49273
	.95226	
	.95226	

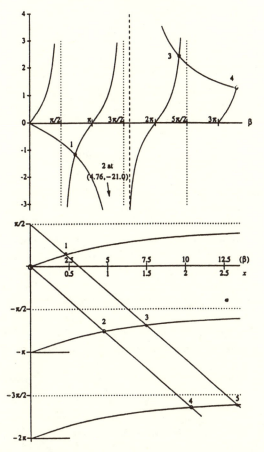

Note that this approach avoids any Newtonian temptation to seize upon the trivial root at the origin.

Exercise

15. First use your favorite "black-box" program or pocket calculator to solve for a first-quadrant root of the equation pair:

$$x^2 - y^2 = 1 \qquad \text{with} \qquad y = \frac{2x}{\pi}\text{atn } x + 0.63600$$

in a straightforward way. Then seek an accurate root, intelligently. (Be warned: this is a "cooked" problem designed to offer some difficulties to uncritical approaches.)

Reconditioning a problem

Most of the examples and exercises in this book are "clean" — they display their shape and most of their difficulties openly. Real-world problems seldom arrive in such good condition; they may need considerable rearrangement and exploration before their true nature is exposed. Here is a modest example.

An engineering problem has produced the equation

$$\frac{0.8474 + 0.3x}{0.8474 + 3.27x} = \cos(0.6697\sqrt{x}) \tag{25}$$

where the numerical values came from physical measurements so may be expected to vary somewhat in subsequent experiments. Both sides of (25) are 1 when x is zero — presumably a solution we do *not* want — and both decline toward zero as x increases. Since the cosine reaches zero and the left side does not, and since the left side starts its descent rather more abruptly than does the cosine, they must cross. But whether the crossing gives a clear decisive root or whether it is one of those glancing, almost tangential crossings that leave us suspicious is not clear without some tedious plotting. Thus, we are impelled to seek a different, hopefully more definitive, formulation.

First, clean up the argument of the cosine by letting $0.6697\sqrt{x} = u$ to get

$$\cos u = \frac{0.8474 + 0.669u^2}{0.8474 + 7.291u^2} = 1 - \frac{6.622u^2}{0.8474 + 7.291u^2}$$

thus removing the 1 explicitly from the fraction. Combining the 1 and the cosine and using the half-angle identity we have

$$1 - \cos u = 2\left(\sin\frac{u}{2}\right)^2 = \frac{6.622u^2}{0.8474 + 7.291u^2}.$$

We can now neutralize the trig function by dividing thru by $2(u/2)^2$ to produce

$$S = \left(\frac{\sin u/2}{u/2}\right)^2 = \frac{13.245}{0.8474 + 7.291u^2}. \tag{26}$$

The left-hand term declines slowly from 1 to 0.810 as u goes from 0 to $\pi/2$ — that is, it is a pseudoconstant. Thus, (26) is pseudolinear in u^2, giving the iteration

$$u^2 \leftarrow \frac{1.817}{S} - 0.1162 \qquad S = \left(\frac{\sin u/2}{u/2}\right)^2 \tag{27}$$

which we can begin by taking $S = 1$. We get the values shown below.

u
1.304
1.408
1.426
1.429
1.430 $\rightarrow x = 4.56$

Note that this formulation avoids the presumably uninteresting root at $x = 0$ that was present in (25). One could, of course, solve (26) via Newton, but there seems no real need for those derivatives. (Sketch both halves of (26) to see why iteration works so efficiently.)

A very transcendental equation

How can the equation

$$F(x) = \int_x^1 \frac{e^{-t}}{t} dt = g(iven) \tag{28}$$

be solved for a given positive g? Since $F(0)$ is infinite (why?) and declines steadily to zero at x equal to 1, the root is isolated. Newton's method seems possible — at worst one can evaluate $F(x)$ by quadratures and the derivative

$$F'(x) = -e^{-x}/x$$

is cheaply available. But the singular geometry near the origin gives pause to our planning; if g is "large" we are fishing in troubled waters with a small x.

Mathematicians will recognize a close connection between $F(x)$ and the Exponential Integral, for which AMS-55 provides both tables and considerable analytical machinery, but one can still explore this problem without those aids.

First "remove" the singular behavior by subtracting off the first term of the exponential series:

$$F(x) = \int_x^1 \frac{e^{-t}}{t}\,dt = \int_x^1 \frac{1}{t}\,dt - \int_x^1 \frac{1 - e^{-t}}{t}\,dt$$
$$= -\ln x - \int_x^1 \frac{1 - e^{-t}}{t}\,dt. \tag{29}$$

This new integral is well-behaved even at $x = 0$, where it reaches its maximum value of about 0.8. Quadratures on this integral would be much more efficient than on (28) when x is small — but we can do better! Extend this integral to zero and subtract off the compensatory integral over $(0, x)$ to get

$$F(x) = -\ln x - \int_0^1 \frac{1 - e^{-t}}{t}\,dt + \int_0^x \frac{1 - e^{-t}}{t}\,dt$$

then replace the constant integral with its numerical value and the last integral with its series — got by substituting the series for e^{-t} and integrating term-by-term. We have

$$F(x) = -\ln x - 0.796599599 + x - \frac{x^2}{2!2} + \frac{x^3}{3!3} - \cdots \tag{30}$$

where the constant can be found by evaluating the series for $x = 1$ (or looking it up in AMS-55). The series converges somewhat faster than that of e^{-x}, making it quite efficient for all values over $(0,1)$.

We propose to solve (28) via Newton's method using (30) when x is not too small, that is, when g is less than 1 or 2. For larger g the dangerous geometry still threatens that solution process, even tho we can evaluate $F(x)$ efficiently. (We prefer not to slide along tangents that are nearly vertical!) Noting that large g means small x, the series in (30) will be small compared to g, so we solve (30) for the logarithm to produce the iteration

$$-\ln x \leftarrow g + 0.796599599 - (x - \frac{x^2}{2!2} + \frac{x^3}{3!3} - \cdots) \tag{31}$$

which should have a slowly varying right side when x is small. Here are the numbers for $g = 2$ and $g = 5$, starting with $x = 0$.

x $(g = 2)$	x $(g = 5)$
0.	0.
0.06101719	3.0378672E−2
0.06479669	3.0471028E−2
0.06503449	3.0471309E−2
0.06504946	3.0471310E−2
0.06505040	
0.06505046	
0.06505047	

The iteration is very efficient, costing little more than one exponentiation to free x from $\ln x$ at each line. (Quadratures take thousands of operations.)

A more sophisticated technique

The iteration (31) is efficient as long as g is greater than 1 but when it is less than 1, x is greater than 0.2 and the *iteration* converges rather slowly. The *series* is still quite efficient, so (30) can still be used in Newton, but there is a nicer way.

Following the principle of giving names to small quantities, let $u = 1 - x$ and $t = 1 - s$, whence $F(x)$ becomes

$$\int_x^1 \frac{e^{-t}}{t}\,dt = \int_0^u \frac{e^{-1+s}}{1-s}\,ds = e^{-1} \cdot \int_0^u \frac{e^s}{1-s}\,ds. \qquad (32)$$

Replace e^s by its series and (28) becomes

$$F(1 - u) = e^{-1}\,[T_0 + T_1 + T_2 + \cdots] \qquad \text{with} \quad T_k = \frac{1}{k!}\int_0^u \frac{s^k}{1-s}\,ds. \qquad (33)$$

The T_k can be evaluated by the recurrence

$$T_k = \frac{1}{k}\left[T_{k-1} - \frac{u^k}{k!}\right] \qquad \text{with} \qquad T_0 = -\ln(1 - u) \qquad (34)$$

whose derivation is not obvious. Even at $x = 0.2$, where $g = 1.0033$, only terms thru T_6 are needed to deliver five correct figures and additional precision follows even more swiftly. Only one transcendental is needed — the logarithm to get T_0.

[Recurrences are not official until chapter 4, but if you want to try deriving this one, begin with

$$\int_0^u \frac{s^k}{1-s} ds$$

and use the identity

$$\frac{s}{1-s} = \frac{1}{1-s} - 1$$

to get a recurrence for the integrals before folding in the factorials.]

Exercise
16. How would you solve the equation

$$\int_x^{\pi/2} \frac{\cos t}{t^2} dt = g(iven)$$

when g is large? And when g is not large?

Efficient versus inefficient algorithms

Altho efficient *solution of equations* is an emphasis of this book, efficiency in *solving a physical problem* is often better sought before an equation is formed — by a judicious formulation of the problem and hence of the algorithm and equations that solve it. We consider a "simple" problem by way of illustration:

> Find the location of the circle with unit radius
> that "sits" stably on top of the curves $y = e^{-x}$ and $y = \ln x$.

(Obviously there are four places where a circle of given radius can be tangent to both of these curves, but we seek only the one that lies entirely above them, as in figure 13.)

If we denote the center of the circle by (a, b) then tangency with the exponential curve at (x_1, y_1) produces the two equations

$$(x_1 - a)^2 + (e^{-x_1} - b)^2 = 1 \qquad \text{and} \qquad -\frac{x_1 - a}{e^{-x_1} - b} = -e^{-x_1} \qquad (35)$$

while the tangency at (x_2, y_2) with the logarithm curve gives two more

$$(x_2 - a)^2 + (\ln x_2 - b)^2 = 1 \qquad \text{and} \qquad -\frac{x_2 - a}{\ln x_2 - b} = \frac{1}{x_2}. \qquad (36)$$

Altho we now have four equations in the four unknowns x_1, x_2, a and b, we do not have an algorithm. From the figure one can guess reasonable values for the four variables, so you might be tempted to just try Newton's method in four variables — especially if you have a computer program that does symbolic differentiation and will set up the 4×4 Jacobian for you. It "ought to work" — meaning that there is no obvious reason why it won't, but don't bet on it. Newton has

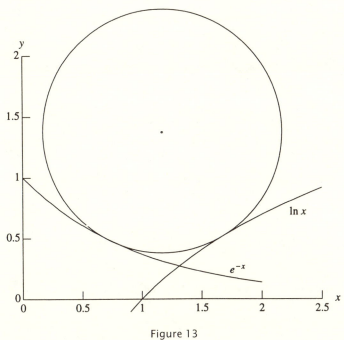

Figure 13

a straying eye and four dimensions gives him a lot of room to look around and find one of the other three solutions. Human geometric intuition is pretty good, so we prefer to constrain the problem to fewer dimensions.

Two loci

Our next approach is to see if we can set up an equation, or equations, that define the locus of the centers of *all* unit circles that are tangent to $y = e^{-x}$ while lying above it (curve L_1 in figure 14) and also equations for the locus of the centers of all unit circles similarly tangent to $y = \ln x$ — curve L_2. If we have equations for these two loci, then finding their intersection is a two-dimensional problem for which our geometric intuition can suggest solution methods.

To get the center of the tangent unit circle when given the point of tangency (x_1, y_1) on the exponential, merely use the slope equation to eliminate the $(e^{-x_1} - b)^2$ term in (35), getting

$$(x_1 - a)^2 \cdot (1 + e^{2x_1}) = 1$$

so

$$x_1 - a = \frac{1}{-\sqrt{1 + e^{2x_1}}}$$

the minus square root being mandated by a glance at the picture where $(x_1 - a)$ is clearly negative. So we have

$$a_1 = x_1 + \frac{1}{\sqrt{1 + e^{2x_1}}} = x_1 + \frac{e^{-x_1}}{\sqrt{e^{-2x_1} + 1}} \tag{37}$$

then

$$b_1 - e^{-x_1} = e^{x_1}(a - x_1) = \frac{1}{\sqrt{e^{-2x_1} + 1}}$$

so

$$b_1 = e^{-x_1} + \frac{1}{\sqrt{e^{-2x_1} + 1}}. \tag{38}$$

Similar algebra yields

$$a_2 = x_2 - \frac{1}{\sqrt{1 + x_2^2}} \tag{39}$$

$$b_2 = \ln x_2 + \frac{x_2}{\sqrt{1 + x_2^2}} \tag{40}$$

for the center of the unit circle tangent to $\ln x$ at x_2.

We are now are in a position to specify an x_1 and an x_2 to generate two points, one on each locus. But then how to adjust x_1 and x_2 so as to move these two points toward coincidence is not clear. We are

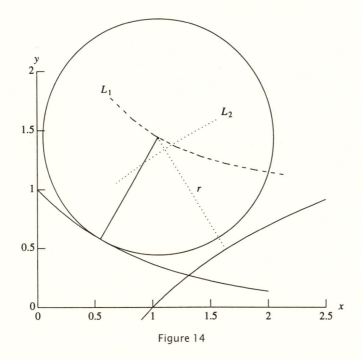

Figure 14

playing blindman's buff in two dimensions. With an interactive computer system we could invoke human pattern recognition as we try various x_1 and x_2 values, but that is scarcely an algorithm.

Newton again (but in 2-d)

We can form the a and b differences to get

$$d_a = a_1 - a_2 = x_1 - x_2 + \frac{1}{\sqrt{1 + e^{2x_1}}} + \frac{1}{\sqrt{1 + x_2^2}} \qquad (41)$$

$$d_b = b_1 - b_2 = e^{-x_1} - \ln x_2 + \frac{1}{\sqrt{e^{-2x_1} + 1}} - \frac{x_2}{\sqrt{1 + x_2^2}} \qquad (42)$$

and now seek to make d_a and d_b simultaneously zero by expanding each equation in a Taylor series in Δx_1 and Δx_2, keep only thru the linear terms, set d_a and d_b to zero and solve for Δx_1 and Δx_2. This is Newton's method in two dimensions. It is better than Newton's method in four dimensions and is efficient for improving x_1 and x_2 once we have values quite close to the solution. But getting those values is still an unsolved problem.

Locus crawling

Altho we can easily generate a point on, say, Locus$_1$, it would be helpful if we could then find how far that point lies from the $\ln x$ curve. But we can! The circle of radius r centered at (A, B) and tangent to $y = \ln x$ gives the equations

$$(x - A)^2 + (y - B)^2 = r^2 \qquad \text{and} \qquad -\frac{x - A}{y - B} = \frac{1}{x}$$

hence

$$x(x - A) = B - \ln x \tag{43}$$

and

$$(x - A)^2 \cdot (1 + x^2) = r^2. \tag{44}$$

If we have A and B, solve (43) for x then substitute in (44) for r^2. Now, instead of a two-dimensional problem we have two one-dimensional problems. The strategy:

a) Given an x_1 (on $y = e^{-x}$), evaluate equations (37) and (38) to get the center (a_1, b_1) of the tangent *unit* circle — a point on Locus$_1$.

b) Find r^2, the square of the distance that (a_1, b_1) is from $y = \ln x$ by identifying a_1 with A and b_1 with B then *solving* (43) for x and substituting it into (44). (r is shown dotted in figure 14.)

c) Since r^2 is clearly a monotone decreasing function of x_1 we merely choose our next value of x_1 smaller if r^2 is too big — and vice versa. After we have two values of $[x_1, r^2]$ we can use False-Position to choose subsequent x_1 values — thus providing a systematic one-dimensional algorithm that solves our problem.

Inside this large iteration we still must solve equation (43) each time. This is easily done by:

1. Iterate

$$x \leftarrow A + \frac{B - \ln x}{x}$$

(but the ×-geometry suggests that convergence may be slow so averaging successive steps may be desirable), or

2. Newton's method on

$$x(x - A) + \ln x - B = 0$$

that is,

$$x \leftarrow x - \frac{x(x - A) + \ln x - B}{2x - A + 1/x}.$$

By either method, three or four iterations should be adequate as we have first approximations from the previous time around the grand cycle.

Exercises

17. Devise a reasonable algorithm to find a circle simultaneously tangent to our friends

$$y = e^{-x} \qquad \text{and} \qquad y = \ln x$$

and also to the ellipse

$$\left(\frac{x}{2}\right)^2 + y^2 = 1.$$

18. Devise a practical algorithm to find the straight line that is doubly tangent to the lower side of the first-quadrant branch of

$$y = 0.1/x + 0.01e^{-(x-3)^2}$$

— a decaying and slightly wobbly hyperbola.

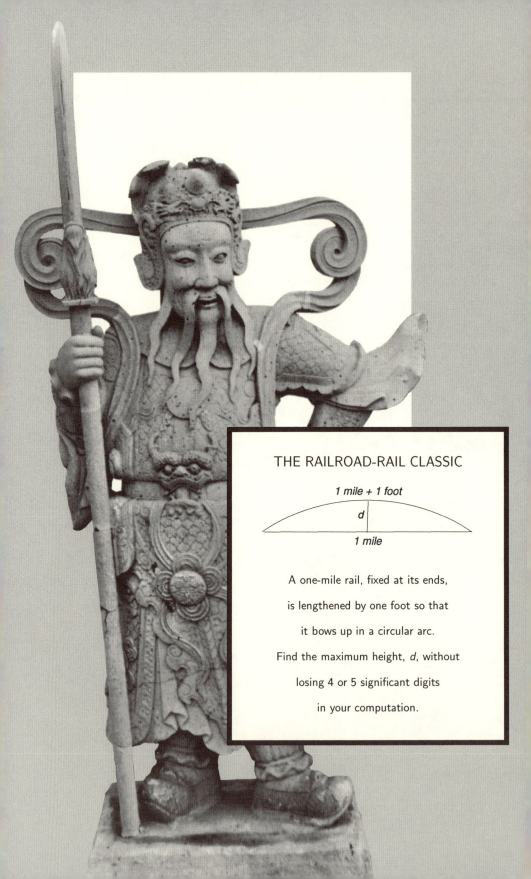

THE RAILROAD-RAIL CLASSIC

1 mile + 1 foot

d

1 mile

A one-mile rail, fixed at its ends,

is lengthened by one foot so that

it bows up in a circular arc.

Find the maximum height, *d*, without

losing 4 or 5 significant digits

in your computation.

Chapter 2

PRESERVING SIGNIFICANT DIGITS

"I will find where truth is hid ..."
Polonius

A persistent problem in scientific computing is the loss of significant figures. We have discussed the simpler examples in chapter 0 and chapter 1 but the malady deserves more attention because it is both subtle and pervasive. Equally important, *the search for these troubles usually leads directly to weak places in your algorithm.*

Occasionally the loss is so drastic that it forces you to recognize it, as in the evaluation of e^{-10} from the series for e^{-x}, but usually the loss is only two to four decimal digits — not the sort of error you notice even if sensitized to the danger. And, of course, the error only occurs for rather small ranges of a parameter, ranges that "aren't going to occur in *my* problem." (How much are you willing to bet against Mr. Murphy?)

A *unique* loss of three digits will seldom destroy the usefulness of an engineering computation. Even if it has been performed in single precision arithmetic, four digits are presumably still good, and unless you are doing high-precision surveying they will probably suffice. If double precision is used, the margin of safety is about fourteen digits — which will get your rocket accurately to Uranus, if you've got your physics right! So why worry? (Note that while double precision costs twice as much *space*, most contemporary scientific computers now provide it with only a quite small incremental cost in *speed*. Thus double precision should always be used unless you are running short of memory.)

The catch is the word *unique*. A long computation may encounter several successive losses of significant digits, which can cumulatively remove many more than three digits. If you are the local numerical guru, you soon encounter otherwise sensible engineers asking, "How can I get quadruple precision in Fortran?" — and you immediately know what the trouble is, even tho fixing it may be difficult. And the fix is *not* quadruple precision!

Extendable-precision software packages, notably in Mathematica^{TM} are useful as diagnostic tools to verify suspicions that precision loss is compromising an algorithm's performance and, more laboriously, to illumine the precise crannies where the cancellations are occurring. They can also be used to evaluate a small number of correct answers to check the new algorithm in which you have hopefully exorcised the devil. For exorcise it you must! You should never run thousands of production iterations needing 40, 60 or 100 digits of precision. If your sense of responsibility is weak, your boss should chastise you severely when he gets the bill! Preventing significant figure cancellations is often a frustrating task — but the rewards are more robust algorithms and greatly increased opportunities to uncover real goofs in your problem formulations. This chapter is an introduction, by example, to the art. The exercises will repay all the effort you choose to expend. (I could add, "Have fun!" — but I'm not that cynical.)

Unfortunately, significant figure losses occur in so many ways that they defy useful classification and lack systematic cures. There are no simple cookbook procedures. Here we can only show examples then urge you to try similar exercises that will help you with your own algorithms. One common geometric configuration, however, will always produce significant figure loss: nearly double roots of an equation — roots that are, of course, draped almost symmetrically around a place where two curves are nearly tangent. Most of the examples in this chapter have that geometry.

An easy tangential geometry

A pair of nearby roots causes most algorithms trouble. Not only does the presence of the other root distract the attention of the algorithm, often causing it suddenly to start after the other root, but the two curves that intersect twice in a small space usually have a nearly parallel geometry there.

To get a stable algorithm that gives precise values for the roots we must first find the tangent (double-root) solution. This part is usually easy because, altho it is another transcendental equation to be solved, the tangent point is an isolated root. Then we must recast our original equation in terms of *deviations* from the tangent point.

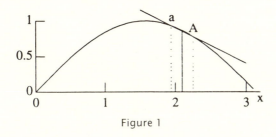

Figure 1

Occasionally this process is trivial, but often some ingenuity, or at least persistence, is needed. We first take a straightforward example

$$\sin x + \frac{x}{2} \; = \; h \; = \; 1.90321 \tag{1}$$

which has two roots near 2 (see figure 1 in which we plot the curve $\sin x$ and the line $1.90321 - x/2$). If we increase h slightly we produce tangency where $\sin x$ has a slope of -0.5, that is, where $\cos x = -0.5$ hence at 2.09440. Altho we have solved the tangency subproblem trivially here, we still need to write its *equation* — in which we use t to represent this critical value of x at the tangent point and h_t for the corresponding parameter value

$$\sin t + \frac{t}{2} \; = \; h_t \; = \; 1.91322. \tag{2}$$

Since h_t is larger than h we prefer to subtract (1) from (2)

$$h_t - h = \frac{t - x}{2} + \sin t - \sin x$$

and let

$$x = t + \delta \qquad \text{and} \qquad h_t - h = \epsilon = 0.01001$$

to produce a positive ϵ:

$$
\begin{aligned}
\epsilon &= -\frac{\delta}{2} + \sin t - \sin(t + \delta) \\
&= -\frac{\delta}{2} + \sin t - \sin t \cdot \cos \delta - \cos t \cdot \sin \delta.
\end{aligned}
\tag{3}
$$

Since δ is small, we can replace $\sin \delta$ by a few terms of its series, as well as $\cos t$ by $-1/2$, to get rid of the linear δ terms

$$\epsilon = -\frac{\delta}{2} + \sin t \cdot (1 - \cos \delta) + \frac{1}{2}\left(\delta - \frac{\delta^3}{3!} + \cdots\right).$$

Replace $\sin t$ by its value $\sqrt{3}/2$, expand $\cos \delta$ and cancel the 1's to give

$$\epsilon = \frac{\sqrt{3}}{2}\left(\frac{\delta^2}{2!} - \frac{\delta^4}{4!} - \cdots\right) - \frac{1}{2}\left(\frac{\delta^3}{3!} - \frac{\delta^5}{5!} + \cdots\right).$$

Our equation is basically *quadratic* — as the local geometry suggests it should be. We can now factor out δ^2 and divide to give the final iteration

$$\delta^2 \leftarrow \frac{2\epsilon}{\sqrt{3}\left(\dfrac{1}{2!} - \dfrac{\delta^2}{4!} + \cdots\right) - \left(\dfrac{\delta}{3!} - \dfrac{\delta^3}{5!} + \cdots\right)}.
\tag{4}$$

The presence of odd powers shows that the root pair is not symmetrical around the tangent point since use of the negative root for δ gives a different iteration from the positive.

Altho we now have a stable iteration, it will not give as precise roots as we might hope because we have *lost two significant figures* in the subtraction to get ϵ so that equation (4) must work with only four-figure data. And if the only information we have is the h of equation (1) there is nothing we can do about it. If, on the other hand, it is ϵ that we are given directly to six figures, then the δ's that equation (4) produces will be good to six figures — always provided we take enough terms of the series. We begin with δ equal to zero to get

δ_-^2	δ_+^2
0.0	0.0
2.31171E−2	2.31171E−2
2.25027E−2	2.38604E−2
2.25102E−2	2.38734E−2
2.25101E−2	2.38736E−2

δ_-	δ_+
−0.150034	0.154511

x_-	x_+
1.94436	2.24891

Altho we can trust only four figures of the δ's, when we add them to the precisely known t they give us five good figures for the x's.

A more typical near-tangency

Look at the classical problem $b = x \cdot \cos x$ pictured in figure 2 with b at 6.36000. The hyperbola b/x intersects the second hump of the cosine curve slightly beyond 2π to give two roots bracketing a point of tangency, t, that will occur if b is increased slightly. To avoid losing significant figures unnecessarily, we need to look more closely at this part of the geometry.

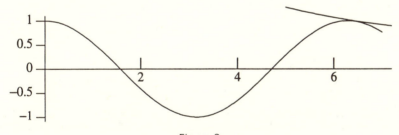

Figure 2

To focus our numerical microscope on one pair of nearly double roots we need to express them as *deviations*, δ, from the easily found tangent abscissa, t, and the *discrepancy*, γ, between b and the corresponding tangential parameter b_t. Since b_t is greater than b we subtract

$$b_t = t \cdot \cos t \quad \text{and} \quad b = x \cdot \cos x = (t + \delta) \cdot \cos(t + \delta)$$

to give a positive γ as

$$\gamma = b_t - b = t \cdot \cos t - (t + \delta) \cdot (\cos t \cdot \cos \delta - \sin t \cdot \sin \delta).$$

Thus far we have not used the equation $t \cdot \sin t = \cos t$ that makes t a *tangential* point. (We solve it in the next section.) We use it now to replace $\sin t$ with $\cos t/t$, giving

$$\gamma = t \cdot \cos t - (t + \delta) \cdot \cos t \cdot \left(\cos \delta - \frac{\sin \delta}{t} \right)$$

thus

$$\gamma/\cos t = t(1 - \cos \delta) + (\sin \delta - \delta \cos \delta) + (\delta \sin \delta)/t$$

and we see that each of the three terms on the right are of the order of δ^2 (and higher powers) — so we have almost rendered the equation into the expected parabolic form

$$c \cdot \gamma = \delta^2.$$

To complete our iterative algorithm, expand $\sin \delta$ and $\cos \delta$, thus

$$\frac{\gamma}{\cos t} = t\left(\frac{\delta^2}{2!} - \frac{\delta^4}{4!} + \cdots \right) + \left(-\frac{\delta^3}{3!} + \frac{\delta^5}{5!} - \cdots + \frac{\delta^3}{2!} - \frac{\delta^5}{4!} + \cdots \right) + \left(\delta^2 - \frac{\delta^4}{3!} + \cdots \right) \bigg/ t$$

then simplify slightly by dividing thru by t and replacing $t \cos t$ by b_t, whence

$$\delta^2 \leftarrow \frac{\gamma/b_t}{\left[\left(\frac{1}{2!} - \frac{\delta^2}{4!} + \cdots \right) + \frac{\delta}{t}\left(\frac{2}{3!} - \frac{4\delta^2}{5!} + \cdots \right) + \frac{1}{t^2}\left(1 - \frac{\delta^2}{3!} + \frac{\delta^4}{5!} - \cdots \right) \right]}.$$

Depending on whether we take the $+$ or $-$ root of δ^2, this algorithm has two solutions — their absolute values not being the same because of the δ term in the denominator. Note that nothing has been thrown away: we may take as many terms of the three series as we wish — tho since δ^2 is small we do not expect to need many. [The zeroth order δ^2 is $\gamma/\cos t/(t/2 + 1/t)$. With t approximately $2k\pi$ this reduces to $\gamma/(k\pi + 1/(2k\pi))$. For $k = 1$ and $\gamma = 0.000144$ we would get a δ^2 of about 0.00660 — but note that this very small γ still gives root separations of about 0.0132 (i.e., 2δ).]

Altho we have solved a problem where the roots lie on the second hump of the cosine, this algorithm is valid for finding root pairs on *any* hump — the only changes being the values of t and b_t that we find from the tangency equation.

As with the simple cosine example of chapter 0, however, the excellent precision we get for our root pair depends directly on knowing γ to comparable precision. If our information about γ is not direct but must be deduced by subtracting b from b_t, then these two data must be known to at least four *additional* significant figures. (They are both approximately equal to $2k\pi$ so we lose four or five figures in the subtraction.) Our numerical microscope cannot add precision to a δ^2 that is directly proportional to an imprecise γ. We would that it could — but it can't!

If we are stuck with b_t and b, then why not save ourselves a lot of algebraic trouble by simply using Newton's method directly on $x \cos x = b$? — I hear you ask. After all, it *is* able to find those roots to the highest precision that is possible. The danger, of course, is that Newton will happily converge to *either* of the close roots and, since the geometry is quite flat in that region, there is a real chance that it may inadvertently end up on the one you don't want — *and you won't know about it!* Our algebraic iteration has no such ambiguity. Good precision in a root is a desirable goal — but getting the *correct* root (with whatever precision) is even more desirable.

Solving the tangency equation

At tangency not only is the hyperbola equal to the cosine, but both have the same *slope* there. Thus we have the equation pair

$$b_t/t = \cos t$$
$$-b_t/t^2 = -\sin t.$$

Dividing to eliminate b_t we have

$$t \cdot \cos t = t^2 \sin t \qquad \text{hence} \qquad \cos t = t \cdot \sin t$$

or the

$$\frac{1}{t} = \tan t$$

shown in figure 3.

Each of these roots is clearly isolated with good first approximations available by inspection. Almost any root-finder will suffice and, since

t typically needs to be found only once (even when several root-pairs are needed in that locale), efficiency in getting t is secondary.

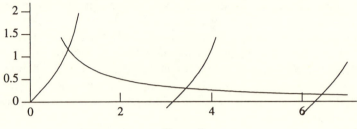

Figure 3

Newton will do nicely, altho if you are fond of stepping iterations the geometry suggests that they also work well for t-values near 2π, 4π, etc. (Only the first root, near 1, is not nice for stepping. Why?) Note that the roots near the odd multiples of π are tangent points only when b_t is *negative* — corresponding to the bottom humps of the cosine in figure 2.

Exercise
1. The student should now solve the similar problem

$$x \cdot \sin x = b$$

for, say, b at 1.818 or perhaps at 7.915 — which give root-pairs near 2.03 and 7.98, respectively.

A tangency with a logarithm

Since the art of obtaining the equation of the differences depends on experience, the student should follow these examples carefully to make sure he understands the maneuvers and the reasons for them and then try some of the numbered exercises (for which hints or answers appear in the back of the book). Here we solve a straight-forward problem that involves a logarithm. We want to find near-tangency roots of $\ln x$ with the hyperbola $r(x + 1/x)$ (figure 4). The strategy is similar to the previous examples, altho the algebraic tactics are somewhat different. We subtract the x-equation

$$\ln x = (r - \epsilon)(x + 1/x)$$

from the tangency version

$$\ln t = r(t + 1/t) \tag{5}$$

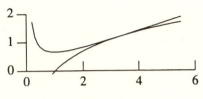

Figure 4

to get

$$\ln t - \ln x = r(t - x + 1/t - 1/x) + \epsilon(x + 1/x). \tag{6}$$

Leaving the small ϵ term on the right, combining the two reciprocals, replacing x by $t + \delta$ in two places and combining the logarithms we get

$$r\left(\delta - \frac{\delta}{xt}\right) - \ln\left(\frac{t+\delta}{t}\right) = \epsilon(x + 1/x)$$

which becomes

$$r\delta\left(1 - \frac{1}{xt}\right) - \ln\left(1 + \frac{\delta}{t}\right) = \epsilon(x + 1/x).$$

Since δ/t is small, we can expand $\ln(1+\delta/t)$ to get a term that should cancel any linear part of the left-hand term, so we simplify our notation by letting $\delta = t\Delta$ to produce

$$r\Delta\left(t - \frac{1}{x}\right) - \Delta + \frac{\Delta^2}{2} - \cdots = \epsilon(x + 1/x) = \Delta\left[r\left(t - \frac{1}{x}\right) - 1\right] + \frac{\Delta^2}{2} - \cdots$$

Now we must use the other tangency equation (slope-equality)

$$\frac{1}{t} = r\left(1 - \frac{1}{t^2}\right) \qquad \text{hence} \qquad r = \frac{t}{t^2 - 1} \tag{7}$$

to make the bracketed terms combinable as

$$\Delta\left[\frac{t}{t^2 - 1}\left(t - \frac{1}{x}\right) - 1\right]$$

thus

$$\frac{\Delta}{t^2 - 1}\left[t^2 - \frac{t}{x} - t^2 + 1\right] = \frac{\Delta}{x(t^2 - 1)}(x - t)$$

and so we get our second δ, hence $t\Delta$, so the equation reads

$$\frac{t\Delta^2}{x(t^2-1)} + \frac{\Delta^2}{2} - \cdots = \epsilon(x+1/x)$$

and a slight simplification comes from using the definition of r to give

$$\Delta^2\left[\left(\frac{r}{x}+\frac{1}{2}\right) - \frac{\Delta}{3} + \frac{\Delta^2}{4} - \cdots\right] = \epsilon(x+1/x)$$

hence the algorithm

$$\Delta^2 \leftarrow \frac{\epsilon(x+1/x)}{\dfrac{r}{x}+\dfrac{1}{2}-\dfrac{\Delta}{3}+\dfrac{\Delta^2}{4}-\cdots} \tag{8}$$

which requires that we have solved the tangency problem for t and r — after which we iterate (8), starting with $x = t$ and $\Delta = 0$.

Tangency requires solution of (5) which, on eliminating r, is

$$\ln t = \frac{t^2+1}{t^2-1}$$

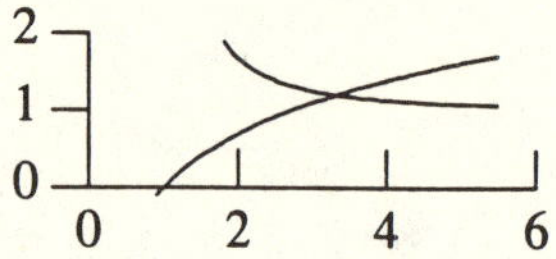

Figure 5

which gives an isolated root somewhere around 3 (figure 5). Using Newton we get $t = 3.31905014$ hence $r = 0.33137171$. (There is a reciprocal root near $t = 0.3$ that introduces no new difficulties.)

A not-so-obvious exponential tangency

Having dealt with a logarithm, let's turn to an exponential intersecting with a cosine. The equation we examine is

$$2e^{-(b+\epsilon)x} = \cos x \tag{9}$$

with the corresponding tangency equations

$$2e^{-bt} = \cos t \quad (\text{and } -b2e^{-bt} = -\sin t \quad \text{hence} \quad b = \tan t) \tag{10a} \tag{10b}$$

By now the force of habit might make you subtract (9) and (10a) — but that would be wrong because the difference of two exponentials is not very malleable. It is easier to beat together two exponentials by division or multiplication. Since cosines are the lesser of our problems here we choose to divide (9) by (10a) to get

$$e^{-\epsilon x} \cdot e^{-b(x-t)} = \cos x / \cos t.$$

Substituting $t + \delta$ for x in the cosine and the second exponential and expanding the cosine, we have

$$e^{-\epsilon x} \cdot e^{-b\delta} = \cos \delta - \tan t \cdot \sin \delta = \cos \delta - b \cdot \sin \delta \tag{11}$$

where we have substituted from the slope tangency equation (10b) for $\tan t$. Since both ϵ and δ will be small, this equation still has the form

approximately 1 = approximately 1

definitely *not* what we want! But if we take the logarithm of both sides we have

$$-\epsilon x - b\delta = \ln[\cos \delta - b \cdot \sin \delta]$$

and we have improved the equation in the sense that both sides now are small — on the right because the argument of the log will be nearly unity.

But we still need to liberate a term linear in δ from the logarithm (hopefully a $b\delta$) to cancel the one already present outside. We need to expand the log in a series; hence we must put it into the form $\ln(1 \pm \text{small})$. So we add and subtract unity to get

$$-\epsilon x - b\delta = \ln[1 - (1 - \cos \delta) - b \cdot \sin \delta] \tag{12}$$

in which the middle term of the argument begins with $\delta^2/2$ and the right one with $b\delta$. To simplify our manipulations and notation we rewrite (12) as

$$-\epsilon x - b\delta = \ln\left[1 - \left(\frac{1 - \cos \delta}{\delta^2}\right)\delta^2 - b\left(\frac{\sin \delta}{\delta}\right)\delta\right] = \ln[1 - (C\delta^2 + bS\delta)] \tag{13}$$

where C and S are pseudoconstants with values near 1/2 and 1, respectively. Now expanding, we have

$$-\epsilon x - b\delta = -(C\delta^2 + bS\delta) - (C\delta^2 + bS\delta)^2/2 - (C\delta^2 + bS\delta)^3/3 - \cdots.$$

Taking $-\epsilon x$ to the right and everything else to the left we get

$$C\delta^2 + b\delta(S - 1) + (C\delta + bS)^2\delta^2/2 + (C\delta + bS)^3\delta^3/3 + \cdots = \epsilon x \tag{14}$$

in which we have factored out one power of δ from inside the parenthesized terms of the series — leaving them powers of $(C\delta + bS)$ that is roughly equal to $b + \delta/2$.

Since the expression $S - 1$ is

$$\frac{\sin \delta}{\delta} - 1 = 1 - \frac{\delta^2}{3!} + \frac{\delta^4}{5!} - \cdots - 1$$

the second term of (14) is of order δ^3. We can combine the two δ^2 terms and, if desired, the two δ^3 terms, then factor out δ^2 and divide to produce the iterative algorithm

$$\delta^2 \leftarrow \frac{\epsilon x}{C + \dfrac{1}{2}(bS + C\delta)^2 - b\delta\left[\dfrac{1-S}{\delta^2}\right] + \dfrac{\delta}{3}(bS + C\delta)^3 + \dfrac{\delta^2}{4}(bS + C\delta)^4 + \cdots}$$

(15)

with

$$x = t + \delta$$

and the functions of δ^2:

$$C = \frac{1 - \cos \delta}{\delta^2} = \frac{1}{2} - \frac{\delta^2}{4!} + \frac{\delta^4}{6!} - \cdots$$

$$S = 1 - \frac{\delta^2}{3!} + \frac{\delta^4}{5!} - \cdots$$

$$\frac{1 - S}{\delta^2} = \frac{1}{3!} - \frac{\delta^2}{5!} + \cdots.$$

A reasonably efficient implementation will evaluate C, S, $(1 - S)/\delta^2$, x and $(bS + C\delta)$, after which the additional terms of the denominator series are trivially produced to the extent demanded by accuracy requirements. Note that our deliberate creation of pseudoconstants has led directly to the sensible computer program. As usual, the presence of odd powers of δ guarantees that the two roots are not quite symmetrically arranged about t.

Exercises

The following near-tangency problems are proposed in roughly increasing order of manipulative difficulty. Hints or answers are given in the back of the book, but note that often several different forms can be correct. If your result does not agree exactly, it is worth trying to reconcile it with the "official" version before concluding that the book is wrong.

2. How should you find the first root-*pair* of $\arctan x = (\pi/2)\sin x$?

3. Find an iteration for the root-pairs that solve

$$\cos x = x/\sqrt{x^2 + 1}.$$

4. Solve $(b - \epsilon)e^{-x} = \cos x$ where b is the tangency parameter and ϵ is a given small quantity.

5. Find the roots defined by a small ϵ and a tangency parameter b by

$$(b - \epsilon)e^{-x} = \sin x.$$

6. Given a, find r that produces a double root for $r + at^2 = \ln t$. Then find an iteration that solves for the close root-pair of $r - \epsilon + ax^2 = \ln x$ when given a small ϵ.

7. For fixed a (say $a = 6$), find the r, t pair that produces tangency for $(a - t)\ln t = r$. Then, given a small ϵ, find an iteration that produces the nearby roots of

$$(a - x)\ln x = r - \epsilon$$

via their deviations, δ, from t.

8. If b is given, say 2, find the values of r, t that give a tangency (double-root) geometry for

$$t \cdot e^{-bt} \cdot \cos t = r.$$

Then derive an iterative algorithm for finding the root-pair that solves

$$x \cdot e^{-bx} \cdot \cos x = r - \epsilon$$

when a small ϵ is given.

9. Solve $\ln x = (r - \epsilon)(x + 1/x^2)$ given a small ϵ. This is not easy. To encourage you to try, we give a compact form of the iteration here:

$$\Delta^2 \leftarrow \frac{\epsilon(x + 1/x^2)}{\frac{r(3 + 2\Delta)}{x^2} + \frac{1}{2} - \frac{\Delta}{3} + \frac{\Delta^2}{4} - \cdots}.$$

The derivation is in the answers.

Resolution of a subtle but familiar indeterminacy

Every sophomore knows that the indefinite integral

$$\int \frac{dx}{1 + 2bx + x^2}$$

has three closed forms according to whether $|b|$ is less than, equal to or greater than 1 and that these three closed forms seem to have almost nothing in common, involving as they do an arctangent, a rational and a logarithm, respectively. Worse, as b approaches 1 the two transcendental expressions seem not to approach the rational expression.

The computor has the same difficulties, only she is working with the *definite* integral, probably with both positive b and the limits $(0, g)$. Our illustrative integral here

$$\int_0^g \frac{dx}{1 + 2bx + x^2} \tag{16}$$

has a particularly pleasant denominator that can always be produced by changing the dummy variable. (The limits may then turn out differently but the points we make here remain unchanged.) If the algorithm to be programmed permits b to take on values in all three regions, then three expressions must be provided — with a test on b. But b, a REAL quantity, is almost never 1 — just sometimes trying to be and coming perilously close. Why perilously? Because both the arctangent and the logarithmic forms become indeterminate *at* unity and lose significant figures when *close* to unity. The careful programmer needs a *transitional* expression that avoids this indeterminate-form nonsense. We give it below, (20), but the derivations, tho elementary, are instructive and probably interesting, since calculus texts stop short with the closed forms for the indefinite integral. Taking the arctangent form, for $0 \le b < 1$ we write (16) as

$$\int_0^g \frac{dx}{(b+x)^2 + (1-b^2)} = \frac{1}{B} \int_0^g \frac{dx/B}{\left(\frac{b+x}{B}\right)^2 + 1} = \frac{1}{B} \operatorname{atn}\left(\frac{b+x}{B}\right)\Big|_0^g. \tag{17}$$

Having defined $B^2 = 1 - b^2$ and taken a B^2 out of the denominator, we get the second integral which, being of the form $\int du/(u^2 + 1)$, integrates immediately. When b approaches 1, however, B approaches zero, so we are somewhat apprehensive with the form of (17). But on substituting the limits we get two arctangents that can be combined by a possibly familiar identity

$$\text{atn}\left(\frac{b+g}{B}\right) - \text{atn}\left(\frac{b}{B}\right) = \text{atn}\left[\frac{\left(\frac{b+g}{B}\right) - \left(\frac{b}{B}\right)}{1 + \left(\frac{b+g}{B}\right)\cdot\left(\frac{b}{B}\right)}\right] = \text{atn}\left[\frac{gB}{B^2 + b^2 + gb}\right].$$

Noting that $B^2 + b^2 = 1$, we have

$$\frac{1}{B}\text{atn}\left(\frac{gB}{1+gb}\right) \tag{18}$$

for our usual computational form when $0 \le b < 1 - \epsilon$. Now we see that (18) is approaching $0/0$ as $b \to 1$, but we have the arctangent series to resolve the indeterminacy. Denoting the argument of the arctangent by A we have

$$\frac{A}{B}\left[1 - \frac{A^2}{3} + \frac{A^4}{5} - \cdots\right] \quad \text{with} \quad A = \frac{gB}{1+gb} \tag{19}$$

where we have factored out one power of the aggregate variable A. Now the B factor in the denominator disappears and we are left with the *transitional series*

$$\int_0^g \frac{dx}{1 + 2bx + x^2} = \frac{g}{1+gb}\left[1 - \frac{A^2}{3} + \frac{A^4}{5} - \cdots\right]; \quad A^2 = \frac{g^2(1-b^2)}{(1+gb)^2}. \tag{20}$$

Since A goes to zero as B approaches 1 we see that this series gives the analytic solution at $b = 1$. Further, this is a series in A-*squared* and we see that when $b > 1$, A^2 is *negative* (all square roots have conveniently disappeared) and our series (20) now consists of positive terms that remain small as long as b^2 is close to unity. Thus this series is a complete transitional algorithm that accurately evaluates the integral smoothly across the region that is so analytically rocky in calculus texts! We still need three separate computational forms but we can avoid the imprecisions near $b = 1$ by using them over $0 \le b \le 0.95$, $0.95 < b < 1.05$ and $1.05 < b$.

The derivation of the closed logarithmic form for (16) is also mildly interesting. When b is greater then 1 the denominator of (16) has real roots that are *reciprocals*, so we can write it as

$$\int_0^g \frac{dx}{(r+x)(1/r+x)} = \frac{1}{r - 1/r}\left[\int_0^g \frac{dx}{1/r+x} - \int_0^g \frac{dx}{r+x}\right] \tag{21}$$

with

$$r = b + \sqrt{b^2 - 1}$$
$$1/r = b - \sqrt{b^2 - 1} .$$

We have chosen r to be the *larger* root and have separated the original integral by partial fractions. Formal integration into logarithms, to which the limits are then applied, followed by recombination is simple — giving

$$\frac{1}{r - 1/r} \ln\left(\frac{1 + gr}{1 + g/r}\right) \tag{22}$$

an expression that becomes indeterminate when $b = 1 = r = 1/r$. It is possible to manipulate (22) into series (20), but it is not nearly as easy as from the arctangent side. A check for *numerical* agreement between (20) and (22) will probably satisfy most readers.

As with near-tangency geometries, this near-indeterminacy calculation preserves all the accuracy in the *deviation* of b from the critical value, 1. If this deviation, ϵ, is available, the expression $1 - b^2$ should be evaluated prudently. How? (If you don't know, go read chapter 0 again and do some of the Exercises there!)

Another transition-region formula

Probably no second-order differential equation is more discussed in technical classrooms than

$$y'' + 2ay' + by = f(t)$$

the linear equation of damped harmonic (or exponential) motion with a driving force $f(t)$. Most of the discussion concentrates on the homogeneous form

$$y'' + 2ay' + by = 0 \tag{23}$$

which describes the "transient" motion that usually dies out, leaving the "steady-state" behavior. Curiously little is said about the steady-state — probably because analytic solutions are practical for only a few $f(t)$. We shall not break with that tradition.

For given parameters a and b, equation (23) has the solutions

$$y = C_1 \sin ct + C_2 \cos ct \qquad c = \sqrt{b - a^2} \qquad \text{if } a^2 < b$$
$$y = C_1 e^{-at} + C_2 t e^{-at} \qquad\qquad\qquad \text{if } a^2 = b$$
$$y = e^{-at}[C_1 e^{+dt} + C_2 e^{-dt}] \qquad d = \sqrt{a^2 - b} > 0 \qquad \text{if } a^2 > b$$

corresponding to oscillatory, critically damped and overdamped behaviors. The a and b come from the physics of the system, while the arbitrary constants C_1 and C_2 are usually chosen to make the equation match the *initial conditions*, that is, the values of $y(0)$ and $y'(0)$.

But what should you do if the rather imprecise physical parameters are *almost* $b = a^2$? Which of the three forms should we use? The beginner's instinct is to avoid the middle form — it's too specialized. ("My system parameters are certainly not b equal to a^2 *exactly*. Besides, it looks sort of funny with that t in there." Or some such feeling.) So he chooses the exponential form — while wondering if the oscillatory might not perhaps be preferable. ("My experiment didn't *seem* to oscillate!")

When he starts to fit the C_1 and C_2 he will differentiate to get

$$y' = -ae^{-at}[C_1 e^{dt} + C_2 e^{-dt}] + de^{-at}[C_1 e^{dt} - C_2 e^{-dt}]$$

leading to the fitting equations

$$y_0 = C_1 + C_2$$

$$y_0' = -a(C_1 + C_2) + d(C_1 - C_2)$$

hence

$$ay_0 + y_0' = d(C_1 - C_2)$$

so finally

$$2C_1 = y_0 + \frac{ay_0 + y_0'}{d}$$

$$2C_2 = y_0 - \frac{ay_0 + y_0'}{d}$$

(24)

where d is small (and might even be zero)! Of course if the model is even close to reality $ay_0 + y_0'$ is *also small* — and by subtraction — yet another trap for the beginner.

On the other hand, if we multiply the exponential form of the solution by $2e^{at}$ and substitute (24) we get

$$2ye^{at} = \left[(y_0 + \frac{ay_0 + y_0'}{d})e^{dt} + (y_0 - \frac{ay_0 + y_0'}{d})e^{-dt}\right]$$

$$= y_0(e^{dt} + e^{-dt}) + \frac{ay_0 + y_0'}{d}(e^{dt} - e^{-dt}).$$

Substitute a few terms of the exponential series and we see that small d offers no problems. The first parenthesis is essentially 2 while the second is $2dt$ — making the equation nearly independent of d. If greater precision is desired, further terms of the series can be kept to give

$$y = e^{-at} \left[y_0 (1 + \frac{d^2 t^2}{2!} + \cdots) + (a y_0 + y_0')t(1 + \frac{d^2 t^2}{3!} + \cdots) \right] \qquad (25)$$

an expression in which the troublesome d appears only as its *square*. Since

$$d^2 = a^2 - b$$

it makes no difference whether $a^2 - b$ is positive, zero or negative — (25) holds smoothly over the previously troublesome transition region between oscillatory and overcritically damped behaviors. Of course, like all series, it is inefficient to use this form for large values of td, but for values less than, say, 7.9 it works rather well.

Complex square roots

Arithmetic performed on complex numbers is a minefield for significant figure loss. Consider, for example, the simple operation of squaring the complex number $2.0 + 2.01i$ where the two numbers are known to seven figures. The real part of the result is, of course,

$$(2.0)^2 - (2.01)^2 = 4.0 - 4.0401 = -0.0401$$

and there went two digits! (Transforming to polar form before squaring will lose the same information and cost about 100 times as many computer operations because of the transcendental function evaluations.) The difficulty is inherent in the statement of the operation — precision has already been lost if we must work with the numbers 2.0 and 2.01. If, however, the problem happens to arise in the form "square $[a + (a + \epsilon)i]$" with a and ϵ both given to seven figures, we can do it accurately because *we* know the real part to be

$$a^2 - (a + \epsilon)^2 = -\epsilon(2a + \epsilon)$$

in which no precision is lost via this alternate form. And, of course, there is nothing special about squaring that produces this difficulty; it is a gene that is recessive in all complex multiplications, waiting for the proper mating to produce its disaster.

This example should not deter you from doing complex arithmetic. But if mysterious losses are occurring in some crucial spot you should remember that, unlike real multiplication, complex multiplications *can* lose information and are thus are among the potential villains.

Complex square roots are particularly dangerous if done incorrectly. *All* square roots of small numbers make those numbers larger, thus often moving a previously unimportant imprecision into a more troubling digit position — but complex square roots require special care. The *efficient* algorithm naturally avoids polar form (unless polar forms are natural to the problem and are thus already present). From

$$\sqrt{z} = \sqrt{x + iy} = U + iV$$

one can easily derive

$$r = \sqrt{x^2 + y^2} \qquad U = \sqrt{\frac{r + x}{2}} \qquad V = \mathrm{sgn}(y)\sqrt{\frac{r - x}{2}} \qquad (26)$$

which only requires three real square roots. But that subtraction in V can be noisy if y is small — while if x is negative it is the addition in U that can give trouble. Fortunately we also have

$$U \cdot V = \frac{y}{2} \qquad (27)$$

so the proper algorithm uses (26) to compute whichever of U or V is safe, then uses (27) to get the other — thereby avoiding *unnecessary* degradation of the information in z.

A small case study

Problems that arrive on the desk of a local numerical "expert" are seldom in ideal condition — at least from his point of view. The major difficulties are often ones of accurate communication: the notation is unfamiliar; the original formulators of the problem are unavailable; the ultimate purpose of the computation is obscure. You are presented with a piece of a larger problem with which somebody has been having trouble — usually involving insufficiently precise answers achieved at exhorbitant computational costs. We conclude this chapter with a real (albeit moderately clean) example.

Here is part of a real computational problem — but COMPLEX as well as REAL — that arose from a mathematical model of a diffraction grating that is absorbing part of the incident light and, of course, reflecting the rest. This part of a larger computation landed on your author's desk via a common friend after the physicists* who formulated it began to use what they (correctly) felt was excessive computer time in finding the first forty roots of a transcendental equation for each of a potentially large set of exploratory physical parameters. Worse, for some of these parameter sets, some of the roots are nearly double and the physicists, for reasons I do not find entirely convincing, insisted on knowing the distinct values even when they differed only in the eighth significant figure. They had not always been able to achieve this separation using double-precision Fortran. Their inquiry was about quadruple-precision — altho amid speculations as to the availability of a supercomputer, they were also reported to admit some embarrassment about computing costs.

The equation (28) is as originally given, the parameter and variable names having physical significance to their fond parents but presenting an intimidating opacity to this numerical analyst. (There are really two equations here, differing only in the value given to τ, representing magnetic and electric fields.)

$$0 = \cos(k_0 d \sin\theta) - \cos(r\beta d)\cos[(1-r)\alpha d]$$
$$+ \frac{1}{2}\left[\frac{\tau\alpha}{\beta} + \frac{\beta}{\tau\alpha}\right]\sin(r\beta d)\sin[(1-r)\alpha d] \tag{28}$$

with

$$\alpha = \sqrt{k_0^2 - \Lambda^2} \qquad \beta = \sqrt{\epsilon k_0^2 - \Lambda^2} \qquad \tau = \left\{\begin{array}{l}\epsilon \text{ for H problems}\\ 1 \text{ for E problems}\end{array}\right\}.$$

Unlike many itinerant problems, this one arrived bearing some explicit computational information. The physicists had found roots, Λ^2, for the set of parameters shown here:

$r = 0.5$

$d = 1050$

$\epsilon = -23.4$

$k_0 d = 2\pi * 1050/700 = 9.4247780$

$\left(\dfrac{k_0 d}{2}\right)^2 = 22.2066099$

$\left(\dfrac{k_0 d}{2}\right)^2 \cdot (1 - \epsilon) = 541.8412816 = T.$

They also had supplied a plot of the right side of (28) against Λ^2 that looked roughly like figure 6. One glance shows that there are two

*Ping Sheng, R. S. Stepleman and P. N. Sanda; "Exact Eigenfunctions for Square-wave Gratings," *Phys. Rev. B.* 26 (1982), 2907.

regions here with quite different behaviors. To the left the roots seem regularly spaced and mostly (but perhaps not all) real, the amplitude of the oscillations is modest, and they go on forever.

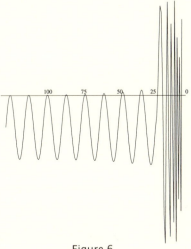

Figure 6

To the right the amplitudes seem enormous and they stop suddenly. Such differences almost certainly demand different root-finding algorithms. The regions clearly correspond to values of β that are real (left) and pure imaginary (right).

The grand strategy

Altho their sample calculations were based on a real given value of ϵ, the physicists also wished to be able to solve (28) when ϵ is complex — a change that makes all the roots complex. This fact, together with the occasional closeness of some root-pairs, makes Newton's method a two-dimensional search that can easily bounce from one root to another. Since the roots were to be used as the basis for a series expansion, it is important that they *all* be known, and be known in their proper order. A bouncing Newton is therefore bad! Likewise, any kind of exhaustive search over a two-dimensional grid for places where the right side of a complex (28) becomes zero is not only expensive but still quite capable of missing close pairs of roots when the search grid is too coarse — which, sooner or later, it will always be.

To minimize the two-dimensional difficulties when ϵ is complex, I proposed to find all forty roots for the nearest real ϵ, then add a *small* imaginary component and solve again for the forty roots by Newton's method using the previous roots as starting values. This process is then repeated with a larger imaginary component to ϵ, the roots refined by Newton, etc., until the actual complex ϵ of interest is reached. Since each Newton process has a good starting value, it should converge in three or four cycles each time. And it should seldom lose its root as it is being "walked" out into the complex plane. Indeed, since all forty roots are being advanced in parallel, it is possible to check at each step to make sure Newton hasn't bounced to a close neighbor by verifying that all forty roots are still distinct. (If trouble arises, you need only fall back one major cycle then advance the imaginary part of ϵ by a smaller increment.)

Taming the notations

Before we seek algorithms, the notational turgidity needs to be reduced. Dimensionless groups of names should be replaced by single names, especially where they are arguments of sines and cosines. It also helps reduce manipulative errors if variable and parameter names usually hold *positive* numerical values. Thus we define:

$$-\epsilon = \sigma \qquad -\Lambda^2 = k_0^2 \lambda \qquad p = \cos(k_0 d \sin\theta)$$

and also

$$\left\{ \begin{array}{l} \alpha d = k_0 d\sqrt{\lambda+1} = 2C \\[2mm] \beta d = k_0 d\sqrt{\lambda-\sigma} = 2B \end{array} \right\} \quad \text{so} \quad \left\{ \begin{array}{l} C^2 - B^2 = \left(\dfrac{k_0 d}{2}\right)^2 \cdot (1+\sigma) = T \\[3mm] \lambda = \dfrac{4B^2}{(k_0 d)^2} + \sigma \end{array} \right\}.$$

$$(29)$$

The electric (E) equation now reads

$$0 = p - \cos B \cos C + \frac{1}{2}\left[\frac{C}{B} + \frac{B}{C}\right] \sin B \sin C \qquad (30)$$

with λ for its (well-hidden) independent variable. Temporarily writing the last term as

$$\frac{1}{2}(C^2 + B^2)\frac{\sin B}{B}\frac{\sin C}{C}$$

shows that (30) is *even* in both B and C — so we need worry only about positive values. From (29) we see that for $0 < \sigma < \lambda$:

1. B is smaller than C but *both increase with* λ.

2. The sum $C + B$ will increase quickly with λ.

3. The difference $C - B$ will *decrease slowly* with increasing λ as shown by

$$C - B = T/(C + B). \qquad (31)$$

4. There is no limit on C and B, even tho they must approach each other as λ increases.

[When $0 < \lambda < \sigma$, then B and β are pure imaginary but all the terms of (30) remain real. This range of λ produces the large oscillations, B being small in magnitude and a denominator in (30).]

Using the identities

$$\cos(C \pm B) = \cos C \cos B \mp \sin C \sin B$$

and letting

$$g = [C/B + B/C]/2 \geq 1 \qquad \text{for real B} \qquad (32)$$

equation (30) becomes

$$0 = p + \frac{g - 1}{2} \cos(C - B) - \frac{g + 1}{2} \cos(C + B) \qquad (33)$$

and we are well on our way to creating a small variable as the argument of the first cosine. Finish the transformation by letting

$$C + B = 2H$$

$$C - B = 2K$$

and then use the identity

$$\cos 2x = 1 - 2 \sin^2 x$$

to produce

$$0 = 2p + (g - 1)(1 - 2 \sin^2 K) - (g + 1)(1 - 2 \sin^2 H)$$

or

$$0 = 2(p - 1) - 2(g - 1) \sin^2 K + 2(g + 1) \sin^2 H.$$

Dividing,

$$\sin^2 H = \frac{g-1}{g+1} \sin^2 K + \frac{1-p}{g+1} \tag{34}$$

with the last term lying on the range (0,1). Noting that

$$\frac{g-1}{g+1} = \frac{C/B + B/C - 2}{C/B + B/C + 2} = \frac{C^2 + B^2 - 2BC}{C^2 + B^2 + 2BC} = \left[\frac{C-B}{C+B}\right]^2 = \left(\frac{K}{H}\right)^2 \tag{35}$$

our final E-equation for real B is

$$\sin^2 H = \left[\frac{K}{H} \sin K\right]^2 + \frac{1-p}{g+1}. \tag{36}$$

Note also that

$$g+1 = \frac{2BC + C^2 + B^2}{2BC} = \frac{2H^2}{BC}$$

hence

$$\frac{1}{g+1} = \frac{H^2 - K^2}{2H^2} = \frac{1}{2}\left[1 - \left(\frac{K}{H}\right)^2\right].$$

The iterative algorithm

$$\left.\begin{array}{l} K \leftarrow \dfrac{T}{4H} \\[2mm] H \leftarrow \pm\arcsin\sqrt{\left(\dfrac{K}{H}\sin K\right)^2 + \dfrac{1-p}{g+1}} + j\pi \\[2mm] B \leftarrow H - K \\ C \leftarrow H + K \\ (g+1) \leftarrow 2H^2/(BC) = 2H^2/(H^2 - K^2) \end{array}\right\} \tag{37}$$

is efficient because changes in $\sin K$ are sharply damped by the relative flatness of that curve. Note that the two lines evaluating B and C need only be used after the iteration has converged.

As with all iterations, this one is helped by good starting values. A glance at the plot (figure 7) of both halves of (36) with $p = 1/2$ and $p = 1$ shows that the root-pairs are separated by $H = j\pi$. Adequate first approximations would be $H_{j\pm} = (j \pm \frac{1}{4})\pi$. The case of $p = 1$, however, allows a simplification of our algorithm by permitting us to take the square root of both sides of (36). This improves the quality of the intersections of half of the roots when they lie close to $j\pi$. Finally, any implementation of (37) should calculate the *deviations* of

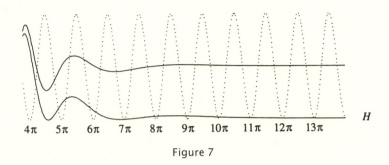

$$4\pi \quad 5\pi \quad 6\pi \quad 7\pi \quad 8\pi \quad 9\pi \quad 10\pi \quad 11\pi \quad 12\pi \quad 13\pi$$

H

Figure 7

the roots from $j\pi$ rather than only H. A typical calculation of the root just above 7π when $p = 1$ gives the deviations, in units of π:

> 0.0
> 0.0109783
> 0.0117947
> 0.0118550
> 0.0118595
> 0.0118598 $\rightarrow$ 22.028407   for H

a quite feasible calculation performed efficiently here on a simple six-figure pocket calculator.

The H-equation for real B and β

If we now look at the magnetic equation, the principal difference is a large negative value for τ in the coefficient of the sine terms of (28). Making the same variable changes as for the E-equation but defining

$$G = \frac{1}{2}\left[\frac{\sigma C}{B} + \frac{B}{\sigma C}\right] \qquad \text{with} \qquad \sigma = 23.4$$

we get

$$\sin^2 H = \frac{G+1}{G-1}\sin^2 K - \frac{1-p}{G-1} \tag{38}$$

where G is large. Again the p term is small, smaller even than in (34), but the coefficient $(G+1)/(G-1)$ is slightly *larger* than unity. Thus altho the $\sin^2 K$ curve still consists of only a few slow oscillations (the relation $K = T/(4H)$ still holds), these oscillations can now rise *above* the maxima of $\sin^2 H$, giving complex-conjugate pairs of roots in the region of the $\sin K$ maxima — altho many of the roots will remain real.

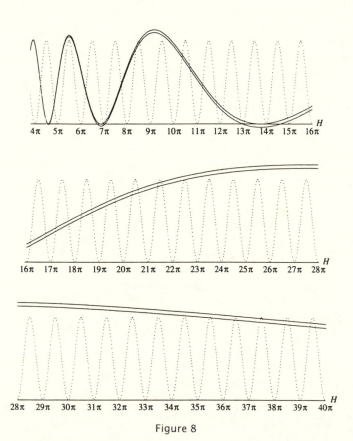

Figure 8

Figure 8 shows two right sides of (38), the upper solid curve being for $p = 0.5$ while the lower is for $p = 1$. Visually, it is clear that complex root-pairs occur near 5.5π, 9.5π and then from 22.5π thru 36.5π — but none thereafter as the solid curve sinks slowly but irrevocably toward zero.

The algorithm (37) still works with the obvious modification from

$$\frac{G+1}{G-1} = \left(\frac{\sigma C + B}{\sigma C - B}\right)^2$$

to provide the coefficient of $\sin^2 K$. Of course you need reliable complex square-root and complex arcsine functions. I found those in my computer's Fortran to be seriously defective* so I had to write my own. Be careful; test your functions!

As figure 8 shows, each real root occupies its own interval of length $\pi/2$, giving good first approximations like $(j \pm 0.25)\pi$ for our iterative algorithm. When the roots turn complex, however, as near 9.5π and in the 25π region, each complex pair "uses up" *two* such intervals. Thus, when this algorithm is seeking a complex root there is a wrong interval-sign combination that will cause it to "converge" to a pseudoroot complex pair — *alternating* between a complex number and its conjugate on successive iterations. The other interval-sign combination gives the actual root, which obviously gives itself back on every iteration after the process has converged. (If restarted with the conjugate of the correct root, the conjugate — which is also a root — will similarly reproduce itself every time.) If you are getting complex conjugates on alternate iterations from a single starting value, this is not a solution. Contrast the data for $j = 22$ and a positive square root with those for $j = 23$ using a negative root:

$j = 22+$	$j = 23-$
(.50000000, −.0250684)	(−.5000000, +.0838239)
(.49875086, −.0639937)	(−.4958349, −.0641698)
(.49681174, −.0640274)	(−.4968221, +.0642960)
(.49680320, −.0639312)	(−.4968124, −.0642477)
(.49680796, −.0639304)	(−.4968148, +.0642480)
(.49680801, −.0639306)	(−.4968148, −.0642479)

Thus $H = (22.49680801, \pm.0639306)$ is the correct root pair but $(22.5031852, \pm.0642479)$ is not.

The E-equation — with B pure imaginary

Returning to the electrical equation but this time with $0 < \lambda < \sigma$, we find that B is a pure imaginary. To keep the notation simple, let

$$B = iB_i$$

*When the argument was in the third quadrant, the double-precision complex square root returned the *conjugate* of the correct root and *stripped the minus sign off of the imaginary part of the argument!* That's "seriously defective!"

after which equation (30) becomes

$$0 = p - \cos C \cdot \cosh B_i + \frac{i}{2}\left[\frac{C}{iB_i} + \frac{iB_i}{C}\right]\sin C \cdot \sinh B_i$$

thus

$$0 = p - \cos C \cdot \cosh B_i + \frac{1}{2}\left[\frac{C}{B_i} - \frac{B_i}{C}\right]\sin C \cdot \sinh B_i \tag{39}$$

with

$$C^2 + B_i^2 = T = 541.8 \tag{40}$$

Both C and B_i range over $(0, \sqrt{T} = 23.2775)$, tho in opposite directions, so that when C is large B_i is small — and *vice versa*. Thus they are good variables for determining the roots. Divide (39) by $\cosh B_i$ to get

$$0 = \frac{v}{\cosh B_i} - \alpha \; ;C + \frac{1}{2}[C^2 - B_i^2]\frac{\sin C}{CB_i}\left(\frac{\sinh B_i}{\cosh B_i}\right). \tag{41}$$

For all but the smallest values of B_i the $\tanh B_i \approx 1$ and $\cosh B_i \gg 1$, and p is a cosine. If we only need (41) to produce a set of approximate roots to be refined by Newton, we can ignore the p term and the $\tanh B_i$ factor. Then we have the approximate equation

$$\cos C = \frac{C^2 - B_i^2}{2CB_i}\sin C \tag{42}$$

which becomes

$$\tan C = \frac{2CB_i}{C^2 - B_i^2} = \frac{2CB_i}{2C^2 - 541.8} = \frac{CB_i}{C^2 - 270.9}. \tag{43}$$

As C increases, B_i decreases symmetrically. Thus CB_i, while not constant, varies more slowly than either C or B_i and $CB_i \gg 0$. (For these parameters $130 < CB_i < 230$.) Except very close to the critical value, 16.5, the denominator factor $C^2 - 270.9 = (C + 16.5)(C - 16.5)$ also varies more slowly than C – *but it changes sign once*. Over most of its range, $\tan C$ changes *faster* than C, often a lot faster. Thus we have an iterative algorithm:

$$\left.\begin{array}{l} B_i \leftarrow \sqrt{541.84 - C^2} \\ C \leftarrow j\pi + \arctan(CB_i/(C^2 - 270.92)) \end{array}\right\} \tag{44}$$

that corresponds to moving vertically to the hyperbola then horizontally to the tangent curve in figure 9. The arctangent is a small variable, being the deviation from $j\pi$; it should receive its own variable name in any program. For $0 < C < 16.5$ the root lies on the lower branch of the hyperbola and the deviation will be negative; for $16.5 < C < 23.28$ the root is on the positive branch. Fortunately, since the arctangent function is odd, the sign reversal in its argument takes care of things without our intervention.

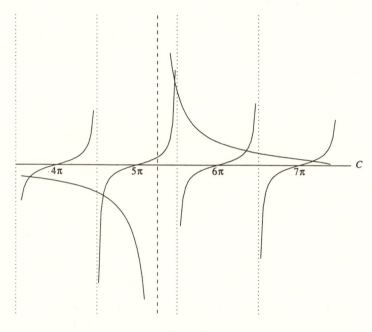

Figure 9

Altho generally there is one root near each integer value of π for which starting values of zero for the arctangent suffice, it is clear from the figure that there are *two* associated with 5π, one below and one above 16.5. But the algorithm will find them when started properly.

The H-equation — with B pure imaginary

Altho this fourth equation introduces nothing new, we include the algorithm for completeness. Making the same variable changes as in the last section and ignoring the p-term and $\tanh B_i$ as before, we get

$$\tan C = -\frac{\sigma C B_i}{(\sigma^2 + 1)C^2/2 - 270.9} \qquad \text{with} \qquad B_i = \sqrt{541.84 - C^2}$$

(45)

and again both B_i and C lie on $(0, 23.3)$. The only difference is that, for $C > 1$, the first term of the denominator of (45) is always much larger than 270.92, so no sign reversal occurs. (But there is a spurious root at the origin that should be avoided.) Figure 10 shows that each of the seven roots lies on its own branch of the tangent curve, somewhat to the left of $j\pi$, and is real. The obvious iteration succeeds and — like the previous equations — will not tax even a pocket calculator.

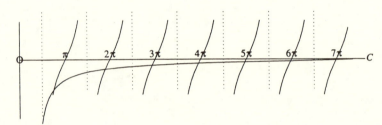

Figure 10

Postlude — *moderato*

Most of the precision losses that are cured in this chapter have the same geometric cause — two nearly parallel curves having two intersections close together. From a dispassionate mathematical perspective the treatment is monotonously the same: Find the crucial parameter value that makes the curves tangent, then express the problem in deviations from this special geometry. Expand in series, whence the linear terms cancel and an iterative formula for the now-dominant quadratic term emerges. But, as the examples show, the necessary manipulations are *not* all alike. Logarithms need to be massaged differently from cosines. Like all arts, this one needs a bit of practice — hence the exercises.

"Should one use computer algebra packages to expand everything around the tangency point?" is a legitimate question. Occasionally there is no other option, but as a general practice it has its own difficulties. Consider the trivial problem of eliminating the linear terms from

$$(1 - x) - \left(\frac{2 + x}{2 + 3x}\right). \qquad (46)$$

We get

$$\frac{(1 - x)(2 + 3x) - (2 + x)}{2 + 3x} = -\frac{3x^2}{2 + 3x}$$

which is a pleasantly compact expression. If, however, we dump the fraction of (46) into an algebraic series machine it becomes, by long division,

$$1 - x + \frac{3}{2}x^2 - \frac{9}{4}x^3 + \frac{27}{8}x^4 - \cdots$$

so our "result" is the infinite series

$$-\frac{3}{2}x^2 + \frac{9}{4}x^3 - \frac{27}{8}x^4 + \cdots.$$

Of course this series can be explicitly summed to yield our compact schoolboy result — but the odds are against that step being attempted by a person who is unwilling to look at the problem instead of just dumping it into a universal algebraic machine.

As you may also have detected, we prefer, wherever possible, to expand only what is necessary by using Taylor's Series with Remainder — thus avoiding losses inherent in truncating an infinite series. We can view our trivial problem as an example by "expanding" the fraction, by division, into

$$1 - x + \frac{3x^2}{2 + 3x}$$

— this being a Taylor Series with Remainder. Some algebraic packages can be persuaded to do this too, but that rather smacks of wheeling up a cannon to shoot a mouse.

Finally, we expand only the crucial factors. A series expansion of a complicated expression often converges less quickly (if at all) and also is inherently more elaborate. Our process gives results that are easier to comprehend visually, as well as being both more precise and more efficient.

Exercise
(Do not tackle this all-too-realistic problem unless you are willing to spend a lot of time. Some of the geometries are not obvious and

you must guard against false solutions. Also, answers may require very precise equation solving. We provide some analytic help and hints in the answers section — but not complete results. Explore!)

10. Consider the surface

$$z = (0.6 + x^2)(4 + x)(x^2 + 4y^2)/8 \qquad (-4 < x, y < 4)$$

which forms a lopsided vase, symmetric in y, with a local bottom at the origin. Near the origin the horizontal cross-sections (z constant) are ellipses with x-semiaxes twice as long as the y — while the vertical sections thru the origin are parabolic. But since the surface falls back to zero again along the line $x = -4$, the vase has its left side bent out and over, forming a sort of spout above $z \approx 11$. (Figure 11 and the contour map, figure 12, each depict only half of the vase.)

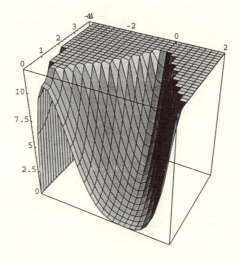

Figure 11

We would like to know where a spherical ball will be stably supported if placed inside this vase. Obviously a tiny ballbearing will sit at the bottom, stably supported at the *single* point (0, 0, 0). A larger ball will get stuck before reaching that bottom, probably supported at *two* points $(x_2, \pm y_2, z_2)$.

But as the radius of the ball increases further, the contours become

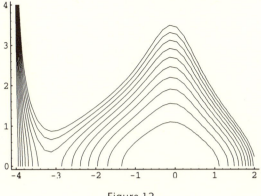

Figure 12

less like ellipses and also less symmetrical in x so that support occurs at *four* points $(x, \pm y, z)_{left}$ and $(x, \pm y, z)_{right}$. And finally, for a really large ball, the center of the ball will lie to the left of all four "support" points $(x_{center} < x_{supports})$, forcing the ball to roll out of the vase.

Devise algorithms to find the support points for balls of given radii. Trickier (and just a bit tedious): What are the critical radii that divide the support types: 1 point from 2, 2 from 4, and 4 from "won't stay in the vase?" And after all that is under control, you might like to try to find the 2-point supports for a sphere whose radius *squared* is 0.1736111120 — using a pocket calculator with no more than twelve-digit precision. [I get: $x = -0.425956736563E{-}9$, $y = \pm 0.291875569006E{-}4$ and $z = 0.102229617334E{-}8$.]

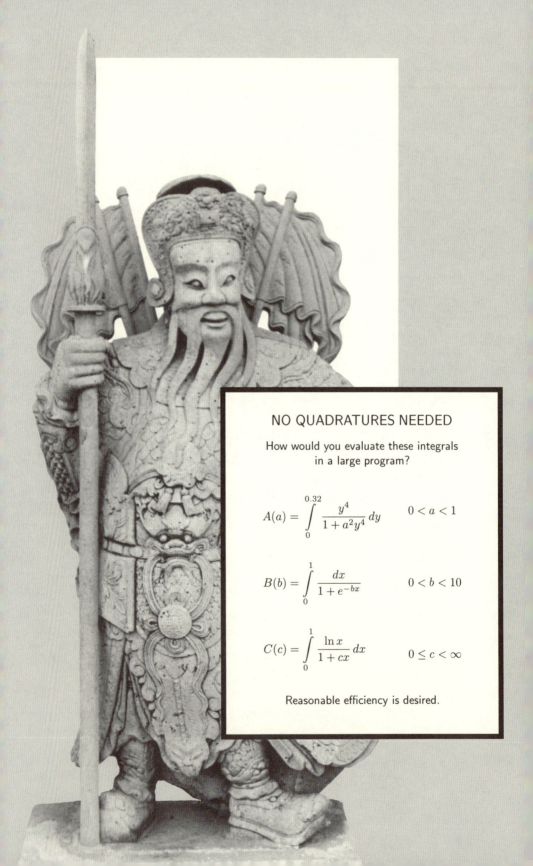

NO QUADRATURES NEEDED

How would you evaluate these integrals
in a large program?

$$A(a) = \int\limits_{0}^{0.32} \frac{y^4}{1 + a^2 y^4}\, dy \qquad 0 < a < 1$$

$$B(b) = \int\limits_{0}^{1} \frac{dx}{1 + e^{-bx}} \qquad 0 < b < 10$$

$$C(c) = \int\limits_{0}^{1} \frac{\ln x}{1 + cx}\, dx \qquad 0 \leq c < \infty$$

Reasonable efficiency is desired.

Chapter 3

QUADRATURES

A strategic dilemma

The numerical evaluation of definite integrals is one of the oldest numerical techniques. Newton, Gauss, Bessel and a host of lesser names are attached to "general" and specialized formulæ that approximate areas under curves — each with some claim to superiority when applied to the appropriate integrand. Today's scientist encounters only the *trapezoidal, Gauss* and *Simpson's* rules, with perhaps *Romberg's* extension of the trapezoidal, but is usually unaware of (or has long forgotten) the limitations that restrict their effective use. Those limitations are simple, but important:

> *Every short piece of the curve under which you are seeking the area must be accurately approximatable by a polynomial of low degree — usually a straight line or a parabola.*

But most integrands that need quadratures *are not polynomials* and, at least in some regions, *behave in ways that polynomials do not* — like going vertically, or approaching a vertical or horizontal asymptote. This unpleasant fact poses a strategic dilemma both to the designer of any black-box quadrature program and to the engineer who shuns such prosthetics in favor of doing her own thing with the standard tools:

> Should special quadrature algorithms be implemented for each nonpolynomic geometry — or should each obstreperous integrand be altered so that its geometry becomes plausibly polynomic before being dumped into the standard Romberg algorithm? (Of the two individuals, the black-box designer has the harder job since he must detect nasty user geometries automatically then, still automatically, decide which of his various algorithms had best be used.)

Since neither of these choices is attractive to someone who merely wants an answer, the majority of naive computors simply dump their function into a Simpson rule — geometry-be-damned — thus getting answers that are often terribly expensive and frequently inaccurate. Worse, they get no warning that their results are shaky. At best, numerical quadratures are costly computations. Each point on an integrand usually requires a transcendental function evaluation and several hundred points can be needed — thousands if the geometry is nonpolynomic — just to produce one area. These methods do not usually complain (unless the user has been crass enough to make them divide by zero somewhere) — they simply keep on subdividing the region, evaluating more points. In an inner program loop the costs can be enormous.

As with all genuine dilemmas, this one offers no clearly superior choice. Our technical world is filled with people who need integrals evaluated — preferably without thought or worry — and very capable numerical analysts have laboriously constructed "general" integrators in an effort to satisfy this very real demand. As you probably have already suspected, I liken such efforts to designing a universal crutch to fit all the world's cripples — it might work much of the time, but seldom well. In my persistent effort to get people to examine the problem at hand, I clearly opt for some thought about the shape of that problem and, in quadratures, for pasteurizing the nonpolynomic behavior so that one standard algorithm will do the job accurately and efficiently. The standard algorithm is Romberg quadratures, explained in a somewhat cookbook fashion in the next section. The rest of this chapter then shows how to tame unpleasant integrands so that they integrate nicely. If this approach does not appeal, I cannot argue; Go in Peace — and use some "universal" crutch. Mine is the way less often taken.

Romberg quadratures

In 1955 Werner Romberg published an inexpensive add-on algorithm that takes a sequence of *trapezoidal* rule results to construct much more accurate approximants for the same integral. The trapezoidal areas must be constructed from step sizes h, $h/2$, $h/4$, ..., that is, halving the interval each time — which is the sensible procedure even if only the trapezoidal rule were to be used.* Then a triangular

k	0	1	2	3	4
h	T_{00}				
$h/2$	T_{01}	R_{11}			
$h/4$	T_{02}	R_{12}	R_{22}		
$h/8$	T_{03}	R_{13}	R_{23}	R_{33}	
$h/16$	T_{04}	R_{14}	R_{24}	R_{34}	R_{44}

$$\begin{array}{|c|c|} \hline b & \\ \hline c & d \\ \hline \end{array}$$

$$\frac{4^k \cdot c - b}{4^k - 1} \to d_k$$

array is constructed from the first column (the trapezoidal estimates) according to the somewhat unusual weighted-average rule shown in the figure, k being the column to which the *result* d_k belongs. This rule suffices to produce all the other numbers. The approximants increase in precision both downward and to the right with the last, R_{kk}, being the best. The gain with most integrands is spectacular. If you are not yet familiar with this Romberg quadrature algorithm, try it with something not too drastic — like the integral of $\tan x$ from 0 to $\pi/3$.

---

*Halving permits full use of the already computed ordinate-sums — requiring only evaluation of the new ordinates.

Trapezoidal quadratures

The trapezoidal rule is simplicity itself, being

$$\int_a^b f(x)dx \approx$$

$$h\left(\frac{f_0(a)}{2} + f_1(a+h) + f_2(a+2h) + \cdots + f_{n-1}(a+(n-1)h) + \frac{f_n(b)}{2}\right)$$

with

$$h = (b-a)/n$$

which arises directly from figure 1 — the area under the curve $f(x)$ having been replaced by the n trapezoids constructed from the $n+1$ ordinates. (Altho n may be any positive integer, I use a power of 2, allowing an automatic interval-doubling algorithm to start from the aesthetically pleasing single trapezoid $[f(a)/2 + f(b)/2] \cdot (b-a)$ with n being 1.)

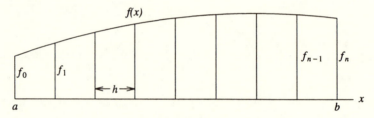

Figure 1

As n increases, this quadrature formula obviously approaches the area of figure 1 from below — and would approach from above if $f(x)$ were concave upward over the range. It also approaches the areas under most curves *slowly* — so slowly that it is seldom used alone. If high accuracy is desired, you will seldom get it by running the trapezoidal rule at finer and finer intervals, h. If you try that, the rounding errors of your machine will start to build up, intruding into the approximants from the right once the number of ordinates gets into the thousands.

It is an interesting experiment to run a trapezoidal algorithm that refines the interval until your patience (or computer budget) is exhausted on $1/(1+x^2)$ over $(0,1)$ and $(0,8)$ to see at what point the rounding errors of your machine become disruptive by virtue of their excessive cumulation. Not only will the approximants fail to converge to the correct (analytic) value, they will usually end up by *diverging* as the rounding errors take over. This description is necessarily vague because computer rounding effects vary widely with the problem. Still, this experiment is one way to obtain a feeling for how your machine's rounding errors can influence lengthy computations with REAL numbers.

Systematic creep in quadrature abscissae

When implementing quadrature algorithms, you should beware a common computational booby-trap: the evaluation of a sequence of equally spaced abscissae, x_i, from the all-too-obvious formula

$$x_{i+1} = x_i + h \qquad i = 0, 1, 2, \cdots. \tag{1}$$

Since h is almost always a constant computed with limited precision, it is *wrong* by some constant ϵ. Thus, even tho x_0 is correct, x_1 is wrong by ϵ, x_2 is wrong by 2ϵ, $\cdots$ and x_{1000} is wrong by 1000ϵ — which is almost certainly noticeable even if ϵ is only an original rounding error.

Many areas that require numerical evaluation have a shape like figure 2, with the major contribution occurring at one end of the range. If (1) is used to get the equally spaced abscissae at which to evaluate the ordinates, they will all be shifted slightly in the same direction — the one at the right being shifted the most. Hence all the *ordinates* will also be wrong in the same direction — either all too large or all too small, according to whether ϵ is positive or negative. Further, with the geometry shown, the ordinates that are most in error are the ones that are contributing the most to the area.

The problem can be avoided by computing x_k from the formula

$$x_k = (b - a) * k/n \tag{2}$$

(but not $k/n * (b - a)$, please — at least not in Fortran, where the leading k/n will monotonously produce zero if you have forgotten to declare k or n to be REAL). The use of (2) inserts only three rounding errors into each x — even in x_{1000} — and since they will be random effects they will largely cancel.

Efficient evaluation of trapezoidal ordinate sums

Most general quadrature programs seek an area by computing an approximate area using a coarse interval, then cutting the interval in half to get the next approximant. If these two estimates of the area do not agree to the precision desired, the interval is again halved, etc. With this strategy one need never re-evaluate an ordinate — all earlier computations being still useful in the next approximant. This can be seen from figure 2 in which the trapezoidal area from the solid ordinates is

$$T_{solid} = H \times (\text{Sum of Solids with end ordinates weighted } 1/2)$$

while the next approximant is

$$T_{all} = h \times (\text{Sum Dotteds } + \text{ Sum Solids, ends weighted } 1/2).$$

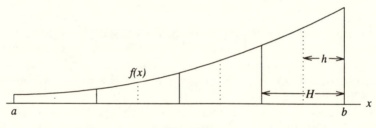

Figure 2

Thus you need keep only the *ordsum* (a single floating-point number) and n (the number of *intervals*) in addition to the constant *range* whose value is $(b - a)$. The efficient algorithm becomes:

a) Update the ordinate sum via
$$ordsum \leftarrow ordsum + \text{sum of dotted ordinates.}$$
b) Update n
$$n \leftarrow 2 \cdot n.$$
c) Calculate
$$T_n = range \cdot ordsum / n.$$

(Note: n is the number of *intervals* in the sum. It is not the number of *ordinates*, which is always *odd* in this algorithm.)

The large cost of quadratures comes from the large number of ordinate evaluations, each of which usually requires the evaluation of a transcendental function or at least a square root. Thus you should never recompute old ordinates. Likewise, you should always use the ordinates already evaluated.

These efficiency strictures rule out *Gaussian* quadratures in systematic refinement algorithms. Gaussian quadratures evaluate ordinates at very unevenly spaced abscissae. They should be used *only* when the required number of ordinates is *known in advance* — when they can be very efficient for near-polynomic integrands. (Numerical analysis texts give space to Gaussian quadratures out of all proportion to their usefulness because of the cute theorems that are embedded in their theory.)

Slightly nervous integrals

Faced with getting a numerical value for

$$\int_0^{\pi/2} \frac{\sin x}{x} dx$$

via a quadrature program, even the inexperienced computor will realize that she must make special provision for the value of the integrand at zero. If she does not, the computer will remind her very quickly that it does not know how to evaluate 0/0. So she will probably write a function something like

```
function f(x)
if x=0 then f = 1.0
    else f = sin(x)/x
return.
```

Assuming she does not omit some grammatical nicety of her programming language, this construct will probably work — but it betrays a touch of computational naivety and lacks solidity. The naivety lies in testing x, a REAL (floating-point) number, for *equality* with zero. Testing anything REAL for equality to *anything* is dangerous because of the rounding properties of the arithmetic organ. If any arithmetic has been performed, one is seldom sure just what the least significant bits of the result now are.

The real objection, however, lies in the observation that "nearly zero / nearly zero" is not a good way to compute "nearly one"! We discussed this difficulty in chapter 0 with indeterminate expressions and the same principles hold here. We should use a few terms of the series for sin x and divide out the x explicitly to produce the (pseudocode) function

```
function f(x)
if |x|<0.1 then f = 1.0 - x^2(1.0 - x^2/20.0)/6.0
               else f = sin(x)/x
return
```

which will deliver at least nine significant figures for f no matter what reasonable value of x is supplied. If greater precision is wanted, the next term of the series can be included[*] or the limit at which this approximation is invoked could be reduced.

Sick Integrals — integrands with vertical asymptotes

Consider evaluating

$$\int_0^{\pi/2} \frac{\cos x}{\sqrt{x}}\, dx \tag{3}$$

with any quadrature algorithm that replaces small pieces of the integrand with small pieces of a polynomial. Over much of the range of integration this replacement encounters no problems, but near the origin the geometry doesn't fit — no polynomial ever tried to go *vertically*. And there is the associated arithmetic problem that *at* the lower limit the integrand is infinite.

If the integrand had been

$$\int_0^{\pi/2} \frac{1}{\sqrt{x}}\, dx = 2\sqrt{x}\Big|_0^{\pi/2} = 2\sqrt{\pi/2} \tag{4}$$

the nearest freshman would integrate it analytically — probably forgetting how once he had had to make a change in the dummy variable

[*] At $x = 0.1$ it is only 1.98E−10.

of integration to get the result in (4) that now comes automatically. The change of variable, of course, was

$$x = u^2 \quad \text{with} \quad dx = 2u\, du \tag{5}$$

whence

$$\int_0^{\pi/2} \frac{1}{\sqrt{x}}\, dx = \int_0^{\sqrt{\pi/2}} \frac{2\not{u}}{\not{u}}\, du = 2\sqrt{\pi/2}. \tag{6}$$

Looking at the second integral in (6) we see that its integrand is *very* polynomic — being merely the constant 2. Even the trapezoidal rule will have no trouble with that! The change (5) in the dummy variable has *removed the singular geometry.* Of course it also works for (3)

$$\int_0^{\pi/2} \frac{\cos x}{\sqrt{x}}\, dx = 2 \cdot \int_0^{\sqrt{\pi/2}} \cos(u^2)\, du$$

and altho this integral is not analytically integrable, any numerical quadrature algorithm will now have no trouble with it — the cosine being a very polynomial-like curve. Vertical slopes and infinities have simply disappeared.

The Sick Integral has been Pasteurized.

Since most of the integrals that require treatment before numerical evaluation have illnesses of this type, we examine several more before asking the reader to try the exercises. So look next at

$$\int_0^1 \frac{\sin x}{\sqrt{1-x}}\, dx$$

where the sine has no essential role except to prevent analytic integration; the troubles occur in the denominator. Here the infinity comes at the upper limit, 1, and — as with transcendental equations — *trouble spots should be moved to the origin.* So we let

$$x = 1 - u \qquad dx = -du$$

to get the integral

$$-\int_{u=1}^0 \frac{\sin(1-u)}{\sqrt{u}}\, du = \int_{u=0}^1 \frac{\sin(1-u)}{\sqrt{u}}\, du$$

in which the minus sign from the differential has been absorbed by interchanging the new limits of integration. Now we have a square-rootish problem like the previous integral and the cure is the same; let

$$u = w^2 \qquad\qquad du = 2w\,dw$$

whence the integral becomes

$$2 \cdot \int_{w=0}^{1} \sin(1 - w^2)\,dw$$

whose geometry is quite benign.

Another integral

$$\int_0^1 \frac{\cos x}{\sqrt{x(1 - x)}}\,dx$$

has trouble at both limits. In such situations divide-and-conquer by splitting the integral into two, since the medicines that cure the two illnesses will probably interfere with each other. The exact point of splitting is irrelevant — 1/2 seems pleasant here. We get

$$\int_0^{1/2} \frac{\cos x}{\sqrt{x(1 - x)}}\,dx \;+\; \int_{1/2}^{1} \frac{\cos x}{\sqrt{x(1 - x)}}\,dx$$

and now the cures should be obvious. In the first integral let $x = u^2$ to produce

$$2 \cdot \int_{u=0}^{1/\sqrt{2}} \frac{\cos u^2}{\sqrt{1 - u^2}}\,du$$

while in the second integral the substitution $x = 1 - u$ will move the problem to the new origin in

$$\int_{u=0}^{1/2} \frac{\cos(1 - u)}{\sqrt{(1 - u)u}}\,du\,.$$

(Again, note the interchange of limits to absorb the negative sign from the differential.) Then let $u = w^2$ to produce

$$2 \cdot \int_{w=0}^{1/\sqrt{2}} \frac{\cos(1 - w^2)}{\sqrt{1 - w^2}}\,dw$$

and we note that the argument of the square root remains safely away from zero — ranging between 1/2 and 1. All infinities have disappeared. One integral with two vertical asymptotes has been replaced with two placid integrals — and we here have been unusually lucky in that they can be combined because they share the same limits and have the same denominators. So we need only provide a function for the integrand

$$2 \cdot \frac{\cos w^2 + \cos(1 - w^2)}{\sqrt{1 - w^2}}$$

that fans of obscure trigonometric identities will further combine to get

$$4 \cos\left(\frac{1}{2}\right) \cdot \int_0^{1/\sqrt{2}} \frac{\cos(w^2 - 1/2)}{\sqrt{1 - w^2}}\, dw$$

thereby cutting the computational costs nearly in half.

Another "removable" singularity

The integral

$$\int_0^2 \frac{e^{-x}}{\sqrt{4 - x^2}}\, dx \tag{7}$$

has troubles at its upper limit. Students in a calculus course will immediately think of the transformation

$$x = 2\cos u \qquad \text{hence} \qquad dx = -2\sin u\, du$$

which produces

$$\int_{u=0}^{\pi/2} e^{-2\cos u}\, du \tag{7p}$$

— the minus again being absorbed by the limit interchange. And it works! The singularity in the integrand has been *removed* by the change in the dummy variable of integration. (Most transformations in integral calculus are to remove singular behavior, altho this point is seldom made in those courses.)

But the careful reader will probably have realized that the trouble in (7) is being caused by only *one* of the factors of its denominator. On writing (7) as

$$\int_0^2 \frac{e^{-x}}{\sqrt{(2 + x)(2 - x)}}\, dx$$

we see the familiar square-rootish problem. The cure? Let's coalesce the two transformations into one with

$$2 - x = u^2 \qquad dx = -2u\,du$$

hence

$$\int_0^{\sqrt{2}} \frac{e^{u^2-2}2\cancel{u}}{\sqrt{4-u^2}\cdot\cancel{u}}\,du \;=\; 2e^{-2}\cdot\int_0^{\sqrt{2}} \frac{e^{u^2}}{\sqrt{4-u^2}}\,du \tag{8}$$

with our momentary fears for the new denominator vanishing when we realize that it never becomes smaller than $\sqrt{2}$. But the integrand does have an asymptote; even tho it is a bit off-stage at 2, the influence can be sensed in the (solid) graph. It is reaching a bit too eagerly for the sky (figure 3).

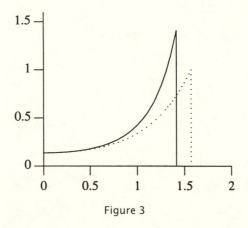

Figure 3

Which form of singularity removal is preferable? It's the surgeon's choice. One can argue that since a square root is computationally cheaper than a cosine, (8) is more efficient, but the *shape* of the integrand of (7p) (dotted in the figure) is somehow less rambunctious. *That*, unfortunately, is not a mathematical argument; only a numerical experiment can show whether there is a significant difference here.

More important, when trying to decide the nature of your current integrand's singularity, be sure to see if it makes geometric sense in your physical problem. (It just might have arisen from an incorrect minus sign!)

Exercises

Pasteurize these integrals so that conventional quadratures can be efficiently employed.

1. $\int_0^\pi \frac{\sin x}{\sqrt{x}}\, dx$

2. $\int_0^{\pi/2} \frac{\cos x}{\sqrt{\pi/2 - x}}\, dx$

3. $\int_0^{\pi/2} \frac{\sin x}{\sqrt{\pi/2 - x}}\, dx$

4. $\int_0^{\pi/2} \frac{\pi/2 - x}{\sqrt{\sin x}}\, dx$

5. $\int_0^{\pi/2} \frac{\sin x}{x\sqrt{x}}\, dx$

6. $\int_0^2 \frac{\arctan x}{\sqrt{x(2 - x)}}\, dx$

7. $\int_0^1 \frac{dx}{\sqrt{\arctan x}}$

8. $\int_0^{\pi/2} \frac{\pi/2 - x}{\sqrt{\cos x}}\, dx$

Logarithms near zero

Logarithmic functions behave well when their arguments are near unity, or larger, but they go to negative infinity at zero. [It is the $\ln(1 + x)$ function that has the good power series, useful for small x and for resolving indeterminacies in $\ln(1 + x)/x$ at $x = 0$.] Integrals such as

$$\int_0^{1.2} \frac{\ln x}{e^{-x} + x}\, dx \qquad (9)$$

pose a nasty problem for numerical quadratures because most of the area lies in a big negative spike that has the y-axis for its left boundary. We know that the area is finite because this integral is not significantly different in its behavior near zero from

$$\int_0^1 \ln x\, dx = x \cdot \ln x \Big|_0^1 - \int_0^1 x\, \frac{dx}{x} = -1$$

which we learned to integrate by parts in calculus — and we also learned there that x goes to zero faster than $\ln x$ goes to $-\infty$. But how should we handle (9) where the denominator, tho geometrically calm over the range of integration, effectively prevents integration by parts to remove the logarithm?

The crucial tool comes from the observation that $x^n \cdot \ln x$ goes to zero with x for any positive power, n (even with fractional powers, altho they are not of immediate interest). Look at the graphs of $x \cdot \ln x$, $x^2 \ln x$ and $x^3 \ln x$ in figure 4. Of course they all cross the axis at 1, but it is their behavior at zero that concerns us. $x \cdot \ln x$ has a vertical

Figure 4

slope at the origin — not polynomic — but the other two go horizontal there. $x^3 \ln x$ *stays flat* for an appreciable distance — indeed, it never gets farther than $-.1226$ from the x-axis between zero and one. If we change the dummy variable by the substitution $x = w^4$ then

$$\int_0 f(x) \ln x \, dx = \int_0 f(w^4) \ln(w^4) \cdot 4w^3 dw = 16 \int_0 f(w^4) \cdot w^3 \cdot \ln w \, dw$$

so we have abolished the spike and produced a very polynomic geometry — always assuming that f is a quiet function.

Altho the geometry is now under control, one still dare not evaluate the transformed integrand *at zero* — the computer doesn't know that w^3 will win. But *near zero* our new integrand is so small that we can afford to ignore the small piece of the area under it between 0 and ϵ.*
Table 1 shows the value of $16\epsilon^3 \ln \epsilon$ as well as the *area* $16 \int_0^\epsilon x^3 \ln x \, dx$.

ϵ	$16\epsilon^3 \ln \epsilon$	Area
0.0001	$-1.47\text{E}{-}10$	$-3.78\text{E}{-}15$
0.001	$-1.11\text{E}{-}7$	$-2.86\text{E}{-}11$
0.01	$-7.37\text{E}{-}5$	$-1.94\text{E}{-}7$

Table 1

*This is one of the very few places in which I recommend *avoiding* a trouble spot by ϵ. Usually we exorcise the devil rather than see how close we can come without getting burnt!

It is clear that we can afford to set our integrand to zero whenever the argument is less than an ϵ chosen to satisfy our accuracy needs.

Returning to (9), the transformation $x = w^4$ yields

$$16 \cdot \int_{w=0}^{1.2^{1/4}} \frac{w^3 \ln w}{[e^{-x} + x]_{x=w^4}} \, dw$$

the notation being in harmony with the quadrature pseudo-function that we would write for the integrand:

```
real function f(w)
   x = w4
   if w < 0.001 then f = 0.
               else f = 16.0*w3*ln(w)/(exp(-x)+x)
   return.
```

Horizontal asymptotes

Consider the integral

$$\int_1^\infty \frac{e^{-x}}{x+1} \, dx \qquad (10)$$

which, despite its simple appearance, has no closed analytic form. The integrand is benign enough — nearly horizontal after x is 2 or 3, becoming vanishingly small quite quickly. There seems no need to ask Romberg to integrate out to infinity, even if he had the time to try. Would a reduced upper limit of 10 be reasonable instead? Probably not; e^{-10} is only 4×10^{-5}. But surely $x = 20$ is far enough.

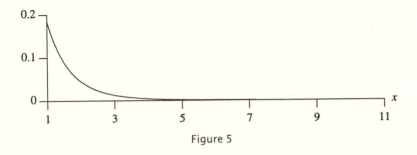

Figure 5

When we look at this proposal from Romberg's viewpoint, however, something seems wrong. Most of the area under the integrand in figure 5 lies in the range $1 \leq x \leq 3$, yet we are asking Romberg to spend the bulk of his computational energy on a quite thin tail out to the right. The process will work, but surely is inefficient. We are again fighting an infinity, altho this time it lies in a limit rather than in the integrand. Our difficulty can be removed, or perhaps we should say *moved*, by using a *reciprocal* transformation. Let

$$x = 1/y \qquad dx = -dy/y^2$$

whence (10) becomes

$$\int_0^1 \frac{e^{-1/y}}{(1+y)} \cdot \frac{dy}{y}$$

so now Romberg deals with a very human-sized range of integration, but leaves *us* with the responsibility to protect him from the troubles at zero. There are two troubles: we must not ask for the integrand to be evaluated when y is zero nor, more significantly, when $e^{-1/y}$ is so small that the *computer cannot represent it* in its floating-point format.

This problem is called *underflow* and is machine-dependent, but a rule-of-thumb says that requests for e^{-40} are getting dangerously close to underflow for many double-precision (REAL*8 in Fortran) representations. (But my pocket HP-28 handles e^{-300} with complete nonchalance.) Some computers just replace underflown numbers with zero and go blithely on — a behavior that would accommodate us here, but one that can produce dangerous errors in other computations and so is generally frowned upon. A better reaction for the computer is to give a warning, replace by zero, and go on — but that makes the output look bad, inducing freshmen to seek the command that turns the warning off!

A function that should keep everybody happy here is

```
real function f(y)
 f = 0
 if y < 0.025 then return
 f = exp(-1/y)/(y+1)/y
return
```

since the *if* guarantees that the nontrivial value of f is computed only when $1/y$ is less than 40, so Romberg will waste little energy on unproductive regions of the integrand.

Let's now pretend that you don't know how to integrate

$$\int_0^\infty \frac{\arctan x}{x\sqrt{x}}\,dx$$

analytically (it's a real mess that is almost certain to lose a few factors of 2 for you!) so numerical quadratures are to be used. Troubles exist at both limits so split into

$$\int_0^1 \frac{\arctan x}{x\sqrt{x}}\,dx + \int_1^\infty \frac{\arctan x}{x\sqrt{x}}\,dx$$

then reciprocate the dummy in the second integral to bring it onto the range (0,1) as

$$\int_0^1 \frac{\arctan(1/y)}{\sqrt{y}}\,dy$$

which, on using the reciprocal properties of the arctangent, becomes

$$\int_0^1 \frac{\pi/2 - \arctan y}{\sqrt{y}}\,dy = \frac{\pi}{2}\cdot 2 - \int_0^1 \frac{\arctan y}{\sqrt{y}}\,dy.$$

The remaining integrals both have indeterminacies at the origin. In addition, one has a vertical asymptote there while the other merely has a vertical *slope* — neither geometry being polynomic. Treating the square-root problems, we get

$$\int_0^1 \frac{\arctan x}{x}\frac{dx}{\sqrt{x}} = 2\int_0^1 \left(\frac{\arctan u^2}{u^2}\right)du$$

and

$$\int_0^1 \arctan y\,\frac{dy}{\sqrt{y}} = 2\int_0^1 (\arctan u^2)\,du$$

that now offer no numerical difficulties if we remember to evaluate the first integrand from the first four terms of the series

$$1 - \frac{(u^2)^2}{3} + \frac{(u^2)^4}{5} - \frac{(u^2)^6}{7}$$

whenever u is small, say $u < 0.1$.

Exercises

Here are some integrals with vertical and horizontal asymptotes for you to make amenable to numerical quadratures.

9. $\displaystyle\int_0^{37} \frac{\arctan x}{x\sqrt{x}}\, dx$

13. $\displaystyle\int_1^{37} \frac{\arctan x}{\sqrt{4+x^2}}\, dx$

10. $\displaystyle\int_0^{\infty} \frac{e^{-x}}{1+x^2}\, dx$

14. $\displaystyle\int_1^{\infty} \frac{\ln x}{x\sqrt{1+x}}\, dx$

11. $\displaystyle\int_0^1 \frac{\ln x}{\sqrt{x(1+x)}}\, dx$

15. $\displaystyle\int_1^{37} \frac{\arctan x}{\sqrt{x^2-1}}\, dx$

12. $\displaystyle\int_1^{\infty} \frac{\ln x}{\sqrt{2+x^3}}\, dx$

16. $\displaystyle\int_0^1 \frac{\ln x}{\sqrt{x(1-x)}}\, dx$

Subtracting off a singularity

Thus far we have considered integrands that become infinite but with *finite area* under them — the removable singularity. Now we turn to integrands that become infinite so strongly that the area under them is also infinite *if one goes all the way to the vertical asymptote*. Altho in that limiting case these integrals do not exist, they still must often be evaluated for limits close to the asymptote, where the highly non-polynomic geometry of the integrand precludes the effective use of standard quadratures.

For example, the familiar integral

$$\int_\epsilon^1 \frac{dx}{x} = -\ln \epsilon \tag{11}$$

has a finite value only as long as ϵ remains larger than zero. The geometry of $1/x$ is dangerously nonpolynomic and *no change in the dummy variable will render this integral pleasant,* as the singularity is not "removable." Of course here we have an analytic closed form, but let us now look at a similar integral that does not. Consider

$$\int_\epsilon^1 \frac{e^{-x}}{x}\, dx. \tag{12}$$

For this kind of integral we usually try to *subtract the singularity off* — by which is meant subtracting off a simpler integral that has a closed form and *that goes to infinity at the same rate (and place) as our actual integral*. Since e^{-x}/x behaves like $1/x$ when x is near zero, (11) has the same kind of singular behavior as (12). Thus we subtract it off and add it back again to produce

$$\int_\epsilon^1 \frac{e^{-x}}{x}\, dx = \int_\epsilon^1 \frac{1}{x}\, dx - \int_\epsilon^1 \frac{1 - e^{-x}}{x}\, dx. \tag{13}$$

Our problem has now become

$$\int_\epsilon^1 \frac{e^{-x}}{x} dx = -\ln \epsilon - \int_\epsilon^1 \frac{1 - e^{-x}}{x}\, dx \tag{14}$$

in which the new integrand declines slowly from 1 to 0.63 over the range (0,1). Quadratures encounter no problems if we provide an alternate evaluation for small x by using a few terms of the e^{-x} series. Thus, use

$$\frac{1 - e^{-x}}{x} = 1 - \frac{x}{2!} + \frac{x^2}{3!} - \frac{x^3}{4!}$$

for, say, $x < 0.05$ to preserve five significant figures. For more precision, keep more terms (or reduce the threshold).

Singular behavior can sometimes be subtracted off in more than one way. Look at

$$\int_0^{1-\epsilon} \frac{\sqrt{1 + x}}{1 - x^3}\, dx = \int_0^{1-\epsilon} \frac{\sqrt{1 + x}}{(1 - x)(1 + x + x^2)}\, dx \tag{15}$$

that near 1 almost turns into

$$\approx \frac{\sqrt{2}}{3} \int^{1-\epsilon} \frac{dx}{1 - x} = -\frac{\sqrt{2}}{3} \ln \epsilon + \text{ordinary stuff.} \tag{16}$$

We therefore have the choice of subtracting off this elementary integral or the slightly more complicated

$$\frac{1}{3} \int^{1-\epsilon} \frac{\sqrt{1 + x}}{1 - x}\, dx. \tag{17}$$

Both of these possible subtrahends have closed analytic forms, altho one is rather harder to derive — or find!

In practice it is usually better to move the singularity to the origin first. Let $1 - x = u$ in (15) to produce

$$\int_\epsilon^1 \frac{\sqrt{2-u}}{u(3 - 3u + u^2)}\, du. \tag{18}$$

Then subtracting the more complicated representation of the singularity gives

$$\int_\epsilon^1 \frac{\sqrt{2-u}}{3u}\, du + \int_\epsilon^1 \frac{\sqrt{2-u}}{3u}\left[\frac{1}{1 - u + u^2/3} - 1\right] du \tag{19}$$

and the second integral becomes

$$\int_\epsilon^1 \frac{\sqrt{2-u}}{3u}\left[\frac{u - u^2/3}{1 - u + u^2/3}\right] du = \frac{1}{3}\int_\epsilon^1 \frac{\sqrt{2-u}(1 - u/3)}{1 - u + u^2/3}\, du \tag{20}$$

which, after dividing out u, has no problems for quadratures (even at zero). The first integral in (19) may take a bit of work, but after letting $2 - u = v^2$ to get

$$\frac{2}{3}\int_1^{\sqrt{2-\epsilon}} \frac{v^2}{2 - v^2}\, dv = \frac{2}{3}\int_1^{\sqrt{2-\epsilon}} \left[\frac{2}{2 - v^2} - 1\right] dv$$

it can be found to become

$$\frac{2\sqrt{2}}{3} \ln\left[\frac{\sqrt{2} + \sqrt{2-\epsilon}}{\sqrt{2}+1}\right] - \frac{2}{3}(\sqrt{2-\epsilon} - 1) - \frac{\sqrt{2}}{3}\ln\epsilon \tag{21}$$

which isolates the singular behavior in the last term.

The simpler subtrahend turns (18) into

$$\frac{\sqrt{2}}{3}\int_\epsilon^1 \frac{du}{u} + \frac{\sqrt{2}}{3}\int_\epsilon^1 \left[\frac{\sqrt{1-u/2}}{1 - u + u^2/3} - 1\right]\frac{du}{u} \tag{22}$$

and altho the integral with the singularity is now trivial, the other requires sophisticated manipulation. The square bracket can be written as

$$\left[\frac{(\sqrt{1-u/2} - 1) + u - u^2/3}{1 - u + u^2/3}\right] = \left[\frac{\frac{-u/2}{1+\sqrt{1-u/2}} + u - u^2/3}{1 - u + u^2/3}\right].$$

Note the gambit of multiplying and dividing the parenthesized expression by $(\sqrt{1-u/2}+1)$ to free the $-u/2$ term. Now the denominator factor of u in (22) cancels, leaving the final expression

$$-\frac{\sqrt{2}}{3}\ln\epsilon \;+\; \frac{\sqrt{2}}{3}\int_{\epsilon}^{1}\frac{\frac{-1/2}{1+\sqrt{1-u/2}}+1-u/3}{1-u+u^2/3}\,du \tag{23}$$

where the remaining integral is well-behaved, again even at zero.

It is a revealing exercise to try your favorite quadratures program on the previous integrals (18), (20) and (23) with $\epsilon = 0.001$ to get a feeling for the relative efficiencies (and accuracies) they exhibit. [The integral (18) is 3.70902246 when $\epsilon = 0.001$.]

Exercises
Pasteurize these integrals so that conventional quadratures can be efficiently employed. Most have singular behavior that needs to be subtracted off. ϵ is presumed positive but quite small.

17. $\displaystyle\int_{\epsilon}^{\pi/2}\frac{\cos x}{x}\,dx$

18. $\displaystyle\int_{\epsilon}^{\pi/2}\frac{\sin x}{x^2}\,dx$

19. $\displaystyle\int_{0}^{\pi/2}\frac{\sin x}{x\sqrt{x^2+b^2}}\,dx$
    for b near 0

20. $\displaystyle\int_{\epsilon}^{\pi/2}\frac{\sin x}{x^2\sqrt{x^2+b^2}}\,dx$
    as $b \to 0$

21. $\displaystyle\int_{0}^{G}\frac{\ln x}{1+x}\,dx$

22. $\displaystyle\int_{\epsilon}^{\infty}\frac{\ln x}{x\sqrt{x+b}}\,dx$
    Split at 1.

23. $\displaystyle\int_{1}^{\infty}\frac{\ln x}{\sqrt{b^2+x^2}}\,dx$

24. $\displaystyle\int_{0}^{\infty}\frac{\ln x}{\sqrt{x}(b^2+x^2)}\,dx$
    Again, split at 1.

Subtracting off an obscure singularity

Some nearly singular integrals require fairly sophisticated treatment. So skip this section if you don't feel that sophisticated, mathematically; otherwise, consider

$$\int_0^1 \frac{e^{-x}}{\sqrt{|x^2 - b^2|}} \, dx \qquad 0 < b < 1 \tag{24}$$

which clearly has problems at $x = b$. The absolute value can be got rid of by splitting at b into

$$\int_0^b \frac{e^{-x}}{\sqrt{b^2 - x^2}} \, dx + \int_b^1 \frac{e^{-x}}{\sqrt{x^2 - b^2}} \, dx \tag{25}$$

and now the treatments seem fairly familiar — square-rootish substitutions of $b - x = u^2$ and $x - b = v^2$ or perhaps the standard trigonometric abolishments for these denominators. So what's the problem?

The problem arises as b approaches zero. If it ever *gets* to zero then (24) is

$$\int_0^1 \frac{e^{-x}}{x} \, dx$$

— which is *infinite*.

If you want proof, split this at an a small enough so that $e^{-a} \approx 1$, then

$$\int_0^1 \frac{e^{-x}}{x} \, dx = \int_0^a \frac{1}{x} \, dx + \int_a^1 \frac{e^{-x}}{x} \, dx$$

and this first integral is $(\ln a - \ln 0)$ and $-\ln 0$ is $+\infty$.

Since the integral (not merely the integrand) goes to infinity as b goes to zero, we must subtract off a simpler integral that has the same strength of singular behavior but that can be integrated analytically. But looking at (25), we wonder which integral goes to infinity. Certainly the one on the right; but what about the other? Let's postpone him until later and deal with the devil we know.

To produce an integral that blows up at b equal to zero and blows up at the *same rate* as

$$\int_b^1 \frac{e^{-x}}{\sqrt{x^2 - b^2}} \, dx \tag{26}$$

we need only freeze the exponential at e^{-b} — the value of x at which the integrand has its asymptote. Subtracting and adding this integral to (26) we get

$$e^{-b} \cdot \int_b^1 \frac{dx}{\sqrt{x^2 - b^2}} - \int_b^1 \frac{e^{-b} - e^{-x}}{\sqrt{x^2 - b^2}} \, dx. \tag{27}$$

The term on the left integrates immediately to

$$e^{-b}\left[\ln(1 + \sqrt{1 - b^2}) - \ln b\right]$$

while the right-hand integral can be improved by $x - b = v^2$ to yield

$$2e^{-b} \cdot \int_0^{\sqrt{1-b}} \frac{1 - e^{-v^2}}{\sqrt{2b + v^2}}\, dv \qquad (28)$$

which offers quadratures no unusual problems. (Note that for small v^2 the numerator series begins with v^2, so even if b were zero the denominator v could be cancelled out.)

The first integral of (25) yields to $x = b\sin\theta$ to give

$$\int_0^b \frac{e^{-x}}{\sqrt{b^2 - x^2}}\, dx = \int_0^{\pi/2} e^{-b\sin\theta}\, d\theta \qquad (29)$$

from which we see that its maximum value, $\pi/2$, would occur if b ever went to zero.

Summarizing, the difficult integral (24) has been converted into the sum of two tame integrals plus two explicit terms, one of which contains the singular behavior when b approaches zero:

$$\int_0^{\pi/2} e^{-b\sin\theta}\, d\theta + 2e^{-b}\int_0^{\sqrt{1-b}} \frac{1 - e^{-v^2}}{\sqrt{2b + v^2}}\, dv + e^{-b}\left[\ln(1 + \sqrt{1 - b^2}) - \ln b\right].$$

Bounds, approximations, and "unimportant" terms

Sometimes a small additive term in an integrand can be discarded to permit a closed-form approximation of the integral. Consider the function

$$G(b, c) = \int_c^\infty \frac{dx}{1 + b^2x^2 + e^{-x}} \qquad \text{for} \quad b, c \geq 2. \qquad (30)$$

Accurate evaluation by quadratures is not difficult, but we note that when $b = c = 2$ the exponential is a quite small part of the denominator. It is no more than 0.135 added onto at least 17.0 — and its proportional contribution decreases rapidly with increases in either b or c.

We can get a lower bound on G by fixing e^{-x} at e^{-c} and an upper bound by throwing the term away. Both bounds are, of course, arctangent functions:

$$\frac{1}{b\sqrt{1+e^{-c}}}\left[\frac{\pi}{2}-\arctan\frac{bc}{\sqrt{1+e^{-c}}}\right] < G(b,c) < \frac{1}{b}\left[\frac{\pi}{2}-\arctan(bc)\right]$$

$$0.1218185 < 0.12231150 < 0.12248933$$

where the correct value of $G(2,2)$ comes from quadratures of (30) after inverting the dummy variable. If you do not need more than three or four figures, the upper bound will suffice.

But with this integrand we can do better. Rewrite (30) factoring out $(1+b^2x^2)$ and expand the other factor:

$$G(b,c) = \int_c^\infty \frac{dx}{(1+b^2x^2)\left[1+\frac{e^{-x}}{1+b^2x^2}\right]}$$

$$= \int_c^\infty \left[\frac{1}{1+b^2x^2} - \frac{e^{-x}}{(1+b^2x^2)^2} + \frac{e^{-2x}}{(1+b^2x^2)^3} - \ldots\right]dx. \quad (31)$$

The first term is our upper bound while the corrections are exponentially small and decrease rapidly. We need only the first correction and will even treat it rather cavalierly by discarding the 1 in its denominator to produce

$$\int_c^\infty \frac{e^{-x}}{b^4x^4}\,dx$$

which is one form of the Exponential Integral. Let $cx = y$ then

$$\frac{1}{b^4}\int_c^\infty \frac{e^{-x}}{x^4}\,dx = \frac{1}{b^4c^3}\int_1^\infty \frac{e^{-cy}}{y^4}\,dy = \frac{E_4(c)}{b^4c^3}$$

whence, using the approximation (5.1.52) in AMS-55, becomes

$$\frac{e^{-c}}{b^4c^3(c+4)} = 0.00017621$$

so

$$G(2,2) \approx 0.12231312$$

a remarkably good approximation that allows us to dispense entirely with quadratures. (The second correction in (31) should not be used, as we have already made two approximations in evaluating the first.)

When available, these shenanigans can greatly increase the efficiency of your computation, but you must check carefully to find the parameter ranges over which the approximations meet your accuracy needs. Here, for example, smaller values for c make e^{-x} much more influential. "Unimportant" terms do not always remain unimportant!

"Fine-tuning" a repetitive quadrature

Quadratures are expensive. They are also rather robust in that they seldom give misleading *wrong* answers. Imprecise answers, inefficient answers — yes; wrong answers — no. Thus, if you need only a few values of an integral, the inefficiency is not very important. But all too often a function that sits far down inside the concentric loops of a much larger computation is defined by a quadrature and so is executed thousands of times for various values of its parameters. Then you will be motivated to find ways to save time (and money).

If there is only a single parameter and if accuracy requirements are modest, the best strategy is to precompute a table and implement an interpolation algorithm on it. With two or more parameters and high accuracy needs, the table strategy becomes difficult to carry out, and even if it is possible the table will occupy what used to be considered a lot of memory. (Times, however, have changed. I remember using at least three machines that had memory capacities of 512 "words" to hold all their data *and instructions!*)

A somewhat less effective, but more easily implemented strategy is to break up a single quadrature into several smaller ones. Some experimentation is needed, but often an expensive quadrature is found to have its problems concentrated in one small part of the range of integration. Suppose we have to evaluate

$$S(b, t) = \int_0^t \frac{\sin x}{\sqrt{x^2 + b^2}} \, dx \qquad (32)$$

for various b and t on $(0,1)$. Quadratures are efficient for most parameter values, but when b becomes very small, then troubles appear. A brute-force attack for $t = 1$ but $b = 0.001$ requires Romberg to evaluate 16,000 ordinates to get one nine-decimal-digit area — and thirteen accurate digits are not possible in double precision because of the buildup of rounding errors when more than 16K ordinates are evaluated. This integral is simple enough to invite several alternative evaluation schemes, but suppose that we are not analytically disposed (it's 4 A.M., answers needed yesterday, etc.) so we try integrating it in five quadratures of width 0.2 each. The results appear in table 2 where we see that altho the program is still having some difficulties,

Range	Area		9 dec	13
0.0–1.0	0.945083652	16384	—	
0.0–0.2	0.198558605	4096	8192	
0.2–0.4	0.196904143	8	32	
0.4–0.6	0.101666945	8	16	
0.6–0.8	0.183966783	8	16	
0.8–1.0	0.173987176	8	16	

Table 2

we are at least able to get thirteen digits (if we want them) and the labor to get nine is only one-fourth of that needed by the single quadrature.

More interesting, however, is the question of *why* the small region (0, 0.2) is still having troubles. On that range $\sin x$ is not much different from x, so plot $x/\sqrt{x^2 + b^2}$ with your pocket calculator — or do some algebra if you prefer that to arithmetic — to find out what is going on geometrically here. (If you are completely unmotivated to explore this point, the plot exists back in the Answers — but I hope you will accept the puzzle rather than the solution.)

Range	Area	9 dec	13
0.0 – 0.001	0.000414214	16	64
0.001– 0.01	0.008635607	128	256
0.01 – 0.1	0.089899648	128	512
0.1 – 1.0	0.846134183	64	512
Totals	0.945083652	336	1344

Table 3

After looking at the geometry you might wonder what a set of logarithmic subdivisions might produce. Table 3 gives an encouraging answer. So, with hindsight, our machine's labor has been reduced from 16,000 ordinates to 336 — better than a factor of 48. And we have achieved some insights about how an automatic subdivision scheme might be organized for a function program where b and t can vary.

Since this integral is simple enough for some analytic modifications, another approach also suggests itself. If we write

$$S(t,b) = \int_0^t \frac{x}{\sqrt{x^2 + b^2}}\, dx - \int_0^t \frac{x - \sin x}{\sqrt{x^2 + b^2}}\, dx \tag{33}$$

the first integral is available in closed form while the integrand of the second behaves like $(x^3/6)/\sqrt{x^2 + b^2}$ over the critical region of small x. If we evaluate this version for $t = 1$, $b = 0.001$ in a single quadrature over $(0,1)$ we get the nine-digit area with only thirty-two ordinates!

Range	13 dec
0.0 – 0.001	8
0.001– 0.01	32
0.01 – 0.1	32
0.1 – 1.0	32
Total	104

Table 4

If we are still anxious for thirteen correct digits, it needs 8000 — but when we subdivide this integral into the same four logarithmic intervals of table 3 it takes only 104 ordinates!

Quick graphical quadratures

You frequently need a quick rough approximation to an integral — often to check a newly written computer program. We give here a method that can yield surprisingly good results with very little effort. Like all numerical quadratures, however, the results are best if the integrand has polynomic geometry. We illustrate the method by finding the area

$$\int_0^3 \frac{dx}{1 + x^2}.$$

First plot the integrand at convenient points and, if necessary, enough other points to permit an adequate freehand sketch. Then:

1.a) Pick a set of points that divides the curve into *segments that look parabolic* (or straight). There is no need for any kind of equal spacing. We chose 0, 1/2, 3/2, 5/2, 3 here.

b) Connect adjacent points by chords.

c) Drop ordinates from these dividing points.

2. At the midpoint of each chord, draw a vertical line to the curve and plot the point, A_i, that lies *2/3 of the way from the chord toward the curve*. Use this as the *average ordinate* for this segment — which is exactly correct for parabolic segments. [The area under this segment is thus (height of A_i) × (segment width), but there is usually no need to evaluate these separate areas — the graphical cumulation process of step 3 being easier.]

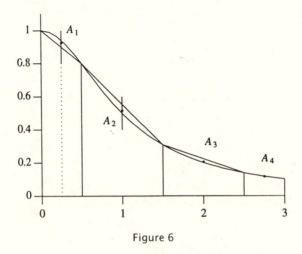

Figure 6

At this stage our procedure has produced figure 6. Here we have shown all the construction lines, but in practice only small parts of them are needed to produce the points A_i from which the final cumulation proceeds. Indeed, the less one can clutter the plot while getting the A_i's the less confusing will be the final stage:

3.a) Connect A_1 and A_2 by a straight line and find the point B_2 on it that lies *halfway horizontally* between the bounding ordinates of segments 1 and 2 — that is, the x coordinate of B_2 will be 0.75 in our example. B_2 is the average ordinate for the first two segments (figure 7). You may now forget about A_1 and A_2.

b) Connect B_2 with A_3 by a straight line and find the point B_3 on it that lies *halfway horizontally* between the bounding ordinates of the combined segments 1, 2 and 3 — that is, the x coordinate of B_3 will

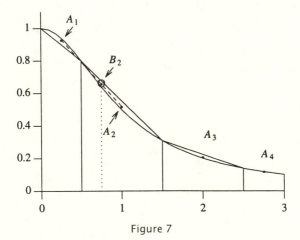

Figure 7

be 1.25 in our example. B_3 is the average ordinate for the first three segments (figure 8). [Again, the cumulated area of the first three segments can be evaluated, if needed, from (ordinate of B_3) × (width of these three segments).]

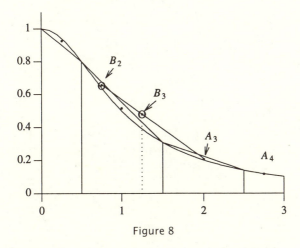

Figure 8

c) Continue as before, connecting the latest B with the next A and thus finding the next B at the middle of the current range. The total area will be (height of the final B) × (width of the region).

In our example the final B_4 appears to have a vertical coordinate of about 0.42 (figure 9). Thus, we estimate the total area to be

$$0.42 \times 3.0 = 1.26.$$

The true area is $\arctan 3.0 = 1.2490$.

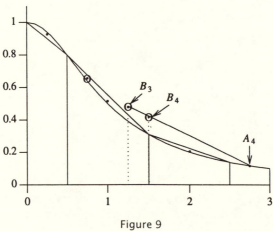

Figure 9

This technique will usually give two correct significant figures and frequently almost three. It is much faster to *do* it than to *describe* it!

Exercises

This miscellany of Sick Integrals is presented as your final exam in the subject. Some are easy; some are not — and they are randomly mixed! As with all exams, peeking at the answers is not encouraged, altho Open Book is certainly an option. ϵ is presumed positive but quite small; B is big — perhaps 137.

25. $\displaystyle\int_0^{\pi/2} \frac{1 - \cos x}{x^2 \sqrt{x}}\, dx$

27. $\displaystyle\int_\epsilon^{\pi/2} \frac{dx}{1 - \cos x}$

26. $\displaystyle\int_0^1 \frac{dx}{\sqrt{(1 - x^2)(1 - b^2 x^2)}}$
for $0 < b < 1$

28. $\displaystyle\int_b^{\pi/2} \frac{\sin x}{\sqrt{x^2 - b^2}}\, dx$
for $0 < b < 1$

29. $\displaystyle\int_0^{\pi/2} \frac{\cos x}{\sqrt{|x^2 - b^2|}}\, dx$

for $0 < b < \pi/2$

30. $\displaystyle\int_0^{1-\epsilon} \frac{dx}{\ln x}$

31. $\displaystyle\int_0^\infty \frac{\ln(1+x)}{x\sqrt{x}}\, dx$

32. $\displaystyle\int_0^B \frac{\arctan x}{\ln(1+x)}\, dx$

33. $\displaystyle\int_0^B \frac{\ln x}{\sqrt{3+x^2}}\, dx$

34. $\displaystyle\int_\epsilon^{\pi/2} \frac{dx}{\tan x(\pi/2 - x)}$

35. $\displaystyle\int_\epsilon^\infty \frac{e^{-x}}{\arctan x}\, dx$

36. $\displaystyle\int_\epsilon^{\pi/2} \frac{\cos x}{x\sqrt{1+x}}\, dx$

37. $\displaystyle\int_0^{\pi/2} \sqrt{\frac{\pi/2 - x}{1 - \sin x}} \cdot \frac{dx}{\sqrt{x}}$

38. $\displaystyle\int_\epsilon^{\pi/2} \frac{\cos x}{x\sqrt{x}(\pi/2 - x)}\, dx$

39. $\displaystyle\int_0^B \frac{\ln(1+x)}{\sqrt{x}\arctan x}\, dx$

40. $\displaystyle\int_0^{\pi-\epsilon} \frac{x}{\sin x}\, dx$

ARCHIMEDES, DESPAIR!

There's an old iteration that strives
To deliver the value of π:

$$s_{n+1} = 2^n \sqrt{2\left(1 - \sqrt{1 - (s_n/2^n)^2}\right)}$$

for   n = 2, 3 ...   with $s_2 = 2\sqrt{2}$.

But why does it not quite succeed?
Push some buttons to give it a try.

[Then fix it!]

Chapter 4

RECURRENCE RELATIONS

But hopefully not "vain repetitions."

A typical recurrence relation lets you compute the next function in a sequence of functions from one or two of the most recent — and do it very cheaply. The only familiar recurrence that seems to occur in underclass mathematics connects three adjacent cosines:

$$-\cos(n-1)\theta + (2\cos\theta) \cdot \cos n\theta = \cos(n+1)\theta.$$

If we write down copies of this relation with n set to 1, 2 and 3, respectively, we get

$$-1 + (2\cos\theta) \cdot \cos\theta = \cos 2\theta$$
$$-\cos\theta + (2\cos\theta) \cdot \cos 2\theta = \cos 3\theta$$
$$-\cos 2\theta + (2\cos\theta) \cdot \cos 3\theta = \cos 4\theta$$

and it is clear that having once computed $\cos\theta$, we can then generate the whole succession of $\cos n\theta$ at a cost of one multiplication (by $2\cos\theta$) and one subtraction each. Two arithmetic operations to get something that needs thirty or forty when evaluated directly from its power series is probably the world's greatest computational bargain, tho we might hope to find similar ones. Actually, most of the transcendental functions that sport subscripts (Bessel functions J_n and I_n, Legendre polynomials P_n, Chebyshev polynomials T_n and U_n) have recurrence relations [AMS-55 is full of them] but because these functions are considered esoteric and hence avoided by most undergraduates, recurrence relations remain a mystery to most students.

This chapter is at least partially an attempt to redress the balance by showing how recurrences can be useful (and are used) altho we shall avoid the esoteric functions and concentrate on more homely examples that should occasion no alarms.

Suppose you needed to evaluate either of the integrals

$$\int_0^g \frac{\text{atn}\,x}{b+x}\,dx \quad \text{or} \quad \int_0^g \frac{e^{-x}}{b+x}\,dx$$

for a variety of their parameter values (b, g). A few minutes of effort will convince you that sophomore calculus is inadequate — a closed form eludes you* — and you reluctantly wonder about using rather ponderous quadratures like Simpson. But wait! Both the exponential function and the arctangent have power series that are respectable if x is not too large. Thus, if g is not too big we can replace the transcendentals by their series to produce

$$\left.\begin{array}{l} \displaystyle\int_0^g \frac{\text{atn}\,x}{b+x}\,dx = T_1 - T_3/3 + T_5/5 - \cdots \\[2em] \displaystyle\int_0^g \frac{e^{-x}}{b+x}\,dx = T_0 - T_1/1! + T_2/2! - \cdots \end{array}\right\} \quad \text{with} \quad T_n = \int_0^g \frac{x^n}{b+x}\,dx$$

$$(1)$$

and now calculus seems applicable. T_0 is $\ln(1+g/b)$, T_1 is $g-b\cdot\ln(1+g/b)$, T_2 is ... and hope again starts to fade. It *can* be done — but twenty terms? Human error rates are too high; life is too short.

---

*For good reason, as these integrals have no closed forms.

Or is it? If we write

$$b \cdot T_{n-1} + T_n = \int_0^g \frac{bx^{n-1} + x^n}{b+x} \, dx = \int_0^g \frac{x^{n-1}(b+x)}{b+x} \, dx = g^n/n \quad (2)$$

we suddenly have a recurrence relation that expresses the next T_n in terms of the current T_{n-1} — so we need only 4 arithmetic operations (one to update g^{n-1} to g^n) for each. So we generate the T's, combine them with the series coefficients in (1) and add them up. Try it!

Important Experiment

If you are at all experimentally inclined, you will learn much more from this chapter if you stop reading the exposition here and do a simple experiment on a programmable pocket calculator:

First: Implement the recurrence

$$T_n \leftarrow g^n/n - b \cdot T_{n-1} \qquad \text{with} \qquad T_0 = \ln(1 + g/b)$$

and generate T_n upwards-in-n from T_0. Run it for $g = 0.5$ and various b — including at least 0.3, 0.8, 1.5 and 3.0. Record all the T_n's up to T_{25}.

Second: Implement the same recurrence *downward*

$$T_{n-1} \leftarrow (g^n/n - T_n)/b \qquad \text{with} \qquad T_{25} = 0.0$$

and record all the T's down to T_0. Again hold g constant at 0.5 and run the same b values as before. Compare your values from the two runs.

Since the second experiment starts from a (slightly) wrong value of T_{25}, we might expect our down-in-n values to differ a little from those calculated up-in-n. But some will differ a lot. Like not even the same sign! Where they differ, try to decide which is correct. Use quadratures, if you have the time and curiosity, to find the correct value of (say) T_6 — and thus determine how well the two recurrences actually did.

n	Up	Down
0	.15415068	.15415068
1	.03754795	.03754796
2	.01235616	.01235612
3	.00459818	.00459831
4	.00183045	.00183007
5	.00075864	.00075980
6	.00032826	.00032476
7	.00013129	.00014179
8	.00009441	.00006291
9	−.00006623	.00002827
10	.00029633	.00001284
11	−.00084461	.00000588
12	.00255418	.00000271
13	−.00765314	.00000126
14	.02296377	.00000059
15	−.06888928	.00000027
16	.20666879	.00000013
17	−.62000591	.00000006
18	1.86001801	.00000003
19	−5.58005428	.00000001
20	16.74016190	.00000001
21	−50.22048569	.00000000
22	150.66145325	.00000000
23	−451.98437500	.00000000
24	1355.95312500	.00000000
25	−4067.85937500	.00000000

A Hint

What's going on here? We have a Down recurrence starting with a *wrong* value for T_{25} but generating T_n from it that look resonable, ending with a perfect T_0. The Up recurrence, altho beginning with a correct T_0, produces rapidly deteriorating values that ultimately go negative and then increase in magnitude with alternating signs. If you try this experiment in double precision (but go, try it!), the same pattern emerges, altho it is somewhat slower about it — Up values going negative at T_{19} instead of T_9. That suggests our troubles are coming in from the right end — with double-precision making them travel thru more digits before they can flip the sign.

Now that you have a clue, look again at your numbers for (0.3, 0.5). What do you see? [No, I'm not going to do your homework for you. You must look at your own data.]

We discuss the phenomena you observe in the following sections, but again we urge you to do the experiment first. See if your detective skills can decipher the facts from the evidence before your eyes. (And don't try to blame peculiar behaviors on programming errors — the algorithms are too simple for that to be likely.) But just in case you are worried about your numbers, we give the values we get on running the two algorithms for (b, g) equal to (3, 0.5) in single-precision Fortran.

This behavior, both good and bad, is typical of most common recurrences — stable in one direction (but not always the Down one) and unstable in the other. We examine them analytically in the rest of this chapter. The mathematics is not difficult; the insights it grants will satisfy, so we recommend it. But in all fairness we have to point out that the person in a hurry can test the utility of a new recurrence experimentally without recourse to theory. A recurrence is so simple to program that a few minutes with a programmable calculator will establish the parametric regions for which it is stable, and some closer checking of the stable results will disclose whether they are accurate. Indeed, as a computational tool, recurrence relations shine both by their efficiency and their ease of use. (Too bad they don't always work!)

The divergence problem

When g exceeds unity, this series for the arctangent does not converge. Each succeeding term, g^{odd}/odd, has the previous numerator multiplied by g^2 while its divisor only increases by 2. Sooner or later g^{odd} wins. The typical term, T_n, in our series (1) can easily be bounded by freezing the x in the denominator at its upper and lower limits:

$$\frac{g^{n+1}}{(n+1)(b+g)} \;<\; \int_0^g \frac{x^n}{b+x}\,dx \;<\; \frac{g^{n+1}}{(n+1)(b)}$$

and we see that it suffers from the same growth problem as the arctangent series itself. Thus the behavior of our algorithm when g is even a little larger than unity is clear — divergence only needs g slightly greater than 1 to emerge, and it emerges exponentially!

The instability problem

The problem with larger b's is slightly more subtle. The recurrence computes each T_n from the previous T_{n-1} *multiplied* by $-b$. Thus any error in T_{n-1} is also multiplied by $-b$ before being transmitted into T_n. After n steps, the original errors in T_0 (from both roundings and inaccuracies in the logarithmic function) are multiplied by $(-b)^n$. If b is less than unity they will have shrunk to insignificance, but for b greater than one they will inexorably increase. Since the correct T_n are getting smaller, any *growing* errors become an increasingly larger percentage of the next T — ultimately overwhelming the true value and causing the T_n to alternate in sign. (We stop our algorithm whenever $T_n < 10^{-16}$ — which also acts when T_n becomes negative.) When b is 2, the error growth is rapid, the negative T_n

occurring long before a correct calculation could have produced decent convergence. Thus, at (2, 0.7) the double-precision version of the algorithm stops when n is 33 with only eight correct significant figures in the sum. The larger the b, the sooner disaster strikes, altho very small g and modest accuracy requirements may permit adequate results to emerge first. But to depend on such behavior is to walk a tightrope over Niagara Falls. People do it, but it is not recommended for the beginner.

A quantitative picture of our algorithm's behavior for various (b, g) values is shown in figures 1 and 2 — where the principal entry is the n needed to produce the most accurate value of our integral possible using double-precision arithmetic. The subscript shows the number of digits that were correct. Thus at (0.5, 0.5) we achieve sixteen significant figures at T_{43}, while at (2, 0.5) T_{25} goes negative, leaving our series correct only to ten significant figures. The recurrence for T_n becomes *unstable for b greater than unity.*

b

8	13_7	13_5	15_4	17_1
4	19_7	19_6	23_4	23_2
2	25_{10}	33_8	39_6	51_2
1	41_{16}	75_{16}	217_{15}	x
.5	43_{16}	69_{15}	239_{16}	x

| | .5 | .7 | .9 | 1.1 | g |

Figure 1

1.1	163_{13}	325_7	31_2
1.0	217_{15}	999_7	31_2
0.9	233_{16}	999_7	31_2
	0.9	1.0	1.1

Figure 2

For b less than one, a dramatically different behavior occurs as g passes unity. The series, which reluctantly gave sixteen correct figures at T_{239} for $g = 0.9$ (and was still gamely trying at $g = 1.0$ — but yielding only seven correct figures at T_{1000} when we gave up) suddenly quits in disgust and takes off at $g = 1.1$ — growing without limit, rapidly, after T_{30}.

In the fourth region, with both b and g greater than one, no useful values can be computed. We show the behavior in figure 1, but analysis seems superfluous there!

A closer look at the (1, 1) region is shown in figure 2, where we see that the bad behavior as g passes 1 appears quite suddenly. The effects in the b direction are much more gradual.

Larger b values — a downward recurrence for $b > 1$

When b is greater than one, our computed T_n contains more error than T_{n-1} because we *multiplied* T_{n-1} by $-b$. If, on the other hand, we use the same recurrence, but *in the other direction* — use it to compute T_{n-1} from T_n — we will *divide* by $-b$ and hence *reduce* the error. For this evaluation of our series, we need to start our recurrence out at some large N with a known value of T_N and generate the T's downwards-in-n. Of course we don't know any T_N exactly, but since they become small as n increases, we can take T_N equal to *zero*. We thereby commit an error (the size of the actual T_N) but we know its approximate size from our bounds and we also know that the recurrence will *reduce* that error — so we only have to start out at an N where T_N is smaller than quantities we choose to ignore. Of course we have to be evaluating a series that converges, so g must be less than unity — indeed for efficiency it ought to be not much bigger than 0.5, where an N of 47 will guarantee sixteen significant figures and five figures will need only an N of 13. (If g is 0.8, then an N of 37 is needed to deliver 5 figures. How big should it be for 16?)

If g is not too large we now can evaluate our integral for most positive b. (But what should you do if b is very small? Or zero?) When g is larger than 0.5 or perhaps 0.7, however, we need other algorithms. There are many, but here they would complicate our effort to understand the behavior of recurrence relations. We treat the bigger g's later.

A similar integral

The other integral

$$\int_0^g \frac{e^{-x}}{b+x}\,dx = T_0 - \frac{T_1}{1!} + \frac{T_2}{2!} - \cdots \tag{3}$$

where, as before

$$T_n = \int_0^g \frac{x^n}{b+x}\,dx \quad\text{and}\quad b\cdot T_{n-1} + T_n = g^n/n \qquad (4)$$

seems no different from its arctangent brother — except for the presence of both even and odd terms and of factorials that strengthen the denominators and thereby give more efficient convergence. The recurrence is still stable upwards-in-n for b less than unity and stable downwards-in-n for larger b.

Convergence is clearly the interesting question. If we run our algorithms, we get the data of figures 3 and 4. The main entry is the number of terms, n, at which our algorithm delivers its maximum accuracy while the subscript shows the number of good digits delivered there. As the data show, the up-in-n algorithm gives nearly full double-precision accuracy when both b and g are less than 4, while down-in-n is good for b greater than 4 if g is smaller than b.

b	Up-in-n						
32	8_{11}	10_9	12_8	17_7	x		
16	9_{13}	11_{11}	17_{11}	22_{10}	x		
8	11_{14}	14_{14}	18_{14}	27_{14}	x		
4	13_{16}	16_{16}	21_{15}	28_{15}	x		
2	12_{16}	17_{14}	20_{15}	29_{15}	40_{14}	x	
1	13_{17}	16_{16}	20_{15}	29_{15}	41_{14}	58_{11}	x
.5	12_{16}	16_{15}	20_{16}	29_{15}	43_{16}	60_{11}	x
	.5	1	2	4	8	16	32 g

Figure 3

When g gets bigger than 4, both up and down algorithms degenerate, altho the problem does not appear suddenly at 1 as it does with the arctangent. Why?

Convergence here is much faster than it was in figure 1 because the terms of (3) behave like $g^n/n!/n$ — it only takes thirteen terms to deliver sixteen significant figures when g is 0.5 and even at 0.8 we can still get sixteen digits in fifteen terms. Clearly the convergence is now being provided mostly by the denominator. We can even expect convergence in thirty terms if g is 4, and might hope for forty terms at 8 — but we should be worried because our series is *alternating* in sign and we remember that the series for e^{-x} itself starts to lose significant digits once x exceeds 3. The subscripts in figure 3 show those troubles still to be with us here.

We can include the factorials in our recurrence, thereby simplifying our algorithm and making it easier to analyze. Let $E_n = T_n/n!$; then, dividing the recurrence (4) by $n!$ we find

$$\frac{b}{n} \cdot E_{n-1} + E_n = \frac{g^n}{n!n} \qquad \text{with} \qquad E_0 = \ln(1 + g/b) \qquad (5)$$

and we want

$$E = E_0 - E_1 + E_2 - \cdots = \int_0^g \frac{e^{-x}}{b+x}\,dx. \qquad (6)$$

b	Down-in-n						
32	13_{16}	16_{16}	21_{16}	30_{16}	45_{15}	80_{13}	x
16	13_{16}	17_{16}	22_{16}	34_{16}	65_{15}	x	
8	14_{16}	19_{16}	28_{16}	56_{16}	x		
4	17_{16}	25_{16}	59_{16}	x			
2	24_{16}	46_{16}	x				
1	46_{16}						
	.5	1	2	4	8	16	g

Figure 4

The noise-suppressing multiplier at each step now is b/n — which seems to become helpful (in the upwards iteration) rather quickly, even if b is larger than one. But the *signal* is *shrinking* by the factor E_n/E_{n-1}, that is, by $g(n-1)/n^2$, so that the *relative error* changes by

$$\frac{b/n}{(n-1)g/n^2} = \frac{b}{g}\left(\frac{n}{n-1}\right) \approx \frac{b}{g}.$$

In the down direction this stability factor is g/b and we see it clearly operating in figure 4 where, for $b > g$, our algorithm works — until the cancellation of significant digits finally kills it (these being mostly a result of large g). The upwards algorithm gets killed by significant figure loss from the alternating signs at about g equal to 8 — except when very small b/g prevents the appearance of much error for the figure loss to amplify.

The Exponential Integral

We shall conclude with an integral with an infinite upper limit

$$E(b) = \int\limits_0^\infty \frac{e^{-x}}{b+x}\,dx$$

which is one form of the well-known Exponential Integral — for which a variety of algorithms exist. [See chapter 5 of Abramowitz & Stegun's *Handbook of Mathematical Functions* (AMS-55) — especially equations 5.1.28, 5.1.11, and 5.1.22.] But we are going to develop a more efficient algorithm (at least more efficient for b greater than about 3) based on a homogeneous recurrence. The derivation takes a bit of effort to follow but is rewarding because it is the prototype for a family of recurrence derivations. Understanding will confer both ability and appreciation. [If you only want fast answers, skip to (7).]

Our strategy is to embed $E(b)$ in a sequence of integrals

$$\int\limits_0^\infty \frac{e^{-x}x^k}{(b+x)^{k+1}}\,dx \qquad k = n, n-1, \ldots, 1, 0$$

where the last integral is the one we seek. Define

$$E_{k,m} = \int\limits_0^\infty \frac{e^{-x}x^k}{(b+x)^m}\,dx$$

(which is also a function of b, but since b never changes in our derivation we omit mention of it). Integration-by-parts gives

$$E_{k,m} = \left[\frac{e^{-x}x^{k+1}}{(k+1)(b+x)^m}\right]_0^\infty + \frac{m}{k+1}\int_0^\infty \frac{e^{-x}x^{k+1}}{(b+x)^{m+1}}\,dx + \frac{1}{k+1}\int_0^\infty \frac{e^{-x}x^{k+1}}{(b+x)^m}\,dx.$$

The first term on the right disappears at both limits. The remaining terms give

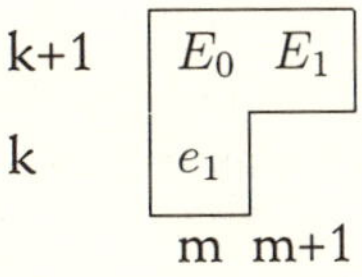

$$(k+1)E_{k,m} = m \cdot E_{k+1,m+1} + E_{k+1,m}$$

which connects three adjacent elements of our (k,m) diagram.

The more simply derived relation (derive it!)

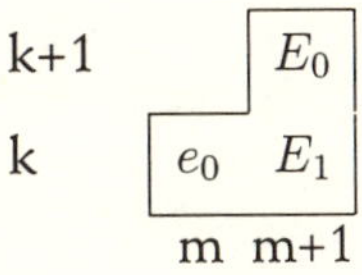

$$E_{k,m} = b \cdot E_{k,m+1} + E_{k+1,m+1}$$

connects the three nearby elements of the lower diagram.

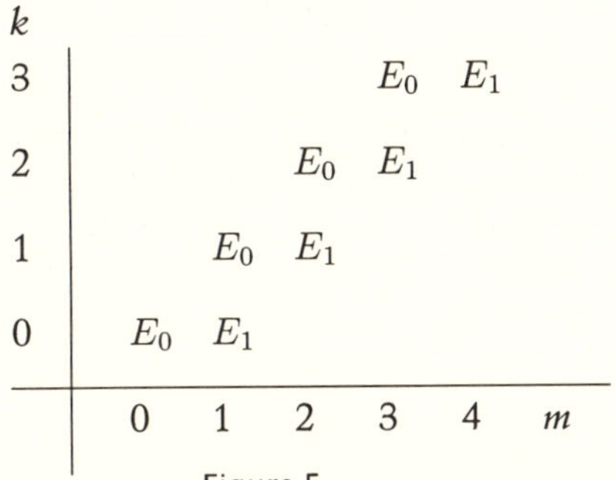

k

3   E_0 E_1

2   E_0 E_1

1   E_0 E_1

0 E_0 E_1

   0 1 2 3 4 *m*

Figure 5

If we simplify our subscript notation by using j where

$$k + j = m$$

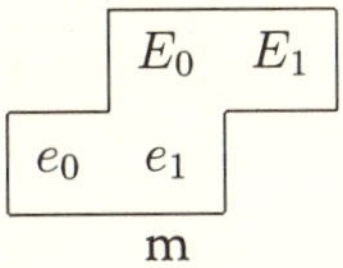

then our last two relations can be rewritten as

$$m \cdot e_1 = m \cdot E_1 + E_0 \quad \text{and} \quad e_0 = b \cdot e_1 + E_0$$

which refer to the 45° elements in figure 5. If we are given two adjacent elements from the same row, then applying these two relations immediately gives us the next two — one row below and one column to the left. Thus we can generate the diagonal staircase of figure 5. Note that this is an algorithm in which each new e_j can immediately replace the old E_j so that no subscripted variables are needed in the computer program.

The definition of our E_j's guarantees that they become steadily smaller as k (and m) increase: the ratio $x/(b+x)$ is clearly less than unity, so $[x/(b+x)]^m$ can be made as small as we wish by taking m large enough. Also, the larger b is, the more quickly the E's shrink. We may therefore start with some suitably large m and take E_1 to be zero there. We might also be tempted to take E_0 on the same row to be zero, but that would be a serious mistake because our algorithm is *homogeneous*, that is, there is no term without an E. If we start with both E_1 and E_0 at zero, then e_1 and e_0 are also zero — as are all the E's generated from them. So we shall let E_1 be zero but take E_0 as $1/m$ — which is an arbitrary value that is wrong by some unknown factor, f. Since E_1 is also wrong by the same factor (fE_1 is zero too!) we are really executing the algorithm

$$(fe_1) = (fE_1) + (fE_0)/m$$
$$(fe_0) = (fE_0) + b \cdot (fe_1). \tag{7}$$

We finally have fe_1 on the bottom row of figure 5 in which every element is multiplied by f. Now if only we knew f, we would have our answer. But *we do know one integral* on the bottom row of our array: at $(0,\ 0)$ we have

$$E_{0,0} = \int\limits_0^\infty e^{-x} dx = 1$$

so the (fe_0) on row 0 is merely f and hence

$$e_1 = (fe_1)/(fe_0).$$

b	.5	1	2	3	4	8	16	32
16	(178)	99	49	33	28	16	9	7
5	(26)	13	7	5	4	3	2	2

Figure 6

Try it! In figure 6 we show the starting value of m necessary to produce sixteen significant figures and also five significant figures as a function of b. [Below b equal to 3 a power series with an additional $\ln(x)$ term (see 5.1.11 in AMS-55) is more efficient when one needs high precision, but if five figures are all you want, the current algorithm wins down to at least $b = 0.5$.]

Large — but not infinite — g

When discussing the integral

$$\int_0^g \frac{e^{-x}}{b + x}\, dx$$

we had to limit g to less than approximately 4 because of the loss of significant figures in the alternating series. Now that we have the infinite integral available, we can cover previously omitted ranges of g. Consider the transformation

$$\int_g^\infty \frac{e^{-x}}{b + x}\, dx \;=\; e^{-g} \int_0^\infty \frac{e^{-y}}{(b + g) + y}\, dy$$

$$x \;=\; g + y\,.$$

Thus

$$\int_0^g \frac{e^{-x}}{b + x}\, dx \;=\; \int_0^\infty \frac{e^{-x}}{b + x}\, dx \;-\; e^{-g} \int_0^\infty \frac{e^{-y}}{(b + g) + y}\, dy$$

so we can evaluate our $(0, g)$ integral as the difference between two $(0, \infty)$ integrals (and the evaluation of one exponential).

The "other" arctangent series

Since the alternating series for the arctangent

$$\text{atn } x = x - x^3/3 + x^5/5 - \cdots$$

lacks the factorials of the sine and cosine series, its useful range is
limited to roughly $|x| < 0.7$. There is, however, another series that is
more robust.

$$\text{atn } x = \frac{x}{1+x^2}\left[1 + \frac{2}{3}\frac{x^2}{1+x^2} + \frac{2\cdot 4}{3\cdot 5}\left(\frac{x^2}{1+x^2}\right)^2 + \cdots\right]$$

converges quite rapidly even at $x = 1$. Indeed, its effective range extends to about $x = 2$, tho it is often better to reformulate an arctangent problem with large arguments in terms of the reciprocal variable. The presence of the $1 + x^2$ in the denominator limits the *algebraic* utility of this series but *numerically* it helps a lot.

As a final example of a useful recurrence we evaluate

$$\int_0^g \frac{\text{atn } x}{\sqrt{1+x^2}}\, dx \qquad 0 \le g \le 1$$

by replacing the arctangent with this series, producing

$$h_0 + \frac{2}{3}h_1 + \frac{2\cdot 4}{3\cdot 5}h_2 + \cdots \quad \text{with} \quad h_n = \int_0^g \left[\frac{x^2}{1+x^2}\right]^n \cdot \frac{1}{\sqrt{1+x^2}} \cdot \frac{x\,dx}{1+x^2}.$$

Noting that

$$d\left(\frac{1}{\sqrt{1+x^2}}\right) = -\frac{1}{\sqrt{1+x^2}}\frac{x\,dx}{1+x^2}$$

integrate by parts to yield

$$h_{n-1} = \left(1 + \frac{1}{2n}\right)h_n + \frac{1}{2n}\cdot\frac{1}{\sqrt{1+x^2}}\left[\frac{g^2}{1+g^2}\right]^n.$$

This recurrence can be evaluated down-in-n if started with n large enough to make $[g^2/(1+g^2)]^n$ negligible, but it also is effective upwards from

$$h_0 = 1 - \frac{1}{\sqrt{1+g^2}}.$$

Similar recurrences are easily found to evaluate all five integrals

$$\int_0^g \frac{\text{atn } x}{\sqrt{1+x^2}}\frac{\sqrt{x}}{x^{k/2}}\, dx \qquad k = 0,1,2,3,4$$

tho for efficiency's sake when $g > 1$ you may want to break the integral into the sum of the integral over (0,1) (a constant) and one over $(1, g)$ in which you then invoke $\pi/2 - \text{atn } 1/x = \text{atn } x$ to produce a closed-form term and a different arctangent integral that can be tamed by a reciprocal transformation.

Exercises

1. If you would like to conduct your own explorations with the embedding technique, you might try

$$\int_0^g \frac{\ln x}{1 + x} \, dx$$

which gives an efficient compact algorithm that also involves a downward recurrence for

$$\int_0^g \frac{x^k}{(1 + x)^m} \, dx.$$

The iterative loop uses only eight arithmetic operations per downward step.

2. Slightly more difficult is

$$\int_0^g \frac{\ln x}{1 + x^2} \, dx$$

by embedding. (But a series expansion of the denominator, followed by term-by-term integration, gives a more efficient algorithm.)

3. The integral

$$\int_0^\infty \frac{e^{-cx}}{(1 + x^2)\sqrt{x}} \, dx$$

will give you practice with an homogeneous recurrence system that requires normalization at its conclusion. [It may help to point out that

$$\int_0^\infty \frac{e^{-cx}}{\sqrt{x}} \, dx = \frac{2}{\sqrt{c}} \int_0^\infty e^{-u^2} \, du$$

an integral that probably has been lurking in your mind since Calculus courses :-)]

RESEARCH PROBLEM

A unit cube is placed in a smooth vase
that is a parabola rotated around its axis.

Specifically, the vase is
$$z = h(x^2 + y^2)$$
where z is the vertical coordinate.

For $h = 0.92$:

1) What configuration does the cube assume
   so that its center is as low as possible?

2) What other equilibrium positions are stable,
   metastable, or unstable?

3) Can you prove that all equilibrium configurations of the cube possess a plane of
   symmetry that contains the vertical
   axis of the vase?

[I believe this conjecture to be true
but know of no proof.]

Chapter 5

CHOOSING AND TUNING
AN ALGORITHM

"If at first you don't succeed ..."
A Scottish spider

"There's more than one way to kill a cat — and some are messier than others." The same is true about solving a physical problem. In this chapter we look at several approaches to a sequence of similar problems, hoping to show how the trials (and rejections) of various algorithms help us avoid the pitfalls with which the rest of this book is principally concerned. We begin with the nearly trivial question: What is the radius of the largest circle that can be squeezed into the first quadrant space bounded above by the ellipse

$$x^2/9 + z^2 = 1$$

and below by the (slightly unusual) hyperbola

$$x \cdot z^2 = 0.01$$

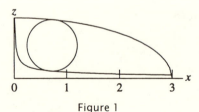

Figure 1

where the form of the hyperbola has been chosen to avoid an $x - z$ symmetry that might urge special algorithmic simplifications — see figure 1. Since we probably would not bother to write a computer program for just one problem, let's generalize the formulas slightly into

$$x \cdot z^2 = c \quad \text{and} \quad ax^2 + z^2 = 1.$$

And again, to get a bit more mileage from our efforts we might also consider how to find the location of a circle of *specified* radius (less than maximal) that is jammed into either "corner" of this same closed space. Since our algorithm presumably will get buried deep inside a big program, it should operate reliably without human guidance — altho at first we may be happy if it works at all.

Before going further, you might profitably consider how you would tackle these jobs. There is no single "right" algorithm — altho some are certainly messier than others.

Parametric searching

The Powerfully Parallel person with computer time to burn will probably observe that the maximal circle has three parameters — the co-ordinates x_c, z_c of the center, C, and its radius, R, while the smaller-circle problem only needs two. In either problem he might decide to lay down a grid of points thruout a reasonable segment of the parameter space and, for each point, test how well the corresponding circle fits. Having localized the answer to a small region of the parameter space, he will subdivide his grid and repeat. Admittedly this procedural description is a bit vague — especially about the fit-testing part — but there is nothing in it that cannot be made precise with a little more work. Since there are more interesting approaches that may also be more efficient, we shall not pursue this one here, but will keep it in mind should it be needed.

The maximal circle

A first formulation of this problem will probably begin with the equations of the hyperbola and the ellipse

$$x_1 z_1^2 = c \qquad\qquad a x_2^2 + z_2^2 = 1 \qquad\qquad (1)\ (2)$$

and normal vectors at the two tangency points (figure 2)

$$[1/x_1 \quad 2/z_1] \qquad\qquad [a x_2 \quad z_2].$$

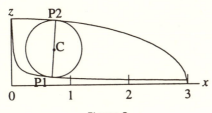

Figure 2

Observing that these normals are also the directions of the supporting radii, we get

$$\frac{x_c - x_1}{1/x_1} = \frac{z_c - z_1}{2/z_1} \quad \text{and} \quad \frac{x_2 - x_c}{a x_2} = \frac{z_2 - z_c}{z_2} \qquad (3)\ (4)$$

(where we have chosen to write these numerators so that they are positive).

We now have four equations for the six unknowns — the coordinates of the center and the two points of tangency, P_1 and P_2. Equating the expressions for the two radii

$$R_1 = (x_1 - x_c)^2 + (z_1 - z_c)^2 = (x_c - x_2)^2 + (z_c - z_2)^2 = R_2$$

gives us a fifth equation, while the maximality condition can be made to produce another. Mathematically speaking, the problem is almost "solved" — but with no algorithm in sight the prospect does not please. One can reduce the number of variables to four but the already quadratic equations rapidly become torturous — suggesting either that our simple three-parameter problem is not simple, or that we need to look for another approach — one that reflects its simplicity. We should certainly look further even tho we might have to return here.

An insight

Looking at figure 2 again, we notice that the tangency points, P_1 and P_2, must lie at the opposite ends of a diameter of the maximal circle, where the slopes of the boundary curves are parallel. (Why?) We can thus temporarily forget the center — formulating our problem in terms of the four coordinates x_1, z_1, x_2, z_2. Further, the upward concavity of the hyperbola facing the downward concavity of the ellipse guarantees that P_1–P_2 is the *only* straight line that is normal to both curves where it intersects them. Finding it is a *one*-parameter search along (say) x_1. Much better than six or even four parameters!

Specifically, starting with x_1: then $z_1 \leftarrow \sqrt{c/x_1}$. If we denote the line P_1–P_2 by $z = m_1 x + b$ then

$$m_1 \leftarrow 2x_1/z_1 \quad \text{and} \quad b \leftarrow -m_1 x_1.$$

Its intersection with the ellipse is given by the *larger** root of a quadratic,

$$x_2 \leftarrow -q + \sqrt{q^2 - p}$$

with

$$q \leftarrow m_1 b/(a + m_1^2) \quad p \leftarrow (b^2 - 1)/(a + m_1^2)$$

whence

$$z_2 \leftarrow \sqrt{1 - ax_2^2}$$

and the slope of the ellipse there is

$$m_2 \leftarrow -ax_2/z_2.$$

The product of the slopes $m_1 m_2$ will be -1 for the line we seek. Since there is only one such line we can use false position — starting values

---

*Geometrically, what point does the other sign give?

being easily available at ϵ and $3 - \epsilon$. For our parameter, $c = 0.01$, the center is $(0.72527, 0.54386)$, the radius 0.424935.

A different approach

Altho we feel that the algorithmic formulation of the maximal circle problem presented above is both straightforward and uncomplicated to implement, other formulations are reasonable and effective. Some people prefer to solve *one* equation for *the* answer.* How might the persistent eliminator do it?

Starting with the equations (1) and (2) of the boundaries at the tangent points, get two more by equating the slopes of the two normals and also equating the slope of the hyperbola's normal to the slope of the line P_1–P_2

$$2ax_1x_2 = z_1z_2 \quad \text{and} \quad 2x_1(x_2 - x_1) = z_1(z_2 - z_1) \qquad (5)\ (6)$$

to produce four equations for the four unknowns. Getting rid of three of them looks difficult. But since the products x_1x_2 and z_1z_2 are prevalent we might do well to change variables, defining the products

$$p_x = x_1x_2 \qquad p_z = z_1z_2$$

and the ratios

$$r_x = x_1/x_2 \qquad r_z = z_1/z_2.$$

Noting that

$$p_xr_x = x_1^2 \qquad p_x/r_x = x_2^2$$

and similarly for the z's, our four equations become

$$p_xr_xp_z^2r_z^2 = c^2 \qquad a\frac{p_x}{r_x} + \frac{p_z}{r_z} + 1 \qquad (7)\ (8)$$

and

$$2ap_x = p_z \qquad 2p_x(1 - r_x) = p_z(1 - r_z). \qquad (9)\ (10)$$

Using (9) to eliminate p_z in (8) and (10) produces

$$2ap_x\left(\frac{1}{2r_x} + \frac{1}{r_z}\right) = 1 \quad \text{and} \quad 1 - r_x = a(1 - r_z). \qquad (11)\ (12)$$

---

*That, of course, is what we were doing above, but it doesn't look like it.

Equations (9) and (12) allow us to eliminate either the z or the x subscripts from our system while (11) can then give an explicit representation of p_x. With these available (7) can be expressed entirely in terms of r_z (or r_x) — one rather complicated equation in one unknown. But which one?

First, which p's and r's are small and which are relatively insensitive when we move P1 a small amount? A glance at figure 2 shows that z_1 is small but z_2 is both near unity and also insensitive. Thus r_z is small (also p_z) while both p_z and p_z/r_z are insensitive. In keeping with our preference for small variables, we solve for r_z. Equation (7) becomes

$$2ac^2 = \frac{[1 - a(1 - r_z)] \cdot r_z^5}{[1 + \frac{r_z/2}{1-a(1-r_z)}]^3}.$$ (13)

Since r_z is small, $1-r_z$ is not sensitive for small changes in r_z. Further, $a = 1/9$, so we see that both expressions in square brackets vary slowly with r_z. This suggests solving for the r_z in the r_z^5 factor to get the iteration

$$r_z \leftarrow \left\{ \frac{2ac^2[1 + \frac{r_z/2}{1-a(1-r_z)}]^3}{1 - a(1 - r_z)} \right\}^{1/5}.$$

For $c = 0.01$ and $a = 1/9$ we obtain

r_z
0.10
0.12376
0.12460
0.124634
0.124635

and working back thru r_x, p_x and p_z we ultimately obtain $x_1 = 0.688195$ and the other original variables, leading to $R = 0.424935$ as before. If you prefer this approach, so be it. It works.

The maximal circle for other c values

We now have two algorithms that will find the tangent points, P_1 and P_2, at opposite ends of a diameter of a circle. They work for a wide range of (c, a) — but is the circle they find always a valid answer to our physical problem?

Consider the shape of the hyperbola as c becomes small: at *zero* it becomes simply the two coordinate axes, so if we support our circle only by a diameter it will be centered at $(0, 1/2)$ with radius $1/2$! For less drastic values, say $c = 0.001$, the circle will sit as shown in figure 3 — most of it in the first quadrant but with a small slice of it to the left of the vertical arm of the hyperbola. For such geometries our simple formulation has been *too* simple.

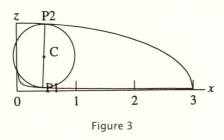

Figure 3

The correct geometry for small c requires *three* tangential supports, two of them on the hyperbola and one on the ellipse, no two of the radii being colinear. For such models we must be able to pick a trial center (x_c, z_c), find the perpendiculars that can be dropped to each boundary curve, and evaluate the distances from the center to each of those possible support points. Then we must juggle the center until all three candidate radii are equal — a two-dimensional search. Note also that the two support points we seek on the hyperbola are separated by a third one down in the sharp "corner" of the hyperbola where its tangent is also perpendicular to the radial direction.

Finally the question arises about the critical value of c that divides our two geometries. Fortunately we can avoid that one if we have the perpendicular radius finder available. We need only start with the two-point algorithm and then, from the center of that circle, find any other possible support points with proper tangents and check that they lie out beyond the radius of the two-point circle.

Dropping a perpendicular
to the hyperbola

Once we turn to the strategy of picking a trial center, C, for our circle, we must be able to find two points, P_j, where each line P_j–

C is perpendicular to the tangent of the hyperbola at P_j. We are, however, interested only in points on the first-quadrant branch of the hyperbola — fourth-quadrant points are to be ignored. Also, when there are three points in the first quadrant, the *middle* point is usually not wanted. Mathematically speaking, we have a simple problem as the equations

$$x_j z_j^2 = c \quad \text{and} \quad 2x_j(x_c - x_j) = z_j(z_c - z_j) \qquad \text{(14) (15)}$$

produce the equation

$$2\frac{c}{z_j^2}(x_c - \frac{c}{z_j^2}) = z_j(z_c - z_j)$$

which is a sextic. If you specify c and (x_c, z_c), standard polynomial solvers will give you all six roots *but you must then select the ones you want* — not always an easy process to program. Fortunately, there is a less error-prone approach.

If we introduce a working parameter, s, and set it equal to both halves of equation (15) we get two quadratic equations

$$2x_j(x_c - x_j) = s \qquad z_j(z_c - z_j) = s$$

hence

$$\left\{\begin{matrix} X_j \\ x_j \end{matrix}\right\} = \frac{x_c}{2} \pm \sqrt{\left(\frac{x_c}{2}\right)^2 - \frac{s}{2}} \quad \text{and} \quad \left\{\begin{matrix} Z_j \\ z_j \end{matrix}\right\} = \frac{z_c}{2} \pm \sqrt{\left(\frac{z_c}{2}\right)^2 - s}$$
$$\text{(16) (17)}$$

so that by choosing an s we generate a point (x_j, z_j) that may or may not be on the hyperbola, that is, may or may not satisfy $x_j \cdot z_j^2 = c$ — and there are four combinations of signs. Terrible! Not at all; helpful, actually.

Looking at our standard three-point configuration, figure 4, we see P_1 has a small x_1 and a big z_1; z_1 is almost z_c. And P_3 is the opposite — big x_3 with small z_3. Thus, denoting the variable from (16) by X_j when the sign is $+$ and by x_j when it is $-$ (and similarly with the z's) the equation to be satisfied at P_1 is

$$x_1 Z_1^2 = c \qquad (18)$$

while P_3 satisfies

$$X_3 z_3^2 = c \qquad (19)$$

(also P_4 is given by $x_4 z_4^2$) and we need to find the s that solves either (18) or (19). We note that s will *always be small* since either x_j or $(x_c - x_j)$ will be small at the P's. And since s is small, both X and Z

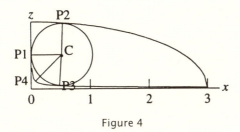

Figure 4

will be insensitive to small changes in it. Further

$$x_j X_j = s_j/2 \quad \text{and} \quad z_j Z_j = s_j$$

so we can eliminate the noisy variables from (18) or (19). Writing

$$c = x_1 Z_1^2 = \frac{x_1 X_1}{X_1} Z_1^2 = \frac{s_1 Z_1^2}{2 X_1}$$

then

$$s_1 \leftarrow \frac{2c X_1}{Z_1^2}$$

should be a stable iteration for s_1 and thus x_1 and Z_1. Similarly, the iteration for P_3 is

$$s_3 \leftarrow Z_3 \sqrt{\frac{c}{X_3}}.$$

We want to emphasize that by shifting our attention repeatedly between the algebra and its geometric implications we have been able to produce algorithms that are *specific for each point*. Thus there is no danger that our iterations will suddenly decide to converge to a different root — one of Newton's favorite pastimes! Further, we do not iterate with the small noisy variables, x_j and z_j, and altho Newton converges somewhat more quickly, our iterations are quite respectable.

For the parameters $c = 0.001$, $x_c = 0.45$, $z_c = 0.52$ we get the values

s_1	s_3
0.0	0.0
3.33E−3	2.45E−2
3.3847E−3	2.279E−2
3.38565E−3	2.2932E−2
3.385669E−3	2.2922E−2
3.385670E−3	2.292164E−2

which yield the coordinates

$$x_1 = 0.003794 \qquad X_3 = 0.422899$$
$$Z_1 = 0.513405 \qquad z_3 = 0.048627$$

hence the radii

$$R_1 = 0.446255 \qquad R_3 = 0.472151$$

which, because we picked the location of C arbitrarily, are not equal.

The original problem
when c is small

When c is small enough for the hyperbola to produce two tangent support points for a circle, we must balance those two radii with each other and also with the perpendicular distance to the ellipse. Since the two arms of the hyperbola are nearly orthogonal, adjusting those radii to be equal can be done easily by changing either x_c or y_c. After then computing the distance to the ellipse, triple agreement can be achieved quickly by moving the center at 45° — rebalancing the radii R_1 and R_3 again should that prove necessary.

To shove a small circle of given radius up into either corner between the ellipse and the hyperbola only requires balancing two radii (but be sure of whether you are computing R_1 or R_3). If you like to be fancy, two-dimensional false position* works well, but simpler methods for successive adjustments of the center will suffice and are easily automated.

*See F. S. Acton, *Numerical Methods that Work,* pp. 374–379.

A transcendental "hyperbola"

Now suppose that the lower curve in our previous problem is the declining exponential

$$z_1 = e^{-cx_1} \tag{20}$$

(instead of the rational function $xz^2 = c$); how would our approach to fitting the maximal circle change?

The basic (sextic) polynomial is now replaced by a transcendental equation — leaving us with fewer manipulative options. But the essential geometry is unchanged: two tangency contacts support the circle from below when the curve is a dogleg (big c) and only one when it declines gracefully (small c). Tangency above with the ellipse

$$ax_2^2 + z_2^2 = 1 \tag{2}$$

remains a single point.

When the exponential declines smoothly enough for the maximal circle to have only two contact points, they still must lie at the opposite ends of a diameter and the previous algorithm still succeeds: Pick a point on the lower curve; find the perpendicular line there, get its intersection with the ellipse, then find the slope of the tangent up there. If that is not perpendicular to the line, move the initial point. (Note, however, that to take our initial point on the ellipse rather than the exponential would require us to solve a transcendental equation to get the point on the lower curve. Doable — but why bother?)

When the exponential is steep enough so that it will support the circle at two points, we again must pick a tentative center for the circle, (x_c, z_c), and find the pertinent perpendiculars, avoiding the middle one to the "corner." The equations are

$$z_j = e^{-cx_j} \qquad \text{and} \qquad x_c - x_j = cz_j(z_c - z_j).$$

We introduce fewer transcendentals by eliminating x_j to get

$$x_c + \ln z_j/c = cz_j(z_c - z_j). \tag{21}$$

For a typical example consider $c = 20$, $x_c = 0.45$, $z_c = 0.52$ whence

$$0.0025(9 + \ln z) = z(0.52 - z)$$

whose two sides are easy to sketch. On the right is a parabola, cutting the axis at 0 and 0.52 with its maximum of 0.676 at 0.26; on the left, a dogleg that crosses the axis nearly vertically at a very small z (1.23E−4) then turning nearly horizontal to pass thru (0.52, 0.021). An enlarged plot of the part below 0.03 shows the two smaller roots at 1.27E−4 and 0.027 while the largest root exists in splendid isolation out near 0.5 at 0.477.

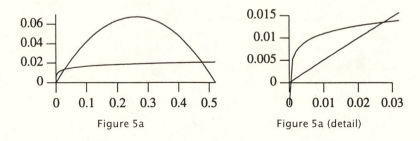

Figure 5a   Figure 5a (detail)

Geometry suggests obvious iterations:

Small root: vertically to the parabola; horizontally to the logarithmic curve.

Middle root: vertically to the logarithmic curve; horizontally to the parabola's left (smaller z) branch.

Big root: vertically to the logarithmic curve; horizontally to the parabola's right (larger z) branch.

Each of these algorithms converges only to its intended root. If started wildly off, they can fail — but they fail spectacularly, so there is no danger of getting an incorrect root that will then be incorporated silently into subsequent calculations. (With poor starting values Newton will usually converge, but to a different root.) As with Newton, we still have the problem of finding suitable starting values, but the window of suitability is about twice as wide for these iterations as it is for Newton, which must be on the correct side of the place where the two curves are parallel — and must even be well away from that spot lest his first jump be out to East Limbo!

For this problem, good starting values for our iterations are obvious from the graph: seek the large root from $z = 0.52$ and the small root from the place the dogleg crosses the z-axis, i.e., $z = e^{-9.0}$. If the middle root is needed, starting our iteration slightly to the right of the small root is clearly safe.

But other configurations can occur that an automatic program must handle properly. A center still at $(0.45, 0.52)$ but with $c = 10$ produces only *one* perpendicular. The sketch of (21) now looks like figure 5b, for which our iteration for the big root will succeed nicely. But we

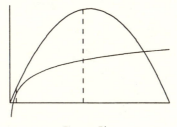

Figure 5b

certainly do not want the program to go looking for other roots! We need a way for the program to decide how many roots exist (and of what types) before seeking them.

The logarithmic dogleg will always enter the first quadrant from the fourth, crossing the z-axis near the origin, and it must exit the stage still rising to the right. It must therefore cross the parabola at least once. If more than one root exists, there must be three (barring the exceptional configurations where the dogleg touches the parabola tangentially to eight significant figures — a phenomenon that is extremely unlikely with a logarithm on the scene).

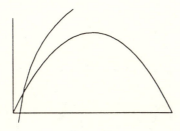

Figure 5c

To distinguish the four possible geometries of our dogleg-parabola plots, we can examine the places where the two curves have the *same slopes* at a common z. There may be none (figure 5c) or two (figures

5a, 5b, 5d). When there are none, the dogleg crosses the parabola only once and at a small z. When there are two critical values of z where the curves are "parallel," we must test whether the same curve lies on top at both. If the dogleg lies on top at both, there is only one root and it is at small z (see figure 5d). If the parabola lies on top at

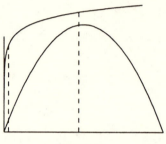

Figure 5d

both z_{crit}, there is only one root but at large z (see figure 5b). And when the dogleg is on top at the smaller z_{crit} but the parabola dominates at the other, there are three roots and they are well separated by the two z_{crit} values (figure 5a).

So...how to find the z_{crit}, if any? Easily: they satisfy the equation got by differentiating *each side* of equation (21)

$$\frac{1}{c^2 z} = z_c - 2z$$

which is

$$\frac{1}{c^2} = z(z_c - 2z).$$

Figure 6

Figure 6 shows the two positions for $1/c^2$ that generate either none or two z_{crit} — depending on whether $1/c^2 > z_c^2/8$ or not.

At this point we finally have enough information to write a computer subprogram that will not go astray. For all positive triples of (x_c, z_c, c) it will discover how many roots equation (21) has, will find them unambiguously then return gracefully.

Query: What does the (unlikely) equality $1/c^2 = z_c^2/8$ imply for the configuration of our dogleg-parabola diagram?

And now that we finally have faced, and answered, the question about which geometry we may have, we also find that we have enough information to supply good first values for Newton's method — if that previously rejected algorithm is still preferred. But, of course, good starting values will help our iterative schemes too. Your choice!

Exercise

1. Explore the three-dimensional problem of the maximal sphere that is bounded above by an ellipsoid $ax^2 + by^2 + z^2 = 1$ and below by the (sort of) hyperbolic surface $z = \frac{c}{x} * e^{-dy}$.

2. Explore the COMPLEX*16 equation

$$e^z = a^2 z^2$$

with detail sufficient to permit the design of a function $E(a, n)$ that will deliver the nth root for the REAL*8 parameter a.

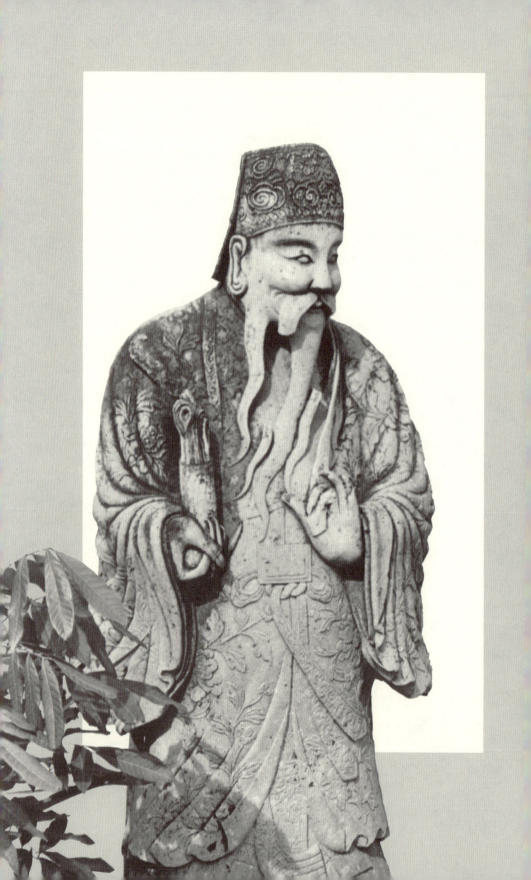

ANSWERS TO MOST OF
THE EXERCISES

Chapter 0
Tools of the Trade

0.0. — An Educational Dalliance
(The answers numbered *zero* refer to the puzzle problems at the chapter fronts.)

My 5-figure calculator computes $\sin 11$ as -1.0570 (using series terms thru $x^{37}/37!$) but my 10-figure device gets an error of only $-3.49\mathrm{E}{-7}$ (using 4 more terms). Your machine may give slightly different errors, depending on its internal arithmetic idiosyncrasies.

0.1. Combine to get $0.5\ln(1 + 1/x)$, then use series.

0.2. When x is large the subtraction is noisy. Do it analytically by multiplying the numerator and denominator by something, then simplify to get $-2\ln(\sqrt{1+x^2}+x)$ — that gives no trouble at all.

When x is small the fraction is (almost-1)/(almost-1). It can be rewritten as

$$\ln\left[1 - \frac{2x}{\sqrt{1+x^2}+x}\right]$$

and the series expansion used. But it is more efficient and elegant to divide by the radical to get

$$\ln\left[\frac{1 - x/\sqrt{1+x^2}}{1 + x/\sqrt{1+x^2}}\right] = -2\left(\frac{t}{1} + \frac{t^3}{3} + \frac{t^5}{5} + \cdots\right) \quad \text{with } t = x/\sqrt{1+x^2}$$

the second expression coming from two applications of the series. If t is really small, only a few terms will be needed.

0.3. Move the trouble to the origin in the first expression by letting $u = \pi/2 - x$. Then, with a series, we get

$$u(1/2! - u^2/4! + u^4/6! - \cdots).$$

The second expression is nearly 1/1. Series disclose it to be *greater* than unity so compute the *deviation*

$$\frac{\cosh x}{2 - \cos x} - 1 = \frac{(\cosh x - 1) - (1 - \cos x)}{2 - \cos x} = \frac{2x^4(1/4! + x^4/8! + \cdots)}{2 - \cos x}$$

which can be evaluated accurately.

0.4. The behaviors are both $2/x$.

0.6. Hint: The crucial identity is $\sinh\dfrac{x}{2} = \sqrt{\dfrac{\cosh x - 1}{2}}$.

0.7. Replace $1 - \cos x$ by $2\sin^2(x/2)$, then factor:

$$2\left[\sin^2\frac{x}{2} - \frac{1}{4}\tan^2 x\right] = 2\left[\sin\frac{x}{2} + \frac{1}{2}\tan x\right]\left[\sin\frac{x}{2} - \frac{1}{2}\frac{\sin x}{\cos x}\right]$$

which becomes

$$\frac{2}{\cos x}\left[\sin\frac{x}{2} + \frac{1}{2}\tan x\right]\left[\sin\frac{x}{2}\cos x - \frac{1}{2}\sin x\right];$$

hence, using $\sin x = 2\sin(x/2) \cdot \cos(x/2)$ and $\cos x = 2\cos^2(x/2) - 1$

$$\frac{2\sin(x/2)}{\cos x}\left[\sin\frac{x}{2} + \frac{1}{2}\tan x\right]\left[2\cos^2\frac{x}{2} - 1 - \cos\frac{x}{2}\right]$$

and the last term factors into $(2\cos(x/2) + 1)(\cos(x/2) - 1)$ — which does it. If, on the other hand, you expand and collect like powers, you (or more probably your computer) should get

$$-\frac{3}{8}x^4 - \frac{3}{16}x^6 - \frac{63}{640}x^8 - \frac{3931}{80640}x^{10} - \cdots$$

which, unfortunately, can only be used for small x — whereas the previous version holds for all values if only we evaluate the final factor appropriately.

0.9. From $b[1 - \sqrt{1 - g}]$ the two forms arise by multiplying above and below by the obvious factor — and by straightforward use of the series for $\sqrt{1 - g}$.

0.11. We need $\arctan(B) = \pi/2 - \arctan(\frac{1}{B})$ hence

$$\frac{\pi}{2} - \left(\frac{1}{B} - \frac{1}{3B^3} + \cdots\right) \qquad \text{where} \qquad B = 485.32.$$

With the other problem you have the choice of looking up a series for $\cot x$ (which begins $1/x$, so direct use is possible if you don't need more than about three terms) or of invoking sines and cosines. Then you get

$$\frac{x\cos x}{\sin x} = 1 - \epsilon$$

so

$$\left(\frac{\sin x}{x}\right) \Big/ \cos x = \frac{1}{1 - \epsilon} = 1 + \frac{\epsilon}{1 - \epsilon}$$

and then

$$\frac{\sin x}{x} - \cos x = \frac{\epsilon\cos x}{1 - \epsilon}.$$

Then series on the left give

$$\frac{2x^2}{3!} - \frac{4x^4}{5!} + \cdots$$

so that finally we have the iteration for x^2

$$x^2 \leftarrow \frac{\epsilon \cos x}{(1 - \epsilon)(2/3! - 4x^2/5! + \cdots)}$$

with x^2 of the order 3ϵ.

0.12. Substitution of a few terms of the series will usually give the behavior as a power of x. But if the expression is nearly a constant, then the next term is often important in finding iteration algorithms. Thus for

$$\frac{\sinh x}{\tan x} = \frac{x + x^3/3! + x^5/5! + \cdots}{x + x^3/3 + 2x^5/15 + \cdots} = \frac{1 + x^2/3! + x^4/5! \cdots}{1 + x^2/3 + 2x^4/15 + \cdots}$$

you will probably wish to write it as

$$1 - \frac{x^2/6 + x^4/8 + (\text{not nice})}{1 + x^2/3 + 2x^4/15 + \cdots}$$

which shows that $1 - x^2/6$ is the behavior near zero.

Chapter 1
Nonlinear Equations

1.0. — A Pillow Problem
(The answers numbered *zero* refer to the puzzle problems at the chapter fronts.)

As a sketch of $-\cos x$ versus $1/(1 + e^{-2x})$ shows, the first pair of positive roots bracket π and lie fairly close to it. Since at the roots the exponential curve is the more nearly horizontal, a successful iteration must move vertically to it, then get the next x by moving horizontally to the cosine — and should begin with a value less than π. Thus student (1) is correct but (2) will diverge. Newton, started at 3.0, will also work, altho not with quadratic efficiency as the next root is rather close.

Altho the precisions offered by both (1) and (3) are probably adequate here, a search for a farther root, say the one just short of 3π, gets a bit dicey (as does this first root if the exponential were, say, e^{-8x}). In its current form each term of our equation has magnitude close to unity, so we prefer to subtract 1 from each of the expressions. We have

$$1 + \cos x = \frac{e^{-bx}}{1 + e^{-bx}}$$

in which the danger has been moved from the equation to the subtraction ($\cos x$ is almost -1) but that can be squashed by replacing x by $3\pi - \delta$ to give $1 - \cos \delta$ on the left. We get the iteration

$$\delta^2 \leftarrow \frac{e^{-bx}}{(1 + e^{-bx})(1/2 - \delta^2/24 + \delta^4/720 + \cdots)}$$

that needs few terms, converges rapidly and, by our choice of sign for δ, even serves for *both* roots near 3π.

1.1a. For small b the small root of $1/(1+x^2) = \cos x - b$ is masked by an equation that equates nearly-one to nearly-one. Expanding both the cosine and the fraction will allow removal of 1 from both sides, but it is somehat more elegant to avoid the series for the fraction. Write

$$1 - \frac{1}{1+x^2} = 1 - \cos x + b$$

thus getting

$$\frac{x^2}{1+x^2} = \frac{x^2}{2} - \frac{x^4}{4!} + \cdots + b$$

hence

$$x^2 \left[\frac{1}{1+x^2} - \frac{1}{2} + \frac{x^2}{4!} - \frac{x^4}{6!} + \cdots \right] = b$$

and the algorithm in x^2 is available immediately by dividing thru by the bracket. As a first approximation, $x = \sqrt{2b}$.

A sketch (yours, presumably) shows that the next root is near $\pi/2$ (with more of them strung out near the crossings of $\cos x$) which is best found by moving the origin there to produce the equation $\sin u = b + 1/[1 + (\pi/2 - u)^2]$. We suggest

$$u \leftarrow \arcsin \left[\frac{1}{1 + (\pi/2 - u)^2} + b \right]$$

altho Newton will also work. For $b = 0.01$ the root is $\pi/2 - 0.4915 = 1.0793$.

1.1b. Tangency questions require the solution of the slope equation

$$\sin t = \frac{2t}{(1+t^2)^2}$$

which can be rewritten as

$$\frac{1}{2} \frac{\sin t}{t} = \frac{1}{(1+t^2)^2}$$

after which, as our sketch clearly shows, there are two possible tangency configurations. For the root near 0.7 we go up to the pseudoconstant then across to the (super)witch several times to yield $t = 0.686928$ with the corresponding $b = 0.093790$.

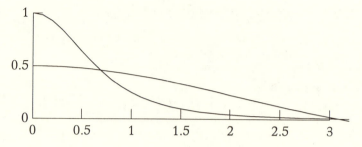

The tangency root out near π is easy after replacing t by $s = \pi - t$ to get

$$s \leftarrow \arcsin[2(\pi - s)/[1 + (\pi - s)^2]^2].$$

which yields $s = 0.05577$ and the $b = -1.0934$.

1.2. Hint: The value 0.09240643 should crop up somewhere.

1.3a. For $b = 1.57$ the root lies near $\pi/2$ where the curves are close together and nearly parallel. Shift the origin via $x = \pi/2 - u$ giving the equation $0.000796 = u - \sin u$ then use series to get rid of u. Factor out u^3. Iterate u^2 via

$$u^2 \leftarrow \frac{(0.000796)^{2/3}}{\left[\dfrac{1}{3!} - \dfrac{u^2}{5!} + \dfrac{u^4}{7!} - \cdots\right]^{2/3}}.$$

Then $u^2 = 2.839484220E{-}2$ and $x = 1.402288635$.

The larger root is near a horizontal part of the cosine. Iterate

$$x \leftarrow 2.0 - \cos x$$

from π or 3.

1.3b. For $b = 0.001$ the direct substitution of the cosine series gets rid of the big terms, allowing an iteration for x^2 — which is seen to be roughly equal to $\sqrt{0.024}$.

For $b = 0.24$ the parabola is *still slightly above* the cosine at $\pi/2$ and both slopes are unity there — a parallel geometry. So shift the origin by $x = \pi/2 + u$ to produce $-\sin u = 1.240 - (\pi/2 + u)^2$ which becomes $u^2 + (\pi u - 2\sin u) - B = 0$ hence $u^2 + 2Cu - B = 0$ with $B = 0.00629944986$ and $C = (\pi/2 - \sin u/u)$. As usual, we need the smaller root. Start near (but not at) zero for very rapid convergence. $u = 0.0109311962$.

1.3c. For $b = 0.01$ close parallel curves at $45°$ suggest subtracting out an x. Since the series for $\tan x$ is inconvenient if more than three terms are wanted, rephrase the equation in terms of the arctangent as $x = \text{atn}(x + b)$ then let $x + b = u$ to get $u - \text{atn}\, u = b$. Now use the systematic series to get an iteration for u^2.

For $b = 10$ we still find the arctangent preferable, but this time for reciprocating the big variable via $u = 1/v$ to get $1/v - \pi/2 + \text{atn}\, v = 10$. Neutralize the arctangent by dividing it by v to produce the pseudo-quadratic $1/v + Av = \pi/2 + 10 = C$ and solve for the smaller root. A convenient form of the iteration is

$$v \leftarrow \frac{(2/C)}{1 + \sqrt{1 - (2/C)^2 A}} \qquad \text{with} \qquad A = \text{atn}\, v/v$$

whence $v = 8.70781489006\text{E}{-3}$; $x = 1.483937275$.

The large root can also be found by the obvious iteration in the large variable, u, or another in x using the original equation. And Newton can be used on either equation.

The student who wants to gain a feeling for the differences between these several methods should execute them in Fortran (or C) — noting that Newton adds the error in the system arctangent function to the pot. [If you evaluate $(\text{atn}\, v)/v$ by its series, the recommended algorithm is algebraic — leaving you at the mercy only of the system square root function which, unlike the arctangent, is almost always correct.]

1.3d. The line $x/10 - 2$ will cross the asymptote of the arctangent at about 35.7, so this root is large and reciprocation is mandated. With $u = 1/x$ and $A = \text{atn}\, u/u$, the pseudoquadratic $(\pi/2 + 2)u - Au^2 = 1$ needs to be solved for its smaller root. Continue as in **1.3c.**

Sketching the root for $b = -0.948$ suggests a tangency problem. So find where the arctangent has a slope of 0.1 by solving $1/(1 + x^2) = 1/10$ to get $x_{tan} = 3$. Since $b_{tan} = -0.94914577$, our problem has one real root on each side of 3. Newton will work, but start him far enough away from 3 so that he will approach each root while going toward 3 (to insure against starting him on a too flat part of the curve). A better technique is to subtract the tangent equation from ours and then express the problem in terms of *differences* from the tangent solution — but that is a subject for chapter 2.

1.3e. (You really shouldn't need help on this one.)

1.3f. For $b = 25$ just reciprocate the variable, neutralize the arctangent and iterate. For $b = .01$ use the series, extract an x and divide by the rest to get an iteration in x^2.

1.3g. Replace both transcendentals by their series when $b = 0.001$, cancel what you can, factor out x^2 and get an iteration. For tangency, solve $e^{-x} = \cos x$ via the iteration $u \leftarrow \arcsin(e^u/e^{\pi/2})$ with $x = \pi/2 - u$. ($x = 1.2926957$ hence $b_{tan} = 0.2361083$.)

1.3h. Solve $2e^{-4x} = x$ via Newton. $r_{tan} = 0.6015738$.

1.4. The small root can be found by the iteration

$$x^2 \leftarrow b^{2/3}/[(1/(1+x^2)) - 1/3!) + x^2/5! - x^4/7! + \cdots]^{2/3}.$$

Newton finds the root in the second quadrant efficiently. Tangency is fixed by

$$\cos t = \frac{(1 - t^2)}{(1 + t^2)^2}$$

whose graph shows tangency possibilities both at zero and just beyond $\pi/2$.

1.5. One answer for small b is

$$x^2 \leftarrow \frac{\sqrt{b}}{\left[\left(\frac{1}{1+x^2} - \frac{1}{12}\right) + 2\left(\frac{1}{6!} - \frac{x^2}{8!} + \cdots\right)\right]^{1/2}}.$$

1.6. Finding where *tangency* can occur will clarify the number-of-roots question. Thus *sketch* $\sin t = 2te^{-t^2}$ probably after recasting it as

$$\frac{1}{2}\frac{\sin t}{t} = e^{-t^2}$$

which clearly shows that tangency can occur near 0.9 and again (tho not for the same b) near 3 (at 0.9147 and 3.14127).

1.7. To decide about roots of $\cos(x + a) = e^{-x^2} + b$ for $a = 0.2$ and various b, it helps to see where, if at all, tangency can occur. Tangency requires equality of slopes, hence

$$\sin(x + a) = 2xe^{-x^2} \qquad (\alpha)$$

in which b has conveniently disappeared. As figure 1.7a here shows, for small a there are two possible tangency locations somewhere near 1 — tho not for the same b — and out near π a third possible tangency location occurs. (What value of b will *that* require: small, large, positive, negative?)

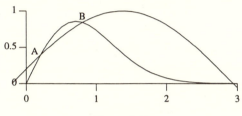

Figure 1.7a

The smallest tangency (point A) will have the exponential curve mostly trapped *below* the cosine lobe — hence for slightly larger b there will be two nearby roots to our equation, plus a third out near $\pi/2 - a$ where the exponential escapes. Tangency configuration B will have the exponential curve entirely *above* the cosine lobe, so a slightly smaller b will give two local roots but no third on the range of our problem.

Altho this answers the original question, it is interesting to note that if a is large enough, the tangency points A and B coalesce and then disappear. How shall we find that maximum a? Clearly this is yet another tangency problem — this time from the requirement that the slopes of the two curves in (α) be equal. We want to solve

$$\cos(x + a) = 2e^{-x^2} - 4x^2 e^{-x^2} \qquad (\beta)$$

together with (α). We can eliminate a by using Pythagoras to get

$$1 = 4e^{-2x^2}[x^2 + (1 - 2x^2)^2].$$

On letting $u = 2x^2$ we get

$$e^u = 4[u/2 + (1 - u)^2]. \qquad (\gamma)$$

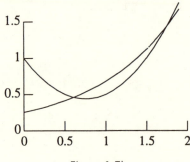

Figure 1.7b

As is obvious from figure 1.7b this sub-problem has two solutions, but it is the smaller, near 0.6, that we need. There the flatter curve is the quadratic, so we can iterate

$$u \leftarrow \ln 4 + \ln[u/2 + (1 - u)^2]$$

to get $u = 0.60595$ and $x = 0.5821$, hence the critical $a = 0.3991$ that brings the points A and B together. Thus, if $0 < a < 0.3991$ there will be two values of b that will make the exponential tangent to the cosine — as discussed above. If we need to find either of those critical b's, given a, we must solve (α) — probably via Newton. (Iteration would require using $y = 2xe^{-x^2}$ in the inconvenient direction!)

1.8. From figure 1.8 it is clear that the first root occurs between e and π and that two subsequent roots occur on each positive hump of the periodic curve until $\ln x$ exceeds e, that is, until x passes $e^e = 15.2 \approx 4.8\pi$. Thus we know that two roots bracket $9\pi/2$ while two

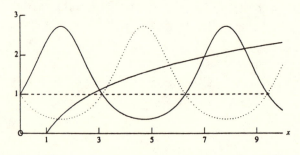

Figure 1.8

others are grouped less closely around $5\pi/2$ — near (say) 2.25π and 2.75π. Newton should succeed nicely if these approximations are used to start him.

But the comparative flatness of $\ln x$ here suggests that "standard iteration" should also work well — with fewer functional evaluations. The equations are:

	x_2
$x_2 \leftarrow 2\pi + \arcsin(\ln(\ln(x)))$	7.07000
$x_3 \leftarrow 3\pi - \arcsin(\ln(\ln(x)))$	7.01851
	7.01348
$x_4 \leftarrow 4\pi + \arcsin(\ln(\ln(x)))$	7.01298
$x_5 \leftarrow 5\pi - \arcsin(\ln(\ln(x)))$	7.01293

The numbers are for x_2.

1.9. Since $\ln x$ increases monotonically without limit, it is clear from figure 1.8 above (where $b = 1$) that increasing b will simply produce more humps that intersect the log curve — with the possibility that the last hump is tangent to it. Thus, there is *no maximum b* beyond which tangencies are impossible. But if b is reduced until the hump at $5\pi/2$ no longer touches the log curve, no tangent geometries can occur for smaller positive b. If b is negative, the periodic curve is essentially shifted back by a half-period (the dotted curve) and we see that the first tangent point can occur on the hump around $3\pi/2$ — an isolated root having occurred between 0.5 and e. Again, there is no maximum on $|b|$ beyond which another tangency cannot occur.

To find these special values of b that produce tangency, we must solve

$$e^{b \sin x} = \ln x \qquad \text{and} \qquad (b \cos x)e^{b \sin x} = 1/x$$

simultaneously. After eliminating b we need to solve

$$\tan x = (x \ln x)(\ln \ln x). \tag{δ}$$

The tangency points, x_k, that fall just shy of $k\pi/2$ when k is odd and greater than 1, can be found by shifting equation (δ) to the local variable $u_k = k\pi/2 - x$. [Only the argument of $\tan x$ need be transformed to the small variable u since $\ln(k\pi/2 - u)$ is still essentially $\ln x$. Altho it then can be expressed as $\ln(k\pi/2) + \ln(1 - 2u/(k\pi))$ no algorithmic advantage follows.] We get the iteration

$$u_k \leftarrow \arctan\left[\frac{1}{x_k \cdot \ln x_k \cdot \ln \ln x}\right]$$

that, for the root near $5\pi/2$, gives the numbers for u_5

$$0.0$$
$$8.52149\mathrm{E} - 2$$
$$8.72381\mathrm{E} - 2$$
$$8.72871\mathrm{E} - 2$$
$$8.72883\mathrm{E} - 2$$
$$8.72884\mathrm{E} - 2$$

for which $b = 0.720507$.

The further u_k converge even more swiftly. Only for u_3 (the first possible tangent when b is negative) is this iteration inefficient — but it still works!

1.10. Hint: The equation can be rewritten as

$$2e^{-\left(\frac{a+b}{2}\right)x}\cosh\left[\left(\frac{a-b}{2}\right)x\right] = 1.$$

1.11. As in the text example, there are still two isolated roots: near the origin and out toward 3.0. The new question is whether a pair of close roots exists near $\pi/2$. That is settled by evaluating the ellipse there to find that it lies at -0.92302. Since the cosine curve reaches $b - 1$, a close root-pair exists if $0 < b < 0.07698$. Finding those roots accurately is a delicate task that we recommend you postpone until you have read at least some of chapter 2.

The small root, obviously sensitive to changes in small b, can be found by a method like the text example. Expose unity by factoring $(1 - y^4)$, then annihilate the dangerous 1 with the cosine series:

$$\frac{x^2/9}{(1 + y^2)(1 + y)} + b = \frac{(2x)^2}{2!} - \frac{(2x)^4}{4!} + \cdots$$

hence

$$(2x)^2 \leftarrow b \Bigg/ \left[\frac{1}{2} - \frac{1/36}{(1 + y^2)(1 + y)} - \frac{(2x)^2}{4!} + \cdots\right].$$

The larger root is not sensitive to changes in small b. It lies well in from 3, where the ellipse is still much flatter than the cosine. So iterate, getting y from the ellipse and x from $\pi - 0.5 \arccos y$. At $b = 0.1$

(not very small) you get the numbers:

$$x$$

2.000
2.790
2.621
2.676
2.661
2.665
2.664

1.12. Surely for *small* b you got

$$\frac{x^2}{4(1+y)} + b = 1 - \cos x = \frac{x^2}{2!} - \frac{x^4}{4!} + \cdots$$

hence the iteration

$$x^2 \leftarrow b \bigg/ \left(\frac{1}{2} - \frac{1}{4(1+y)} - \frac{x^2}{4!} + \frac{x^4}{6!} - \cdots \right)$$

for the small root. And for the root out near 2, a simple stepping of horizontal to the ellipse then vertical to the cosine will work, but in keeping with our penchant for using small variables we recommend introducing u by letting $x = 2 - u$. The ellipse then becomes

$$-u + u^2/4 + y^2 = 0$$

so the iteration is

$$y \leftarrow b + \cos(2 - u)$$
$$u \leftarrow y^2 + u^2/4,$$

beginning with $u = 0$.

Note, however, that when b ceases to remain small, drastic geometric changes occur. For positive b the roots move toward each other, become a close pair (delicate to find), then disappear entirely. (Where?) For negative b the only positive root shrinks steadily toward zero, but our stepping algorithm rapidly becomes inefficient then inapplicable as the cosine curve becomes steeper than the ellipse at their intersection. Finally, as b nears -2, another nearly parallel geometry demands a variant of the small-root algorithm that poses no new difficulties. Until then, because the root is isolated, Newton is probably better for negative b.

1.13. For *b near unity* this problem is similar to exercise **1.12** when its parameter was small. So rewrite our parameter as

$$b = 1 + \epsilon \qquad \text{to get} \qquad y = \epsilon \cos x + \cos x$$

and proceed as before. The small-root geometry is almost the same (so is the algebra because $\cos x \approx 1$), but the root near 2 is different. Because $b \cos x$ crosses the x-axis at $\pi/2$ for all b, this larger root changes very little with b — actually *increasing* slightly toward 2 as b *decreases*. Altho the geometry ensures that this larger root always exists between $\pi/2$ and 2, it also guarantees that stepping will *not* be effective if b grows too large. The cosine curve, whose slope is $-b \sin x$, soon becomes steeper than the ellipse at their intersection — passing the inefficient ×-geometry as b increases. Since this root is firmly localized, Newton seems proper.

Can there be a tangency condition on $0 < x \leq \pi/2$ when b is somewhat greater than unity? Looks unlikely, but to make sure, you can solve for equality of slopes, that is,

$$\frac{x}{4y} = b \sin x \qquad \text{or} \qquad \frac{1}{4y} = b \left(\frac{\sin x}{x} \right).$$

The last form shows there to be no solution, as the right-hand expression remains greater than $2b/\pi$ while that on the left is between 0.25 and 0.404. Thus the small root is unique.

1.14. If we rescale the y-coordinate by a factor of 2, this ellipse becomes a circle — without changing the *argument* of the cosine. Thus, geometrically, we now have a unit circle with a nearly osculatory cosine — both curves having a unit radius of curvature at $x = 0$. This is a close encounter of the second kind; it needs special care lest information be lost. We have

$$x^2 + \left(\frac{b}{2} \right)^2 \cos^2 x = 1$$

which, on defining ϵ by

$$\left(\frac{b}{2} \right)^2 = 1 - \epsilon$$

becomes

$$x^2 - \epsilon \cos^2 x = 1 - \cos^2 x = \sin^2 x$$

hence
$$x^2 - \sin^2 x = \epsilon \cos^2 x$$

or
$$(x - \sin x)(x + \sin x) = \epsilon \cos^2 x.$$

The sine series allows the cancellation of x in the first factor, after which we can factor out an x^3 from it and another x from the second factor to get

$$x^4 \left(\frac{1}{3!} - \frac{x^2}{5!} + \cdots \right) \left(2 - \frac{x^2}{3!} + \cdots \right) = \epsilon \cos^2 x$$

and the iteration for x^2

$$x^2 \leftarrow \cos x \frac{\sqrt{\epsilon}}{\sqrt{(1/3! - x^2/5! + \cdots)(2 - x^2/3! + \cdots)}}$$

which shows x to be approximately $(3\epsilon)^{1/4}$. As always, it is better if ϵ does not have to be computed from b.

1.15. An attempt at plotting these equations suggests that they both seem to approach the $x = y$ line, but from opposite sides. The hyperbola certainly approaches from below and the other equation starts above, remaining above far longer than most will care to plot. But by $x = 1000$ it is very slightly below the 45° line — suggesting a root far out in x.

The small variables $x - y$ and $1/x$ seem appropriate. Letting

$$u = x + y$$

$$v = x - y$$

$$r = 1/x$$

the hyperbola becomes
$$u \cdot v = 1$$

and the reciprocal variable turns the other equation into

$$y = \frac{2}{\pi} x \left[\frac{\pi}{2} - \arctan r \right] + 0.636 = x - \frac{2}{\pi} \frac{\arctan r}{r} + 0.636$$

hence
$$v = \frac{2}{\pi} \frac{\arctan r}{r} - 0.636$$

then

$$v = \left(\frac{2}{\pi} - 0.636\right) - \frac{2}{\pi}\left(\frac{r^2}{3} - \frac{r^4}{5} + \cdots\right). \tag{1}$$

Equation (1) together with

$$u = 1/v \tag{2}$$

and

$$r = \frac{2}{u + v} \tag{3}$$

give an iterative algorithm that can be started with $r = 0$ to produce

r
0.0
1.239544256E − 3
1.238892159E − 3
1.238892845E − 3
1.238892844E − 3   → $x = 807.1723108$.

What does your pocket calculator get?

1.16. If x is near $\pi/2$ the integral (and g) will be small, so change the variables to deviations from $\pi/2$ to get

$$g = \int_{x}^{\pi/2} \frac{\cos t}{t^2}\, dt = \int_{0}^{\pi/2-x} \frac{\sin s}{(\pi/2 - s)^2}\, ds.$$

This integral can be evaluated by a recurrence, but first we would consider the problem of *large g*.

If the integral is to be large, x must be small enough so that the integrand is heading for infinity. Integrate by parts to get

$$g = \frac{\cos x}{x} - \int_{x}^{\pi/2} \frac{\sin t}{t}\, dt.$$

This new integrand has only an indeterminacy and the integral exists even at zero, so extend its lower limit and compensate by subtracting the integral over $(0,\, x)$ — which will be small — to get

$$\int_{x}^{\pi/2} \frac{\sin t}{t}\, dt = 1.37076216816 - \int_{0}^{x} \frac{\sin t}{t}\, dt.$$

Substitute the series for the sine and integrate term by term to get

$$g = \frac{\cos x}{x} - 1.37076216816 + \left(x - \frac{x^3}{3!3} + \frac{x^5}{5!5} - \cdots\right) \qquad (\alpha)$$

a series that is very efficient when $x \leq 1$ and is usable all the way to $\pi/2$, which is how we got that constant. (At 1 it delivers 12 correct digits using terms thru $x^{13}/13!13$ — requiring 54 arithmetic operations.) It is also clear that if g is (say) 2 or 4, most of that must come from the $\cos x/x$ term. Since x is small, $\cos x$ is nearly constant. Thus we try the iteration

$$x \leftarrow \frac{\cos x}{g + 1.37076216816 - \left(x - \frac{x^3}{3!3} + \frac{x^5}{5!5} - \cdots\right)}. \qquad (\beta)$$

Any small change in x will be a very small percentage change in this denominator, so convergence is rapid. This algorithm works well for g over the unusually wide range of $0.1 < g < \infty$.

For $g < 0.1$, x is greater than 1, but we can still evaluate the right side of (α) reasonably efficiently. The iteration (β) fails near $\pi/2$ because $\cos x$ is no longer a pseudoconstant. This suggests that Newton's method is a good choice — especially since the derivative, $-\cos x/x^2$, got from the original form of the equation, does not involve another integral and so is cheap.

Now we don't have to worry about that recurrence method! But, for the curious, it is

$$g = \int_0^u \frac{\sin s}{(\pi/2 - s)^2}\, ds = T_1 - T_3 + T_5 - \cdots$$

with

$$T_k = \frac{1}{k!} \int_0^u \frac{s^k}{(\pi/2 - s)^2}\, ds \qquad \text{and} \qquad u = \pi/2 - x.$$

Then

$$T_{k+1} - \frac{\pi}{k+1} T_k + \frac{(\pi/2)^2}{k(k+1)} T_{k-1} = \frac{u^k}{k(k+1)!}$$

which can be run upward in k from T_0 and T_1 that have closed forms. Indeed, for $u = 0.2030364$, $T_1 = 0.01003608$ and $T_3 = 0.00003576$ — so the evaluation of g is proceeding very rapidly, with T_1 being most of it. Again, Newton is recommended to obtain the small g that you need. (This current u gives $g = 0.01000037$.)

1.17. Given a tentative center (A, B), each of our three curves has a point at which a circle centered at (A, B) will be tangent to it. Usually there will be three different concentric circles, their radii being of different lengths. Since we seek to have these circles coalesce — their radii becoming equal — it seems reasonable to choose the next common center to be equidistant from the three current tangent points. These points form a triangle, hence the point equidistant from them is the intersection of the perpendicular bisectors of the three sides. This algebra is straightforward, as is the by-now-familiar process of finding the tangent points. We get $A = 1.2639700$, $B = 0.5231473$.

1.18. The slope of our perturbed hyperbola is

$$\frac{dy}{dx} = -0.1/x^2 - 0.02(x - 3)e^{-(x-3)^2}.$$

A reasonable algorithm is to choose a tentative slope, say -0.01, for the line, then:

a) Find the *three* points on the upper branch of the hyperbola that have that slope. Number them left-to-right. (If there is only *one* such point you have chosen a very poor tentative slope. Start over!)

b) Take the slope of the line segment ① − ③ as your next trial slope. Go to (a).

We get $y = 0.07777 - 0.012293x$ for the line.

Chapter 2
Preserving Significant Digits

2.0. — The Railroad-rail Classic
The essential information is carried by the half-foot *increment* of rail that was added to the half-mile rail. In units of one mile it is $0.5/5280$. Denoting it by ϵ, our equations are

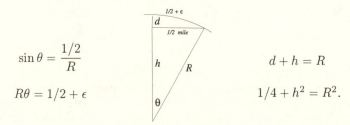

$$\sin\theta = \frac{1/2}{R}$$

$$R\theta = 1/2 + \epsilon$$

$$d + h = R$$

$$1/4 + h^2 = R^2.$$

Using the left pair, create the pseudoconstant $\sin\theta/\theta$ and eliminate R to produce

$$\frac{\sin\theta}{\theta} = \frac{1/2}{1/2+\epsilon} = 1 - \frac{\epsilon}{1/2+\epsilon}.$$

Replace $\sin\theta$ with its series and then cancel the 1's that dominate both sides to get an equation connecting only small quantities,

$$-\frac{\theta^2}{3!} + \frac{\theta^4}{5!} - \frac{\theta^6}{7!} \cdots = -\frac{\epsilon}{1/2+\epsilon}.$$

Then the iteration for the *small* variable θ^2 is

$$\theta^2 \leftarrow 3!\left(\frac{\epsilon}{1/2+\epsilon}\right)\Big/\left(1 - \frac{\theta^2}{4\cdot5} + \frac{\theta^4}{4\cdot5\cdot6\cdot7} - \cdots\right)$$

which converges to $1.13621300\mathrm{E}{-}3$ in three cycles when started from zero. Then R is 14.8361895 and $h = \sqrt{R^2 - 1/4}$ is 14.82776175.

Eliminating R from the right pair of equations gives the pseudo-quadratic for d

$$d^2 + 2hd = 1/4$$

which is expediently solved for the small root by iterating

$$d \leftarrow \frac{1/4 - d^2}{2h}$$

to give $d = 8.42773769\mathrm{E}{-}3$ miles, hence 44.49845 feet.

2.1. Subtract

$$x\cdot\sin x = b - \epsilon$$

from

$$t\cdot\sin t = b$$

to get

$$t\cdot\sin t - x\cdot\sin x = \epsilon.$$

Now let $x = t + \delta$ and use the slope equation

$$\sin t + t\cos t = 0$$

to replace $t\cdot\cos t$ — allowing division thruout by $\sin t$ to get

$$t(1 - \cos\delta) + \sin\delta - \delta\frac{\sin x}{\sin t} = \frac{\epsilon}{\sin t}.$$

Replacing the final x, expanding the sine and replacing the $\cos t$ that then appears, we get

$$t(1 - \cos \delta) + (\sin \delta - \delta \cos \delta) + \frac{\delta \sin \delta}{t} = \frac{\epsilon}{\sin t}.$$

All terms are now quadratic in δ, the final iteration being

$$\delta^2 \leftarrow \frac{\epsilon/\sin t}{t(\frac{1}{2!} - \frac{\delta^2}{4!} + \cdots) + \delta(\frac{2}{3!} - \frac{4\delta^2}{5!} + \frac{6\delta^4}{7!} - \cdots) + (\frac{1}{1!} - \frac{\delta^2}{3!} + \cdots)/t}$$

the odd term showing that the root pairs are not quite symmetrically arranged around the point of tangency.

2.2. A sketch shows that after isolated roots at the origin and near 2, root-pairs occur around the maxima of the sine curve, the first pair being near $5\pi/2$. Shift there with $x = 5\pi/2 + \delta$ to get

$$\cos \delta = \frac{2}{\pi} \arctan x.$$

Both sides being close to unity, subtract from 1 and invert the argument of the arctangent to get

$$1 - \cos \delta = 1 - \frac{2}{\pi}\left(\frac{\pi}{2} - \arctan \frac{1}{x}\right) = \frac{2}{\pi} \arctan \frac{1}{x}.$$

Thus

$$\delta^2 \leftarrow \frac{(2/\pi)\arctan(1/(5\pi/2 + \delta))}{\dfrac{1}{2!} - \dfrac{\delta^2}{4!} + \dfrac{\delta^4}{6!} - \cdots}$$

which gives two more correct digits at each iteration.

2.3. A graph shows that the roots bracket $2k\pi$ closely. To get a small argument for the cosine let $x = 2k\pi + \delta$. Further, since each side of the equation is nearly unity, subtract 1 to produce

$$1 - \cos \delta = 1 - \frac{x}{\sqrt{x^2 + 1}}.$$

Expand the cosine and factor out δ^2 to get

$$\delta^2 \left(\frac{1}{2!} - \frac{\delta^2}{4!} + \frac{\delta^4}{6!} - \cdots\right) = 1 - \frac{x}{\sqrt{x^2 + 1}}.$$

The fraction on the right side can be written $1/\sqrt{1+1/x^2}$ then expanded to get a cancellation of the 1, but it is more efficient merely to put both terms on the right over $\sqrt{x^2+1}$ and resolve the subtraction in the usual way to get

$$\frac{1}{(\sqrt{x^2+1}+x)\sqrt{x^2+1}}$$

then divide by the parenthesized series in δ^2:

$$\delta^2 \leftarrow \frac{1}{x^2+1+x\sqrt{x^2+1}} \cdot \frac{1}{\frac{1}{2!} - \frac{\delta^2}{4!} + \frac{\delta^4}{6!} - \cdots} \qquad \text{with} \qquad x = 2k\pi + \delta$$

and start with $\delta = 0$.

2.4. The tangency equation is

$$be^{-t} = \cos t$$

with the slope equation

$$be^{-t} = \sin t = \cos t$$

so that $t = 1/\sqrt{2}$. Subtracting the tangency equation from the original equation gives

$$b(e^{-x} - e^{-t}) = \cos x - \cos t + \epsilon e^{-x}$$

and letting $x = t + \delta$ gives

$$be^{-t}(e^{-\delta} - 1) - [\cos t(\cos \delta - 1) - \sin t \sin \delta] = \epsilon e^{-x}.$$

Dividing by be^{-t} and its equivalent forms gives

$$-(1 - e^{-\delta}) + (1 - \cos \delta) + \sin \delta = \frac{\epsilon}{b} \cdot e^{-\delta}.$$

The first and third terms will cancel a δ, while the second begins with $\delta^2/2$. Expanding these series and collecting we get several cancellations to produce

$$\delta^2 \left[\frac{1}{2!} - \frac{\delta}{3!} + \frac{\delta^4}{6!} - \frac{\delta^5}{7!} + \cdots \right] = \frac{\epsilon}{2b} \cdot e^{-\delta}.$$

2.5. We leave this one for you to show that it is the same iteration for the deviations as in exercise **2.4**, altho the locations of the tangency points are different.

2.6. Subtract the pair-equation from the tangency equation to get

$$\epsilon + a(t^2 - x^2) = \ln(t/x)$$

so

$$\epsilon = a(x^2 - t^2) - \ln(x/t) = a(x + t)\delta - \ln\left(1 + \frac{\delta}{t}\right).$$

Letting $\Delta = \delta/t$,

$$\epsilon = at^2(2 + \Delta)\Delta - \ln(1 + \Delta).$$

The slope-equality equation at tangency gives $2at = 1/t$ — allowing replacement of at^2 to get

$$\epsilon = (1 + \Delta/2)\Delta - \ln(1 + \Delta).$$

Expanding the logarithm and cancelling the Δ's gives

$$\epsilon = \not{\Delta} + \frac{\Delta^2}{2} - \left(\not{\Delta} - \frac{\Delta^2}{2} + \frac{\Delta^3}{3} - \cdots\right)$$

hence the iteration

$$\Delta^2 \leftarrow \frac{\epsilon}{1 - \dfrac{\Delta}{3} + \dfrac{\Delta^2}{4} - \cdots}.$$

2.7. Tangency requires solution of

$$(a - t)\ln t = r \qquad \text{and} \qquad (a - t)/t = \ln t. \qquad (1)\ (2)$$

Then

$$r = (a - t)^2/t = t \cdot (\ln t)^2.$$

The slope equation (2) happens to be independent of r (for $a = 6$, t is 2.904).

To solve

$$(a - x)\ln x = r - \epsilon \qquad (3)$$

subtract this from (1) to get

$$(a - t) \ln t - (a - x) \ln x = \epsilon.$$

Letting $x = t + \delta$ we have

$$(a - t) \ln t - [(a - t) - \delta] \ln(t + \delta) = \epsilon.$$

To get the argument of the second logarithm in the form of (1 + something small), add and subtract $\ln t$:

$$(a - t) \ln t - [(a - t) - \delta][(\ln(t + \delta) - \ln t) + \ln t] = \epsilon$$

whence

$$(a - t) \ln t - (a - t - \delta) \ln(1 + \delta/t) - (a - t) \ln t + \delta \cdot \ln t = \epsilon.$$

Cancelling, and replacing $(a - t)$ with $t \ln t$, we are left with

$$\delta \cdot \ln(1 + \delta/t) + \delta \cdot \ln t - t \cdot \ln t \cdot \ln(1 + \delta/t) = \epsilon \qquad (4)$$

in which the first term is quadratic in δ but the next two are linear and so must be somehow combined. Notation is simplified by letting $\Delta = \delta/t$, giving

$$t \cdot \Delta \cdot \ln(1 + \Delta) + t \cdot \ln t \cdot [\Delta - \ln(1 + \Delta)] = \epsilon$$

and it is clear that series for the logarithms yield quadratic behavior thruout. The final iteration is

$$\Delta^2 \leftarrow \frac{\epsilon/t}{1 - \frac{\Delta}{2} + \frac{\Delta^2}{3} - \cdots + (\frac{1}{2} - \frac{\Delta}{3} + \frac{\Delta^2}{4} - \cdots) \ln t}.$$

Curiously, this iteration for the deviation Δ does not explicitly contain either a or r.

2.8. Restating the exercise: If b is given, say 2, find the values of r, t that give a tangency (double-root) geometry for

$$t \cdot e^{-bt} \cdot \cos t = r. \qquad (1)$$

Then derive an iterative algorithm for finding the root-pair that solves

$$x \cdot e^{-bx} \cdot \cos x = r - \epsilon \qquad (2)$$

when a small ϵ is given.

This problem is a good example of one where the principles are simple but their execution is apt to be defeated by the messy algebra unless considerable care is exercised. Substitute $x = t + \delta$ into (2) and subtract it from (1) to give

$$te^{-bt}\cos t - (t+\delta)e^{-bt}\cdot e^{-b\delta}[\cos t\cdot\cos\delta - \sin t\cdot\sin\delta] = \epsilon$$

then divide to get

$$t - (t+\delta)e^{-b\delta}[\cos\delta - \tan t\cdot\sin\delta] = \epsilon e^{bt}/\cos t. \tag{3}$$

Since for small δ both $e^{-b\delta}$ and $\cos\delta$ begin like 1, t clearly will disappear, but getting rid of the terms proportional to δ is a bit more complicated. We have not yet used (and it is essential) the fact that t is the *tangential* parameter — that is, it satisfies not only (1) but also the slope equation

$$e^{-bt}\cos t - bte^{-bt}\cos t - te^{-bt}\sin t = 0$$

or

$$\frac{1}{t} - b - \tan t = 0.$$

Now eliminate $\tan t$ in the left side of (3) via

$$\tan t = 1/t - b \tag{4}$$

and encapsule the other transcendentals in pseudoconstants

$$t-(t+\delta)\left[1 - b\delta\left(\frac{1-e^{-b\delta}}{b\delta}\right)\right]\left[1 - \left(\frac{1-\cos\delta}{\delta^2}\right)\delta^2 - \left(\frac{1}{t}-b\right)\delta\left(\frac{\sin\delta}{\delta}\right)\right].$$

Writing this more compactly, we get

$$t - (t+\delta)[1 - \delta bE]\left[1 - \delta\left(\frac{1}{t}-b\right)S - \delta^2 C\right] = \epsilon e^{bt}/\cos t \tag{5}$$

where E, S and C are 1, 1 and 1/2 at $\delta = 0$ with nearby values easily evaluated from their series.

It is clear that on multiplying out the factors the t's will cancel and a careful examination will probably convince you that the first-order δ terms will also disappear. But since an iteration of the form $\delta^2 \leftarrow \epsilon/\delta^2$ will not converge quickly, if at all, the δ^2 terms must also be isolated

— a task that requires considerable care. We take this exercise to show, in some detail, one method of handling the grubby details.

Multiply the square brackets of (5) to get

$$t-(t+\delta)\left\{1-\delta\left[bE+\left(\frac{1}{t}-b\right)S\right]+\delta^2\left[bE\left(\frac{1}{t}-b\right)S-C\right]+\delta^3 bEC\right\}$$
(6)

then expand and put items of the same ostensible order in δ on the same line, simplifying to the right:

$$t-t$$
$$-\delta+\delta[btE+(1-bt)S] \quad = \quad \delta[bt(E-1)+(1-S)(bt-1)]$$
$$\delta^2\left[bE+\left(\frac{1}{t}-b\right)S\right]-\delta^2[bE(1-bt)S-tC] =$$
$$\delta^2\left[bE(1-S)+S\left(\frac{1}{t}-b+b^2tE\right)+tC\right]$$
$$-\delta^3\left[bE+\left(\frac{1}{t}-b\right)S-C\right]-\delta^3 btEC$$
$$-\delta^4 bEC.$$

The t's have disappeared but the "first-order" term is now seen to be composed of a *second*-order term ($E-1$ begins with $-b\delta/2!$) and a *third*-order term ($S-1$ begins with $-\delta^2/3!$) which need to be distributed down to their appropriate rows. The new second-order row reads

$$\delta^2\left\{\left[bE(1-S)+S\left(\frac{1}{t}-b+b^2tE\right)+tC\right]-b^2tG\right\}$$

where

$$G=\left(\frac{1-E}{b\delta}\right)$$

and we see that it actually contains a fourth-order term from $(1-S)$ along with the legitimate second-order items. We have momentary qualms on noting that b^2tES-b^2tG threatens a crucial cancellation, but the fact that G begins with $1/2$ while E and S both begin with 1 shows the threat to be false. And the other terms are solidly present at $\delta=0$.

When programming this iteration, it is a good idea to write small functions now — one for each of the lines of this current schema. Further algebraic manipulation only invites errors. Of course you need also to provide functions for S, E and G — with suitable series evaluations. The final iteration has the form

$$\delta^2 \leftarrow \frac{\epsilon e^{bt}/\cos t}{\text{Coeff. of }\delta^2+\delta\cdot\text{Coeff. of }\delta^3+\delta^2\cdot\text{Coeff. of }\delta^4}$$

where these Coeff's are the (mild) functions of δ mentioned above.

2.9. Subtract $\ln x = (r - \epsilon)(x + 1/x^2)$ from the tangency equation $\ln t = r(t + 1/t^2)$ to get

$$- \ln(1 + \frac{\delta}{t}) = r\left[t - x + \frac{1}{t^2} - \frac{1}{x^2}\right] + \epsilon(x + 1/x^2)$$

then replace r from the slope equation

$$r = \frac{1}{t - 2/t^2} = \frac{t^2}{t^3 - 2}$$

and let $\Delta = \delta/t$ to get

$$- \ln(1 + \Delta) = \frac{t^2}{t^3 - 2}\left[-t\Delta + \frac{(x + t)t\Delta}{t^2 x^2}\right] + \epsilon(x + 1/x^2).$$

Since the logarithm will give a $-\Delta$ we need to get one from the right side. Factor out $t\Delta$ then rephrase $t^3/(t^3 - 2)$ as $1 + 2/(t^3 - 2)$:

$$- \ln(1 + \Delta) = \Delta\left[1 + \frac{2}{t^3 - 2}\right]\left[-1 + \frac{x + t}{t^2 x^2}\right] + \epsilon(x + 1/x^2)$$

$$= -\Delta + \Delta\left[\frac{x + t}{t^2 x^2} + \frac{2}{t^3 - 2}\left(-1 + \frac{x + t}{t^2 x^2}\right)\right] + \epsilon(x + 1/x^2).$$

Now we need *another* Δ factor from within the brackets to expose the quadratic behavior that must lurk quietly somewhere. Remove the common denominator and replace numerator $(x + t)$'s by $t(2 + \Delta)$ to get

$$\frac{1}{t^2 x^2(t^3 - 2)}[t(2 + \Delta)(t^3 - 2) + 2[-t^2 x^2 + t(2 + \Delta)]]$$

then, factoring out a t and expanding

$$\frac{t}{t^2 x^2(t^3 - 2)}[-\cancel{4} - 2\cancel{\Delta} + 2t^3 + t^3\Delta - 2tx^2 + \cancel{4} + 2\cancel{\Delta}].$$

Replacing that last x^2, the bracket simplifies to

$$[2t^3 + t^3\Delta - 2t^3(1 + \Delta)^2]$$

whence factoring out the t^3 and reintroducing r collapses almost everything to

$$-\frac{r}{x^2}[3 + 2\Delta]$$

hence the iteration given with the exercise.

2.10. The Ball-in-the-Vase Problem

Any ball with radius less than the smaller of the two principal radii of curvature of the vase at its bottom will sit there, comfortably supported at that single point. For our vase, the crucial r/c is the one in the y direction that, at the origin, is simply the reciprocal of $\partial^2 z/\partial x^2$, hence 0.41666. ... But since validating other support points requires evaluation of curvatures at general points and since those formulæ are difficult to find, we give them here. For $z = f(x, y)$ let

$$p = \frac{\partial z}{\partial x} \qquad\qquad q = \frac{\partial z}{\partial y}$$

$$r = \frac{\partial^2 z}{\partial x^2} \qquad s = \frac{\partial^2 z}{\partial x \partial y} \qquad t = \frac{\partial^2 z}{\partial y^2}$$

then evaluate

$$K = \frac{rt - s^2}{(1 + p^2 + q^2)^2} \qquad \text{and} \qquad 2H = \frac{r(1 + q^2) - 2spq + t(1 + p^2)}{(1 + p^2 + q^2)^{3/2}}.$$

The principal curvatures (which are the *reciprocals* of the largest and smallest radii of curvature) are the solutions, Θ, of the quadratic equation

$$\Theta^2 - 2H\Theta + K = 0.$$

(These equations are taken from pages 206 and 211 of *Applications of the Absolute Differential Calculus* by A. J. McConnell (Blackie, 1946) — a very readable introduction to tensors and their practical applications.)*

First, some general observations:

> The problem is symmetric in y, that is, it is a function of y^2 rather than of y, so the center of the sphere will always lie in the x-z plane.

---

*For the reader who would prefer a more geometric exposition, the delightful *Space Through the Ages* by Cornelius Lanczos (Academic Press, 1970) provides the same information in chapters III and X.

As the ball increases in size it will, for a while, still have a smaller radius than the r/c of the vase at its extreme excursion from the y axis — hence its support will be two-point at the place where $\partial z/\partial x = 0$. This location will obviously (see the figures) have a *small negative* x-coordinate which will also be that of the ball's center.

Once the ball's r/c exceeds that of the vase at its extreme excursion, the support must be four-point, one on each side of that location — but it is not clear that such support won't occur *sooner* because of the growing nonellipticity of the level lines with their increasingly "pinched" shape in that region.

Equations:

In addition to the vase equation

$$(4 + x)(x^2 + 0.6)(x^2 + 4y^2) = 8z \tag{1}$$

and that of the sphere

$$(x - a)^2 + y^2 + (c - z)^2 = R^2 \tag{2}$$

which has its center at $(a, 0, c)$ and radius R, the conditions of tangency at a point (x, y, z) require the normal vectors there to be colinear:

$$\frac{2x(4 + x)(x^2 + .6) + (x^2 + 4y^2)[(x^2 + .6) + 2x(4 + x)]}{2(x - a)} =$$

$$\frac{8\cancel{y}\,(4 + x)(x^2 + .6)}{2\cancel{y}} = \frac{-8}{-2(c - z)}$$

which can be written

$$(c - z) = \frac{1}{(4 + x)(x^2 + .6)} \tag{3}$$

and

$$(x - a) = \frac{x}{4} + \frac{(x^2 + 4y^2)}{4}\left[\frac{1/2}{4 + x} + \frac{x}{x^2 + .6}\right]. \tag{4}$$

These four equations hold at *one* support point pair, $(x, y^2, z)_{left}$ and a second set at the other, $(x, y^2, z)_{right}$ — a total of eight equations for the eight variables. (They share common values of a and c — and R is given.) So all you have to do is solve them!

If you've been peeking for hints you now have quite a few.

No reasonable person is going to try solving eight nonlinear simultaneous equations if he can possibly help it. The simplest way to reduce the magnitude of this system is to choose a trial value for one of the five variables in our set of four equations, then solve for the other four variables. Clearly x is the variable to neutralize — the other four enter in far fewer and much nicer ways. After a number that can be substituted for x, $(c-z)$, becomes a number that can be inserted in (2). This new version of (2) can be used to eliminate y^2 from (4) — which is now seen to have become a quadratic equation for $(x-a)$! Solve, thereby getting y^2 from the original (2) then z from (1) and finally c from (3). But note that the coefficient of $(x-a)^2$ is small and changes sign in regions of interest, so an unusual form of the quadratic formula is needed. [The quadratic $ax^2 + 2bx + c = 0$ with small a can be solved for its small root via $x = -c/(b + \text{sgn}(b)\sqrt{b^2 - ac})$.] Now all you have to do is look for an x_{left} and an x_{right} that yield the same (a,c) pair — and that is a one-dimensional search. Well, *almost* all. There are still little nagging questions about whether crucial curvatures are compatible. But we leave those investigations to you. If you want to explore an interesting region, we suggest trying R's in the range 0.79 to 0.81 — carefully.

Isn't it time to work on the problem again?

Chapter 3
Quadratures

3.0. — No Quadratures Needed

A) With $a \leq 1$ and $y \leq 0.32$, the second term of the denominator is always less than 0.0105, so expansion of the integrand yields a series that converges rapidly. Expand and integrate term-by-term to get

$$A(a^2) = \int_0^{0.32} [1 - a^2 y^4 + a^4 y^8 - \cdots]\, dy$$

$$= 0.0033554432 \left[\frac{1}{5} - a^2 \frac{(.01048576)}{9} + a^4 \frac{(.01048576)^2}{13} - \cdots \right].$$

Note that we gain at least two additional digits per term.

Closed form? Yes, there is one:

$$\frac{b}{a^2} - \frac{1}{a^{5/2}} \left\{ \frac{1}{4\sqrt{2}} \ln\left[\frac{1 + b\sqrt{2a} + ab^2}{1 - b\sqrt{2a} + ab^2} \right] + \frac{1}{2\sqrt{2}} \arctan \frac{b\sqrt{2a}}{1 - ab^2} \right\}$$

but for $a = 1$ this manages to compute 0.000667207 as the difference of 0.32 and 0.319332793 — not to mention evaluating a log and an arctangent. Poor strategy!

B) When the integrand is this simple it is usually worth exploring for a closed form (sometimes they are cooperative). Here we need only write

$$B(b) = \int_0^1 \left[1 - \frac{e^{-bx}}{1 + e^{-bx}} \right] dx$$

to get

$$B(b) = 1 + \frac{1}{b} \left[\ln(1 + e^{-bx}) \right]_0^1 = 1 + \frac{1}{b} \left[\ln(1 + e^{-bx}) - \ln 2 \right]$$

$$= 1 + \frac{1}{b} \ln \left(\frac{1 + e^{-bx}}{2} \right)$$

which should do quite nicely for all b except 0 and its immediate environs — a region that can be covered by $1/2 + b/8$ with errors less than $b^3/192$.

C) When c is small, expand the fraction $1/(1 + cx)$ and integrate term-by-term to get

$$C(c) = \int_0^1 \frac{\ln x}{1 + cx} dx = -\left[1 - \frac{c}{2^2} + \frac{c^2}{3^2} - \frac{c^3}{4^2} \cdots \right] \quad 0 \le c \le 0.35 \quad (1)$$

which is marginally efficient at $c = 0.5$ (32 terms gives 12 decimals) but reasonable below 0.35 where less than 22 terms suffice.

For $0.35 \le c \le 1$ we can use the fact (AMS-55, p. 69) that $C(1) = -\pi^2/12$, but we must first get the parameter out from the integrand into the limit. Integrate $c \cdot C(c)$ by parts, then let $cx = y$ to get

$$c \cdot C(c) = -\int_0^c \frac{\ln(1 + y)}{y} dy = -\left[\frac{\pi^2}{12} - \int_c^1 \frac{\ln(1 + y)}{y} dy \right].$$

In the new integral let $y = 1 - z$ and separate the $\ln(2 - z)$ term into $\ln 2 + \ln(1 - z/2)$, which gives

$$c \cdot C(c) = -\frac{\pi^2}{12} - \ln 2 \cdot \ln c + \int_0^{1-c} \frac{\ln(1 - z/2)}{1 - z} dz.$$

This last integral can be evaluated by expanding either the logarithm or the denominator with equal effectiveness. We choose the numerator as being simpler. Letting

$$H_n = \int_0^{1-c} \frac{z^n}{1-z} dz \quad \text{hence} \quad H_n = H_{n-1} - \frac{(1-c)^n}{n} \quad \text{with} \quad H_0 = -\ln c$$

we finally have

$$c \cdot C(c) = -\pi^2/12 - \ln 2 \cdot \ln c - \sum_1 \frac{H_n}{2^n n} \quad 0.35 \le c \le 1 \quad (2)$$

which works efficiently over a somewhat wider range of c than (1) — delivering twelve decimals with twenty-one terms for $c = 0.35$ and requiring fewer terms as c increases.

Having covered the $0-1$ range for c, we can invoke the relation

$$c \cdot C(c) + \frac{1}{c} \cdot C(1/c) = -\left[\frac{\pi^2}{6} + \frac{(\ln c)^2}{2}\right]$$

(derivation on request) that allows us to evaluate our integral with $1 \le c < \infty$ via the same integral but with the parameter reciprocated. Thus the two series suffice, the break-even point between (1) and (2) being near 0.35 where each requires about twenty-two terms to deliver twelve decimals. (There are at least eight other series that can be found for this problem, some almost as efficient as these. So you may well come up with a different but satisfactory solution. Also, the answer to exercise 4.1 contains another quite different approach — a recurrence for this integral.)

3.1. The only trouble is at $x = 0$. Since $\sin x$ begins as x there, the net integrand is $\sqrt{x}$ (upstairs) which has an infinite slope there. It is wise to remove that nonpolynomic geometry by the $x = u^2$ substitution to produce

$$2 \int_{u=0}^{\sqrt{\pi}} \left[\frac{\sin x}{x}\right]_{x=u^2} u^2 \cdot du$$

which only needs sympathetic evaluation of $\sin x/x$ when x is small or zero from

$$\frac{\sin x}{x} = 1 - \frac{x^2}{3!} + \frac{x^4}{5!}.$$

(You would keep your calculus instructor happier by writing $\sin u^2/u^2$ — but your computer function surely will begin with $x = u*u$ — and go on from there.)

3.2. The teakettle syndrome: Let $\pi/2 - x = u$ and suddenly you have exercise 3.1!

3.3. Move that trouble to the origin — where the integrand then reads $\cos u/\sqrt{u}$ and we have to do the standard square-root-remove. If you are not the cautious type, you might combine the two steps by letting $\pi/2 - x = u^2$ to produce

$$2 \int_0^{\sqrt{\pi/2}} \cos u^2 \, du.$$

3.4. No need to move — the trouble is already at the origin! Neutralize $\sin x$ via

$$\int_0^{\pi/2} \frac{\pi/2 - x}{\sqrt{\sin x/x}} \frac{dx}{\sqrt{x}}$$

then the usual $x = u^2$ — always remembering to evaluate the $\sin x/x$ via a few terms of its series whenever x is small.

3.5. Almost the same advice as in exercise 3.4 — except that $\sin x/x$ already exists. Evaluate sympathetically after getting rid of $1/\sqrt{x}$ in the usual way.

3.6. Trouble at both limits: Split at 1. The $(0,1)$ integral has a vertical *slope* at the origin; the other has a vertical *asymptote* at 2. They both are obvious square-rootish problems. For the second, use $2 - x = u^2$.

3.7. Neutralize the arctangent (but when x is small, use the series for evaluating $\arctan x/x$) then cure the square root with $x = u^2$.

3.8. Move the problem to the origin, where it becomes

$$\int_0^{\pi/2} \frac{u}{\sqrt{\sin u}} \, du = \int_0^{\pi/2} \frac{\sqrt{u}}{\sqrt{\sin u/u}} \, du = 2 \int_0^{\sqrt{\pi/2}} \frac{v^2}{\left[\sqrt{\sin u/u}\right]_{u=v^2}} \, dv$$

via obvious changes in the dummy variable.

3.9. Two difficulties: the square-rootish singularity at the lower limit and a range of integration that is inefficiently large. (This integral *exists* even when the upper limit becomes infinite. Here it is the computational labor that we would reduce.) Split at 1, then invert the dummy of the larger range to produce

$$\int_0^1 \frac{\arctan x}{x} \cdot \frac{dx}{\sqrt{x}} + \int_{1/37}^1 \frac{\pi/2 - \arctan y}{\sqrt{y}} \, dy.$$

By now the first integral should be familiar. The other splits into two, with the simpler being directly integrable analytically. The final integral needs $y = u^2$ to render it completely docile.

3.10. Infinity is a long way off. Split at 1; invert the big range:

$$\int_0^1 \frac{e^{-x}}{1+x^2} \, dx + \int_0^1 \frac{e^{-1/y}}{1+y^2} \, dy = \int_0^1 \frac{e^{-x} + e^{-1/x}}{1+x^2} \, dx$$

getting a fortuitous recombination into a single integrand — altho evaluating it will require some code that resembles

```
function f(x)
t = 0
if x>0.025 then t = exp(-1.0/x)
f = (exp(-x) + t)/(1.0 + x*x)
return.
```

3.11. Substituting $x = w^4$ gives the integrand $16w \cdot \ln w / \sqrt{1 + w^2}$ — which is still a bit dicey near zero. $x = w^6$ is better but $x = w^8$ is our recommendation (see table 1 in chapter 3) — thus allowing the range of quadratures to be limited safely away from the origin since the active part of the numerator is $w^3 \cdot \ln w$.

3.12. It's a long way ... so reciprocate and deal with

$$-\int_0^1 \frac{\ln y}{\sqrt{2y^2 + 1}} \frac{dy}{\sqrt{y}}$$

whose principal features should be familiar from exercise 3.11.

3.13. Sure an' 37 ain't infinity — which is just as well because this integral doesn't exist if the upper limit ever gets there (consider $\int^\infty \frac{\pi/2}{x} dx$ to see why) — but it's still a long way out. Subtract off the potentially singular behavior to get

$$\int_1^{37} \frac{\pi/2}{\sqrt{4+x^2}} dx - \int_1^{37} \frac{\pi/2 - \arctan x}{\sqrt{4+x^2}} dx =$$

$$\frac{\pi}{2} \ln\left[\frac{37 + \sqrt{4+37^2}}{1+\sqrt{5}}\right] - \int_{1/37}^{1} \frac{\arctan y}{y\sqrt{4y^2+1}} dy$$

in which the last integral is well-behaved — the $(\arctan y/y)$ being unity at zero and stably evaluable nearby from a few terms of the obvious series. [If you are still confused, *do* the transformation $x = 1/y$ (you need the practice!) and remember that $\pi/2 - \arctan x = \arctan 1/x$.]

3.14. Invert; then

$$-\int_0^1 \frac{\ln y}{\sqrt{y(y+1)}} dy,$$

being almost exercise 3.11, needs the $y = w^8$ treatment to squeeze all significant area out of the region near $w = 0$. (That "extra" minus came from $\ln(1/y) = -\ln y$, the minus from the differential having been absorbed by the interchange of the limits of integration.)

3.15. Troubles at 37 (potential) and 1 (actual). Subtract off the big part and invert — in either order — to get

$$\frac{\pi}{2} \int_1^{37} \frac{dx}{\sqrt{x^2-1}} dx - \int_{1/37}^{1} \frac{\arctan y}{y\sqrt{1-y^2}} dy =$$

$$\frac{\pi}{2} \ln(37 + \sqrt{1368}) - 2\int_{u=0}^{6/\sqrt{37}} \left[\frac{\arctan y}{y\sqrt{1+y}}\right]\Bigg|_{y=1-u^2} \cdot du$$

the last integral arising from the square-rootish substitution $y = 1-u^2$ explicitly carried out only where it is needed, with a reminder for the program writer appended to the bracket.

3.16. Troubles at both limits. The origin looks manageable with $x = w^8$. So split somewhere (we use 1/2) then move the upper limit trouble to the origin by $1 - x = v$ to get

$$\int_0^{1/2} \frac{\ln x}{(1-x)\sqrt{x}}\, dx + \int_0^{1/2} \frac{\ln(1-v)}{v\sqrt{1-v}}\, dv.$$

Now invoke the series for $\ln(1-v)$ to cancel the denominator v whenever v is small.

3.17. At zero this integral goes to infinity like $\int_0 dx/x = -\ln 0$, so subtract it and add it to give

$$\int_\epsilon^{\pi/2} \frac{dx}{x} - \int_\epsilon^{\pi/2} \frac{1-\cos x}{x}\, dx = \ln\left(\frac{\pi}{2\epsilon}\right) - \int_\epsilon^{\pi/2} \frac{1-\cos x}{x}\, dx.$$

The integrand now goes to zero at the origin like $x/2$ and ascends gently to $2/\pi$ at $\pi/2$. One merely needs to tell the integrand function to evaluate it from

$$x\left[\frac{1}{2} - \frac{x^2}{4!} + \frac{x^6}{6!}\right]$$

when x is small, say, $x < 0.1$. Most of the area under the infinite spike that was in the original integral is now in the logarithm's argument.

3.18. Near zero $\sin x/x$ is unity, so subtract off the *remaining* $1/x$ to get

$$\int_\epsilon^{\pi/2} \frac{dx}{x} - \int_\epsilon^{\pi/2} \left[1 - \frac{\sin x}{x}\right]\frac{dx}{x}$$

which has the same $\ln(\pi/2\epsilon)$ as exercise 3.17 but a different well-behaved integral for quadratures. The series for small x is

$$x\left[\frac{1}{3!} - \frac{x^2}{5!} + \cdots\right].$$

3.19. If b is not close to zero, quadratures are easy since $\sin x/x$ is quite polynomic in its geometry and the root factor does not disturb the shape. But for small b the integrand starts to sense that an asymptote is about to appear when b gets to zero. So subtract off the integrand with x set to zero in the root and in the $\sin x/x$, getting

$$\int_0^{\pi/2} \frac{1}{b}\, dx - \int_0^{\pi/2} \left[\frac{1}{b} - \frac{\sin x/x}{\sqrt{x^2 + b^2}}\right] dx =$$

$$\frac{\pi/2}{b} - \int_0^{\pi/2} \frac{x^2 + b^2 - b^2 S^2}{b\sqrt{x^2 + b^2}\left[\sqrt{x^2 + b^2} + bS\right]}\, dx$$

where $S(x) = \sin x/x$. The numerator can be written

$$x^2 + b^2(1 - S)(1 + S)$$

and we note that both terms have x^2 behavior because the series for S begins with 1. Making this more noticeable by defining $s2x(x) = (1 - S)/x^2$ our integral becomes

$$\frac{1}{b}\left\{ \frac{\pi}{2} - \int_0^{\pi/2} \frac{x^2\left[1 + b^2 \cdot s2x \cdot (1 + S)\right]}{x^2 + b^2 + b \cdot S \cdot \sqrt{x^2 + b^2}}\, dx \right\}.$$

But numerical tests soon make us uneasy: for $b = 0.001$ it takes 16K ordinates to yield nine significant figures and even these are produced via $(1.5707 - 1.5629)/0.001 \approx 7.86$ — a loss of three digits in the subtraction. Looking back at the integrand, we see that altho it begins at zero it rises rapidly, being roughly $1/(2 + \sqrt{2})$ when $x = b = 0.001$,

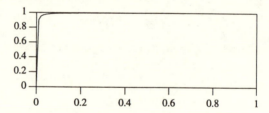

and continues up to 1 very quickly. We ought to do better!

The singularity of the integrand is better represented by $1/\sqrt{x^2 + b^2}$, so we get

$$\int_0^{\pi/2} \frac{dx}{\sqrt{x^2 + b^2}} - \int_0^{\pi/2} \left[1 - \frac{\sin x}{x}\right] \frac{dx}{\sqrt{x^2 + b^2}} =$$

$$\ln\left[\frac{\pi/2 + \sqrt{(\pi/2)^2 + b^2}}{b}\right] - \int_0^{\pi/2} \frac{x^2 \cdot s2x(x)}{\sqrt{x^2 + b^2}}\, dx.$$

At $b = 0.001$ this quadrature gives nine digits with 4K ordinates or thirteen digits with 32K — and *no* loss of significant digits in the subtraction! Clearly the better way.

3.20. To subtract off the singular behavior it would seem that either $1/(xb)$ or $1/(x\sqrt{x^2 + b^2})$ can be used — both being analytically integrable and representative of the behavior of the integrand as x gets close to zero. The first leads to

$$\frac{1}{b}\left\{\ln\left(\frac{\pi/2}{\epsilon}\right) - \int_0^{\pi/2} \frac{x\left[1 + b^2 \cdot s2x \cdot (1 + S)\right]}{x^2 + b^2 + b \cdot S \cdot \sqrt{x^2 + b^2}} dx\right\}$$

and we see that this integrand will have problems similar to those of the first attempt of exercise 3.19. (Actually slightly worse: at $\epsilon = b = 0.001$ it needs 32K ordinates for nine correct digits — losing one in subtraction.)

The second choice of subtrahend gives

$$\int_\epsilon^{\pi/2} \frac{\sin x/x}{x\sqrt{x^2 + b^2}} dx = \int_\epsilon^{\pi/2} \frac{dx}{x\sqrt{b^2 + x^2}} - \int_\epsilon^{\pi/2}\left[1 - \frac{\sin x}{x}\right]\frac{dx}{x\sqrt{b^2 + x^2}}$$

$$= -\frac{1}{b}\ln\left[\frac{(b + \sqrt{(\pi/2)^2 + b^2})}{(b + \sqrt{\epsilon^2 + b^2})} \cdot \frac{\epsilon}{\pi/2}\right] - \int_\epsilon^{\pi/2} \frac{x \cdot s2x(x)}{\sqrt{x^2 + b^2}} dx$$

which produces nine digits with 8K ordinates and no loss of significant digits by subtraction when $\epsilon = b = 0.001$. If ϵ is 0.01, the yield is much more generous with 8K ordinates producing thirteen digits while only 2000 are needed for 9.

3.21. Split at 1 and tame the logarithm at the origin in the usual way, by letting $x = w^4$. Reciprocate the dummy in the other part to get

$$\int_{1/G}^1 \frac{-\ln r}{(1 + r)r} dr = -\int_{1/G}^1 \frac{\ln r}{r} dr + \int_{1/G}^1 \frac{\ln r}{r}\left[1 - \frac{1}{1 + r}\right] dr$$

$$= -\frac{1}{2}(\ln r)^2\Big|_{1/G}^1 + \int_{1/G}^1 \frac{\ln r}{1 + r} dr$$

$$= +\frac{1}{2}(\ln G)^2 + \int_{1/G}^1 \frac{\ln r}{1 + r} dr$$

where the final integral is a minor correction to the potentially singular first term.

3.22. Near $x = 0$ the integral over $(\epsilon, 1)$

$$\int_\epsilon^1 \frac{\ln x}{x\sqrt{b+x}} dx$$

acts like

$$\int_\epsilon^1 \frac{\ln x}{x\sqrt{b}} dx.$$

Hence evaluate

$$\frac{1}{\sqrt{b}} \int_\epsilon^1 \frac{\ln x}{x} dx - \int_\epsilon^1 \frac{\ln x}{x} \left[\frac{1}{\sqrt{b}} - \frac{1}{\sqrt{b+x}}\right] dx =$$

$$\frac{1}{2\sqrt{b}}(\ln x)^2 \Big|_\epsilon^1 - \int_\epsilon^1 \frac{\ln x \cdot \not{x} \ dx}{\not{x} \cdot \sqrt{b}\sqrt{b+x}\left[\sqrt{b+x}+\sqrt{b}\right]}$$

hence

$$-\frac{1}{\sqrt{b}} \left\{\frac{(\ln \epsilon)^2}{2} + \int_\epsilon^1 \frac{\ln x}{b+x+\sqrt{b(b+x)}} dx\right\}$$

and the new integrand is OK after canceling that factor of x.
The integral over $(1, \infty)$ can be inverted:

$$-\int_0^1 \frac{\ln y}{\sqrt{y}\sqrt{by+1}} dy$$

then pasteurized by $y = w^8$.

3.23. Integrals like this come to the local "expert" for evaluation — even tho they don't exist! You must recognize them quickly or waste a lot of time. Here the simplest argument is to note that for *large* x part of the integral is approximately

$$\int_B^\infty \frac{\ln x}{x} dx = \frac{1}{2}(\ln x)^2 \Big|_B^\infty$$

which is clearly infinite.

3.24. Having split at 1, the upper integral can have its dummy variable reciprocated to yield

$$-\int_0^1 \frac{\ln r \cdot \sqrt{r}}{b^2 r^2 + 1} dr$$

which will integrate nicely if we further let $r = w^4$. The *lower* integral

$$\int_0^1 \frac{\ln x \cdot dx}{(b^2 + x^2)\sqrt{x}}$$

will need $x = w^8$ to pacify its geometry for most values of b. But for very small b a singularity looms. When b is small, write

$$\int_0^1 \frac{\ln x \cdot dx}{\sqrt{x}(b^2 + x^2)} = \frac{1}{b^2}\int_0^1 \frac{\ln x}{\sqrt{x}}\, dx - \int_0^1 \left[\frac{\ln x}{\sqrt{x} \cdot b^2} - \frac{\ln x}{\sqrt{x}(b^2 + x^2)} \right] dx$$

$$= -\frac{4}{b^2} - \int_0^1 \frac{\ln x}{\sqrt{x}} \left[\frac{1}{b^2} - \frac{1}{b^2 + x^2} \right] dx$$

$$= -\frac{4}{b^2} - \frac{1}{b^2}\int_0^1 \frac{x\sqrt{x} \cdot \ln x}{b^2 + x^2}\, dx.$$

To tame this one we have a choice ranging from $x = w^2$ to w^4, the latter being enough even if b^2 were to go all the way to zero inside the integrand — which, of course, it can't.

3.25. Since $(1 - \cos x)/x^2$ is 1/2 at the origin (if properly evaluated from the series when x is small) the only other problem is $x^{-1/2}$ — easily squashed by letting $x = u^2$.

3.26. (This is the well-known "Complete Elliptic Integral of the First Kind" for which Gauss found an elegant method of evaluation — but we'll assume you didn't know that and will deal with it by non-Gaussian methods.) If b^2 is not close to 1, then it is only the *other* factor in the denominator that is dangerous at the upper limit — and that can be fixed by the usual $1 - x = u^2$. The resulting integrand is rather messy, but it will work if you don't lose a minus sign or factor of 2. But if b^2 is close to unity, it is better to use a Pythagorean transformation, $1 - x^2 = v^2$, first. We get

$$\frac{1}{b}\int_0^1 \frac{dv}{\sqrt{1 - v^2}\sqrt{\epsilon^2 + v^2}} \qquad \text{with} \qquad \epsilon^2 = \frac{1 - b^2}{b^2}.$$

We still have to deal with the square-rootish trouble at the upper limit, but now the problem with small ϵ^2 occurs at the *lower* limit and so is easier to subtract off. Write the integral as

$$\int_0^1 \frac{dv}{\sqrt{\epsilon^2 + v^2}} - \int_0^1 \left[1 - \frac{1}{\sqrt{1 - v^2}} \right] \frac{dv}{\sqrt{\epsilon^2 + v^2}} =$$

$$\ln\left(1 + \sqrt{\epsilon^2 + 1}\right) - \ln\epsilon + \int_0^1 \frac{v^2 \, dv}{\sqrt{\epsilon^2 + v^2}\sqrt{1 - v^2}[\sqrt{1 - v^2} + 1]}.$$

Now deal with the troublesome factor by $1 - v = u^2$ (there is no need to propagate the substitution explicitly) to get

$$\ln\left(1 + \sqrt{\epsilon^2 + 1}\right) - \ln\epsilon + \int_0^1 \frac{v^2}{\sqrt{\epsilon^2 + v^2}[\sqrt{1 - v^2} + 1]}\bigg|_{v=1-u^2} \cdot \frac{2du}{\sqrt{2 - u^2}}.$$

Most of the original integral lies in the $-\ln\epsilon$ term when b^2 is very close to 1.

3.27. Obviously singular at zero, like $2/x^2$, subtract this singularity off to get

$$2\int_\epsilon^{\pi/2} \frac{dx}{x^2} - \int_\epsilon^{\pi/2}\left[\frac{2}{x^2} - \frac{1}{1 - \cos x}\right] dx$$

whose second term has the form, for small x

$$2\int_\epsilon^{\pi/2} \frac{\frac{x^4}{4!} - \frac{x^6}{6!} + \cdots}{x^2(1 - \cos x)} dx = 2\int_\epsilon^{\pi/2} \frac{\frac{1}{4!} - \frac{x^2}{6!} + \cdots}{\left(\frac{1 - \cos x}{x^2}\right)} dx.$$

3.28. If b is not close to zero the only problem is the common square-rootish one that is eassily solved by letting $x - b = u^2$. But for dangerously small b values, subtract off the equivalent integrable integrand:

$$\int_b^{\pi/2} \frac{\sin x - \sin b}{\sqrt{x^2 - b^2}} dx + \sin b \int_b^{\pi/2} \frac{dx}{\sqrt{x^2 - b^2}}$$

which becomes

$$2\int_b^{\pi/2} \frac{\cos\left(\frac{x+b}{2}\right)\sin\left(\frac{x-b}{2}\right)}{\sqrt{x^2 - b^2}} dx + \sin b \left[\ln\left(\pi/2 + \sqrt{(\pi/2)^2 - b^2}\right) - \ln b\right].$$

The potentially singular behavior is located in $-\sin b \cdot \ln b$. The new integrand can be pasteurized by letting $x - b = u^2$ — which will leave a factor of $\sin(u^2/2)$ upstairs to overpower the $\sqrt{u^2 + 2b}$ down at $u = 0$, even if b were zero.

3.29. Split at b to get rid of the absolute values:

$$\int_0^b \frac{\cos x}{\sqrt{b^2 - x^2}}\, dx + \int_b^{\pi/2} \frac{\cos x}{\sqrt{x^2 - b^2}}\, dx.$$

The first integral has only the standard square-rootish problem at its upper limit (fix with $b - x = u^2$), but the second approaches infinity as b goes to zero. Subtract the limiting form of the integrand (when $x = b$) to get

$$\cos b \int_b^{\pi/2} \frac{dx}{\sqrt{x^2 - b^2}} - \int_b^{\pi/2} \frac{\cos b - \cos x}{\sqrt{x^2 - b^2}}\, dx$$

which becomes

$$\cos b \cdot \ln\left[\frac{\pi/2 + \sqrt{(\pi/2)^2 - b^2}}{b}\right] - 2\int_b^{\pi/2} \frac{\sin(\frac{b-x}{2})\sin(\frac{b+x}{2})}{\sqrt{x^2 - b^2}}\, dx\,.$$

On letting $x - b = u^2$, this integral becomes

$$-2 \cdot 2 \int_0^{\sqrt{\pi/2 - b}} \frac{\sin(\frac{u^2}{2})\sin(\frac{u^2 + 2b}{2})}{\sqrt{u^2 + 2b}}\, du\,.$$

The integrand is well-behaved — tending toward u^4/u as b goes to zero.

3.30. Near zero the geometry is not flat. Use $x = w^3$ to help smooth it enough so that you can avoid the limit. Near 1 a singularity arises since $\ln x$ is $\ln(1 - u) = -(u + u^2/2 + \cdots)$ there. If we have split at 1/2 to separate the troubles, then let $u = 1 - x$ to get

$$\int_\epsilon^{1/2} \frac{du}{\ln(1 - u)} = -\int_\epsilon^{1/2} \frac{du}{u} + \int_\epsilon^{1/2}\left[\frac{1}{u} + \frac{1}{\ln(1 - u)}\right] du$$

$$= -\ln\left(\frac{1/2}{\epsilon}\right) + \int_\epsilon^{1/2} \frac{\ln(1 - u) + u}{u \cdot \ln(1 - u)}\, du.$$

When u is small, the new integrand behaves like

$$\frac{u^2}{2u \cdot u} = \frac{1}{2}$$

— clearly well-behaved if evaluated with T. L. C.

3.31. Analytically integrable! (It's 2π.)

3.32. Despite its forbidding appearance, this integrand remains remarkably smooth — staying near its initial value of 1 (use series near zero) even beyond $x = 2$, then declining slowly, more-or-less forever. (At $x = 500$ it is still about 0.25.) Thus, the geometry will not offer problems to quadratures in its present form. If you prefer, you can scale the limits by letting $x = Bu$, but the effect is purely cosmetic. This is one of very few integrals over a large range with an arctangent in which inversion does *not* help. Indeed, it makes trouble!

3.33. Split at 1. The $(0, 1)$ part needs $x = w^4$ to permit us to avoid the zero limit without ignoring significant area, but it is otherwise tame. The $(1, B)$ area becomes infinite with B so the singular behavior needs to be subtracted. First invert to move the trouble to the origin in

$$-\int_{1/B}^{1} \frac{\ln r}{\sqrt{3r^2+1}} \cdot \frac{dr}{r}$$

which can then be written as

$$-\int_{1/B}^{1} \ln r \cdot \frac{dr}{r} + \int_{1/B}^{1} \frac{\ln r}{r} \left[1 - \frac{1}{\sqrt{3r^2+1}}\right] dr$$

$$= -\frac{1}{2}(\ln r)^2 \Big|_{1/B}^{1} + \int_{1/B}^{1} \frac{\ln r \cdot 3r^2}{r\sqrt{3r^2+1}[\sqrt{3r^2+1}+1]} dr$$

$$= \frac{1}{2}(\ln B)^2 + 3 \int_{1/B}^{1} \frac{r \cdot \ln r}{3r^2+1+\sqrt{3r^2+1}} dr.$$

The new integrand is well-behaved except for its slope when r is small, the potentially infinite part being in $(\ln B)^2/2$. Cure the slope with $r = w^2$.

3.34. Troubles at both limits; split at $\pi/4$ and move the difficulty in the upper integral to the origin with $x = \pi/2 - u$, getting

$$\int_{\pi/4}^{\pi/2} \frac{dx}{\tan x(\pi - x)} = \int_{0}^{\pi/4} \frac{du}{u \cot u} = \int_{0}^{\pi/4} \left(\frac{\sin u}{u}\right) \frac{du}{\cos u}$$

and that problem disappears. The lower integral is toying with real singular behavior which needs to be subtracted off. Write

$$\int\limits_{\epsilon}^{\pi/4} \frac{\cos x\, dx}{\sin x(\frac{\pi}{2} - x)} = \int\limits_{\epsilon}^{\pi/4} \frac{\cos x}{\frac{\pi}{2}\sin x}\, dx - \int\limits_{\epsilon}^{\pi/4} \frac{\cos x}{\frac{\pi}{2}\sin x}\left[1 - \frac{1}{1 - \frac{2}{\pi}x}\right]\, dx$$

which becomes

$$\ln(\sin x)\Big|_{\epsilon}^{\pi/4} - \frac{2}{\pi}\int\limits_{\epsilon}^{\pi/4} \frac{\cos x}{\sin x}\left[\frac{1 - \frac{2}{\pi}x - 1}{1 - \frac{2}{\pi}x}\right]\, dx.$$

This final integral is well-behaved even at zero if $x/\sin x$ is evaluated from the series near there.

3.35. Troubles at both ends; split at 1. At ∞ the arctangent is $\pi/2$ so write the upper integral as

$$\frac{2}{\pi}\int\limits_{1}^{\infty} e^{-x}\left[\frac{\pi/2}{\arctan x} - 1\right]\, dx + \frac{2}{\pi}\int\limits_{1}^{\infty} e^{-x}\, dx$$

then reciprocate:

$$\frac{2}{\pi}\int\limits_{0}^{1} e^{-1/y}\left[\frac{\arctan y}{\pi/2 - \arctan y}\right]\frac{dy}{y^2} + \frac{2}{\pi}e^{-1}.$$

Near zero $\arctan y/y$ absorbs one of the denominator y's and $e^{-1/y}$ is powerful enough of a "zero" to suppress the other for $y < 0.025$.

The other integrand behaves like $1/x$ near the origin, so write it as

$$\int\limits_{\epsilon}^{1}\left[\frac{e^{-x}}{\arctan x} - \frac{1}{x}\right]\, dx + \int\limits_{\epsilon}^{1} \frac{dx}{x}$$

which becomes

$$\int\limits_{\epsilon}^{1} \frac{x \cdot e^{-x} - \arctan x}{x \cdot \arctan x}\, dx - \ln\epsilon.$$

For small x, using series everywhere gives good behavior to the integrand as

$$\frac{-1 + 5x/6 - x^2/6 - 19x^3/120 - x^4/120 + \cdots}{1 - x^2/3 + x^4/5 - \cdots}.$$

3.36. Subtract off the singular part by setting $\cos x$ to its value at zero to get

$$\int_\epsilon^{\pi/2} \frac{\cos x - 1}{x\sqrt{1+x}}\,dx + \int_\epsilon^{\pi/2} \frac{dx}{x\sqrt{1+x}}.$$

The second integral has the closed form

$$2\ln\left[\frac{1+\sqrt{1+\epsilon}}{1+\sqrt{1+\pi/2}}\right] + \ln\left(\frac{\pi/2}{\epsilon}\right).$$

The first is OK if you use series whenever x is small.

3.37. Trouble at both limits — split, then let $\pi/2 - x = u$ (or v^2, if you are foresighted) in the upper one to get

$$\int_0^{\pi/4} \sqrt{\frac{\pi/2 - x}{1 - \sin x}} \cdot \frac{dx}{\sqrt{x}} + \int_0^{\pi/4} \sqrt{\frac{u}{1 - \cos u}} \cdot \frac{du}{\sqrt{\pi/2 - u}}.$$

Remove the square-rootish problem in the first integral via $x = u^2$; rewrite the second as

$$\int_0^{\pi/4} \sqrt{\frac{u^2}{1 - \cos u}} \cdot \frac{du}{\sqrt{u} \cdot \sqrt{\pi/2 - u}}$$

where the cosine is now embalmed in an expression that is $\sqrt{2}$ at the origin (but needs series evaluation near there). The only remaining problem is the $\sqrt{u}$ — and by now you know what to do!

3.38. Split at $\pi/4$. The $(\pi/4, \pi/2)$ part has only indeterminacy troubles at $\pi/2$, so let $\pi/2 - x = u$ to get

$$\int_0^{\pi/4} \frac{\sin u/u}{(\pi/2 - u)^{3/2}}\,du$$

and take care to evaluate $\sin u/u$ properly when u is near (and at) zero. The potentially singular part can be written

$$\int_\epsilon^{\pi/4} \left[\frac{\cos x}{(\pi/2 - x)x\sqrt{x}} - \frac{1}{(\pi/2 - x)x^{3/2}}\right]dx + \int_\epsilon^{\pi/4} \frac{dx}{(\pi/2 - x)x\sqrt{x}}$$

where the singular behavior is in the second integral — which can be integrated analytically after letting $x = v^2$ and then partial-fractioning the new integral into $1/v^2$ and $1/(\pi/2 - v^2)$. The square bracket, being

$$-\left(\frac{1-\cos x}{x^2}\right) \cdot \frac{\sqrt{x}}{\pi/2 - x},$$

is clearly well-behaved after removing the vertical slope at the origin via $x = u^2$ — and remembering to evaluate the cosine fraction via its series if x^2 ever gets very small.

3.39. (If you got this one, you are a certified Doctor for Sick Integrals!) At zero the logarithm and the arctangent are both x, so with careful series evaluation their ratio offers no problem there. The factor of $\sqrt{x}$ requires the usual $x = u^2$ treatment. The real problems arise as B gets large, so split at 1 and invert the upper integral ($x = 1/r$) to give

$$\int_{1/B}^{1} \frac{\ln(1+1/r)}{\arctan(1/r)} \cdot \frac{dr}{r\sqrt{r}} = \int_{1/B}^{1} \frac{\ln(1+r)}{r\arctan(1/r)} \cdot \frac{dr}{\sqrt{r}} - \int_{1/B}^{1} \frac{\ln r}{\arctan(1/r)} \cdot \frac{dr}{r\sqrt{r}}$$

rewritten to give a $\ln(1+r)$ factor that will neutralize one factor of r from the denominator in the first integral. The factor $\arctan(1/r)$ is geometrically benign over $(0,1)$ (and r will not even get to zero). The $\sqrt{r}$ in the denominator needs the usual.

The last integral needs a factor of r upstairs, so subtract off an integral version of its singular behavior:

$$\int_{1/B}^{1} \frac{\ln r}{\arctan(1/r)} \cdot \frac{dr}{r\sqrt{r}} = \frac{2}{\pi} \int_{1/B}^{1} \frac{\ln r}{r\sqrt{r}} dr - \int_{1/B}^{1} \frac{\ln r}{r\sqrt{r}} \left[\frac{1}{\pi/2} - \frac{1}{\arctan(1/r)}\right] dr$$

to produce

$$-\frac{2}{\pi} \cdot 4\left[1 + \sqrt{B}(\ln\sqrt{B} - 1)\right] + \int_{1/B}^{1} \frac{\ln r}{\frac{\pi}{2}\arctan 1/r} \cdot \left(\frac{\arctan r}{r}\right) \cdot \frac{dr}{\sqrt{r}}$$

which still has the factor $\ln r/\sqrt{r}$ to bother us. But $r = w^8$ will crush that! We leave it to you to put the pieces together.

3.40. Near the lower limit the integrand is unity — but should be evaluated from

$$1 \Big/ \left[1 - \frac{x^2}{3!} + \frac{x^4}{5!} - \cdots\right].$$

The real problem is near π, where the integrand and the integral both become infinite. Split at $\pi/2$ then move the trouble at π to the origin by $\pi - x = u$ to get

$$\int_\epsilon^{\pi/2} \frac{\pi - u}{\sin u}\, du.$$

Now we see that the second part of this integral will combine with the

$$\int_0^{\pi/2} \frac{x}{\sin x}\, dx$$

already split off. Thus we have

$$\int_0^\epsilon \frac{x}{\sin x}\, dx + \pi \int_\epsilon^{\pi/2} \frac{du}{\sin u}$$

and the last integral has several closed forms of which

$$\pi \ln \left(\frac{1 + \cos \epsilon}{\sin \epsilon}\right)$$

is probably the most useful here.

Chapter 4
Recurrence Relations

4.0 — Archimedes, Despair!
Since s_n approaches π, $s_n/2^n$ becomes very small, so we have the problem of evaluating $1 - \sqrt{1 - \epsilon}$ accurately. In this form, the recurrence becomes unstable once ϵ shrinks below the precision of REAL 1.0. The cure is to rewrite it as $\epsilon/(1 + \sqrt{1 - \epsilon})$. The computation is beautified, tho not essentially changed, if we redefine the iterate via

$$S_n = \left(\frac{s_n}{2^n}\right)^2$$

then, squaring both sides of the recurrence,

$$S_{n+1} \leftarrow \frac{S_n/2}{1 + \sqrt{1 - S_n}} \qquad\qquad S_2 = 1/2$$

an iteration from which n has disappeared — tho it is needed to recover s_n.

4.1. Integrate

$$L_{k,m} = \int_0^g \frac{x^k \ln x}{(1+x)^m} \, dx$$

by parts to get

$$L_{k,m} = \frac{g^{k+1} \cdot \ln g}{(k+1)(1+g)^m} + \frac{m}{k+1} L_{k+1,m+1} - \frac{1}{k+1} X_{k,m}$$

where

$$X_{k,m} = \int_0^g \frac{x^k}{(1+x)^m} \, dx$$

which, in turn, integrates by parts to give

$$X_{k,m} = \frac{g^{k+1}}{(k+1)(1+g)^m} + \frac{m}{k+1} X_{k+1,m+1}.$$

These two recurrences allow us to proceed downward along the 45° diagonal $k+1 = m$, the final element of which is the integral we seek. Since $L_{k,m}$ approaches zero when both k and m become large, we need only start out far enough. Here is the complete algorithm. Choose a $MaxM$ then set

```
X = L = 0
LNG = ln(g)
G1G = g/(1+g)
GPM = G1G ↑ MaxM
```

then execute

```
for m=MaxM to 1 by -1
X ← GPM/m + X
L ← (GPM*LNG-X)/m + L
GPM ← GPM/G1G
end for
```

to get L. Check the accuracy by testing X against its analytic value $\ln(1+g)$. For $g = 0.8$ you should get better than six correct digits ($L_{0,1} = -0.810942$) with $MaxM = 16$. Altho many other algorithms for this integral are possible (and a few are slightly more efficient), this one is rather good. It delivers 10 significant figures for the starting $MaxM$ shown here:

g	0.3	0.5	0.8	1.0
$MaxM$	13	18	26	30

Each iteration requires eight arithmetic operations. (At the end one logarithm is also needed to get $\ln g$.)

For g greater than 1 this algorithm becomes regressively less efficient — but there is no need to use it there. Since $\int_0^1 \ln x/(1+x)dx = -\pi^2/12$ and since

$$\int_1^G \frac{\ln x}{1+x}\, dx = \frac{1}{2}(\ln G)^2 + \int_{1/G}^1 \frac{\ln x}{1+x}\, dx$$

(a relation that any reader of chapter 3 should be able to derive by subtracting off the singular behavior!) we find

$$\int_0^G \frac{\ln x}{1+x}\, dx = -\frac{\pi^2}{6} + \frac{1}{2}(\ln G)^2 - \int_0^{1/G} \frac{\ln x}{1+x}\, dx.$$

If you want to increase the efficiency still further, the original integral with g in the range $1/2 < g < 1$ can be avoided by using

$$\int_g^1 \frac{\ln x}{1+x}\, dx = -\ln g \cdot \ln\left(\frac{1+g}{2}\right) - \int_0^{1-g} \frac{\ln(1-y/2)}{1-y}\, dy.$$

On replacing $\ln(1-y/2)$ by its series, this latest integral is

$$\sum_{n=1}^{\infty} \frac{H_n}{n \cdot 2^n} \quad \text{with} \quad H_n = \int_0^{h=1-g} \frac{y^n}{1-y}\, dy.$$

The H's are easily and efficiently produced by

$$H_n \leftarrow H_{n-1} - \frac{h^n}{n} \quad \text{with} \quad H_1 = -\ln(1-h) - h.$$

At $g = h = 1/2$ it needs only terms thru H_{12} to deliver 10 significant figures.

4.2. Let

$$L_{k,m} = \int_0^g \frac{x^k \ln x}{(1+x^2)^m} \, dx$$

then integrate by parts to get

$$L_{k,m} = \frac{g^{k+1} \cdot \ln g}{(k+1)(1+g^2)^m} + \frac{2m}{k+1} L_{k+2,m+1} - \frac{1}{k+1} X_{k,m}$$

where

$$X_{k,m} = \int_0^g \frac{x^k}{(1+x^2)^m} \, dx,$$

its recurrence being

$$X_{k,m} = \frac{g^{k+1}}{(k+1)(1+g^2)^m} + \frac{2m}{k+1} X_{k+2,m+1}.$$

These two recurrences link knight's move patterns of the principal iterates. Since we want the (0,1) element, we descend the superdiagonal for which $k+2 = 2m$.

4.3. If you let

$$E_{k,m} = \int_0^\infty \frac{e^{-cx} x^k}{(1+x^2)^m \sqrt{x}} \, dx = \frac{2m}{k+\frac{1}{2}} E_{k+2,m+1} + \frac{c}{k+\frac{1}{2}} E_{k+1,m}$$

you also have the simpler recurrence

$$E_{k,} = E_{k+2,m+1} + E_{k,m+1}$$

and are thus able to extend a group of three adjacent E's in column $m+1$ to three in column m but down by two rows. (Draw the patterns of these two recurrences if subscripts make you dizzy.) The corner (0,0) element, necessary for normalization, is $\sqrt{\pi/c}$.

Chapter 5
Choosing and Tuning an Algorithm

5.0. — The Cube in the Vase

For $h = 0.92$ the stable minimum configuration (which we leave as a puzzle) has its cube center at height 0.893253 while the horizontal-face position, center at 0.96000, is clearly unstable. But there is at least one other stable position — a local minimum — as well as one or two extrema that have less certain stabilities.

If you enjoy this problem, note that you face many other vases! The one with $h = 0.69$ is particularly challenging.

5.1. (This is sufficiently similar to the two-dimensional problem that you should not need help.)

5.2. Take the square root of the equation to get $e^{z/2} = \pm az$, then let $a = b/2$ and $z = 2t$ to produce the two equations

$$e^t = \pm bt \qquad b > 0$$

that are simpler to manipulate. A sketch (figure 5.2) shows that the minus sign always yields an isolated root on the negative real axis while the + sign will yield two positive real roots, separated by unity whenever $b > e$. At $b = e$, these become a double root at 1.

For complex roots let $t = r + is$ to get the equations

$$\left\{ \begin{array}{l} e^r \cos(s) = \pm br \\ e^r \sin(s) = \pm bs \end{array} \right\} \quad \text{hence} \quad \left\{ \begin{array}{l} \tan(s) = s/r \\ r = \ln\left[\pm \dfrac{bs}{\sin(s)}\right] \end{array} \right\}$$

so the real variable, s, is fixed by

$$\ln(b) + \ln\left[\frac{s}{\pm \sin(s)}\right] = \left[\frac{s}{\pm \tan(s)}\right] \quad (= r)$$

as then is r and hence t. A sketch with $b = 1$ produces the periodic picture shown below. Note that the logarithm requires a positive argument, so we take the appropriate sign with the sine factor, for example, a minus when $\pi < s < 2\pi$. Because the tangent curve has a slope of $-s$ where it crosses the axis — hence is nearly vertical there — and soon crosses the quite broad minimum of the logarithmic curve, the roots lie slightly to the left of $(k + 1/2)\pi$. The geometries near zero are easily found by series expansions of the two expressions.

The effect of various b is to shift the logarithmic curves vertically — eliminating the 0th root when b exceeds e (the two real roots then appear) — but not seriously affecting the locations of the other roots. Since these are well separated and have obvious first approximations, Newton is reasonable.

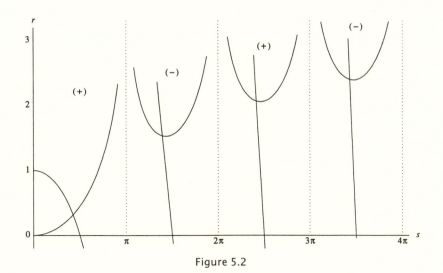

Figure 5.2

But iterative methods are competitive. Shift to a small variable via $s = (k + 1/2)\pi - \delta$ then our equation becomes

$$\ln(b) + \ln \left[\frac{s}{\cos(\delta)} \right] = \left[\frac{s}{\cos(\delta)} \right] \cdot \sin(\delta) \quad (= r).$$

For small δ both $\cos(\delta)$ and s are pseudoconstants and so we solve for the δ in the sine to get the iteration

$$\delta \leftarrow \arcsin \left\{ \ln \left[\frac{bs}{\cos(\delta)} \right] \cdot \frac{\cos(\delta)}{s} \right\}.$$

Starting with $\delta = 0$, six iterations deliver ten-figure accuracy for all roots except the 0th — and that takes thirteen. (All for $b = 1$.) The 0th root is better found by Newton starting with $(\pi/4, \pi/4)$ — unless b is close to e, when chapter 2 techniques should be used: Let $t = 1 + \gamma$ then $e^t = bt$ becomes

$$\gamma = \ln(b/e) + \ln(1 + \gamma)$$

hence the iteration

$$\gamma^2 \leftarrow \frac{\ln(b/e)}{\frac{1}{2} - \frac{\gamma}{3} + \frac{\gamma^2}{4} - \cdots}$$

that will converge to a complex γ if $b < e$ and to a real γ otherwise. Enough!

INDEX